LETTE[FOR VICTORY

By

Martin and Frances Collins

Brewin Books

First published
by Brewin Books, Studley, Warwickshire, B80 7LG
in October 1993

ISBN 1 85858 016 1

British Library Cataloguing in Publication Data.
A Catalogue record for this book is available from the British Library

Typeset by Avon Dataset, Bidford on Avon, Warwickshire, B50 4JH
and made and printed by Cromwell Press.

Contents

Preface

"Mail and morale go hand in hand", so said Lieutenant Jordan, one of the first American officers to be based at the First Base Post Office in Sutton Coldfield, Warwickshire. He was right, imagine how you feel when the postman drops a letter from a friend through your letterbox and imagine how the American soldiers based over here in Britain, thousands of miles from home, felt when they received a letter from friends or family. The importance of having an efficient mail system should not be underestimated in building up morale and aiding the war effort.

The postal troops were amongst the first American soldiers to arrive in Britain in 1942. They set up the First Base Post Office to handle all incoming mail from the States for American troops in Britain, Europe and North Africa and all outgoing mail to the U.S.A. This book records the day to day life of the American Military personnel working at the Post Office in Sutton and also their impact on the Royal Town and its community.

Foreword

By the time the first Americans arrived in 1942, Britain had been at war for almost three years and Sutton had already undergone many changes. The sedate, peaceful Royal Borough, steeped in tradition, had become accustomed to the sight of men and women in uniform – the Territorials, Royal Signal Corp, the R.A.F. Balloon Barrage, Civil Defence and Home Guard. Living with the black-out, gas masks, rationing, long queues and no petrol was the norm. For the most part however, we were still 'very British'. The advent of the G.I.s was a cultural shock. To the older generation it was an event to be approached with apprehension and caution. To the younger element it was novelty and excitement. But, underlying all this, I think, it gave much needed hope to a people who had 'tightened their belts' to the limit.

As the weeks and months progressed, the people of Sutton accepted the influx and, for the most part, revised their opinions of Yanks, which had hitherto been based mostly on American movies and the media. The fun-loving, outgoing G.I.s with their zest for life, shook up the little town and taught us that, once in a while, it's good to let your hair down! Sutton became used to a new type of English language. Certain expressions and usage of certain words on either side, sometimes gave rise to embarrassment and/or amusement. The bonds that were forged between families and the G.I.s remained for a long time, even to the present. Yes, Sutton changed and has, I believe, a lot to owe for its advancement to this episode in history.

– Pearl Lucas (nee Golding) – former resident of Sutton.

v

Chapter 1

The Best Barracks in England

The United States First Base Post Office was activated at Fort Hamilton, Brooklyn, New York on the 1st of May 1942. It consisted of 32 enlisted men and three officers.* Most of these men had been postal workers or clerks in civillian life and were therefore familiar with mailing routines, the filling out of forms and other office duties. Whilst at Fort Hamilton the unit acquired supplies and equipment in preparation for shipment overseas.

By the 4th of June the organisation was ready to embark to a destination unknown. At 12:30 p.m. the men boarded the Motor Ship Tegelberg, a Dutch ship that had recently escaped from the Far East where her sister ship had been sunk. The men's travelling companions were two small army units and a number of women and children who were returning to England after having been evacuated to America and Canada during the blitz earlier in the war.

The vessel was a far cry from a regular troop ship. The meals, cooked by the Javanese crew, were excellent and the services outstanding. Leonard McDermott (one of the 32 enlisted men) noted in his diary at the time:

"We have a nice sun-deck, a library and a radio in the dining room. 'The meals are wonderful! We are served by Chinese waiters who bring us coffee into our bunks at 7:00 a.m. Breakfast is at 8:00, luncheon at noon, tea at 4:00 p.m on deck, and dinner at 7:00 p.m. All excellent meals. Printed menus for luncheon and dinner."

Francis Sullivan (also one of the enlisted men) remembers that in rough seas rims around the tables were raised to keep the meals from sliding off.

During 1942 a large percentage of the American ships attempting to take supplies to England were sunk by German Wolfpacks so it was necessary for the Tegelberg to follow a zigzag course. The trip was still eventful as a British destroyer nearly blew the ship out of the water when the Captain gave the wrong 'signal of the day' as they were passing the West coast of Ireland.

On arrival at Liverpool on the morning of the 16th of June port officials came aboard and inspected the ship's papers, then, about noon, the ship was allowed to enter Liverpool Harbour by going through a series of locks. At 4:15 p.m. the unit disembarked and marched to a British Army Barracks in Fraser Street. On their way the men were shocked to see the destruction that had been caused by the bombing in Liverpool.

Francis Sullivan remembers the barracks clearly. He says it was:

" – a cold building with double decker wire-latticed bunks with folded mattresses. I slept on the upper one and shivered most of the time even though I used my overcoat as a

---

*See Appendix A.

NOTICE.

To make the black-out as effective as possible, the attention of newcoming passengers is drawn to the following:

Before sunset, all windows and portholes of cabins corridors and saloons are closed by ship's personnel. The handles of the cabinwindows will be taken away during the night; one will find them put outside the cabindoors in the early morning.

Smoking on deck after sunset is strictly prohibited, and so is the use of matches, cigaretlighters and flashlights.

No drinks will be served on deck during black-out.

Upon arrival on board, make sure where to find your lifebelt and lifeboatstation.

A lifeboat-drill for the newly embarked passengers is usualy held shortly after departure from a port. This will always be announced via the ship's broadcast. The signal is ringing of the alarmbells throughout the ship. The drill is held on the boatdeck, which is situated on the same level as the sportsdeck.

Realise, that opening windows or portholes during the night, IS A CRIME against yourself, the ship and everyone else in her!!!

MEALHOURS: 1st.class: Breakfast between 7 and 9 a.m.

Lunch from 1 p.m.

Dinner from 8 p.m.

Intermediate class: Breakfast at 8 a.m.

Lunch at noon.

Dinner at 7 p.m.

LIBRARY: Books can be taken by passengers of both classes during the dutyhours of the smokingroom stewards.

SWIMMINGPOOL, SPORTSDECK AND GYMNASIUM are for the use of 1st. class passengers only.

A PASSENGER IS SUPPOSED TO REMAIN IN THE SPACES ASSIGNED TO THE CLASS FOR WHICH HE HAS BOOKED.

Warning notice given to passengers aboard the M.S. Tegelberg.

BALI: Djanger-voorstelling   *Djanger performance*

MONDAY
June 15th 1942.-

V

≡ DINNER ≡

Cream Americaine

◇

Fried Sole
Sauté Potatoes-Lettuce

◇

Roast Ribs of Beef
Purslain-Boiled Potatoes

◇

Ice Cream

◇

Fruit

|||

— To-night clock will be put forward 2.18 min. —

Menu from the M.S. Tegelberg the night it docked in Liverpool.

3

M.S. Tegelberg: 14150 tons, built 1937 by N. V. Nederl. Schps. maats, Amsterdam and owned by N. V. Koninklijke, Paketvraat, maats. Her dimensions were 537.3 × 72.2 × 36.3 and she was registered in Batavia.
(Grenwich Maritime Museum)

blanket and put on my long-johns. I couldn't keep warm, no matter what, so I got out of bed and started dressing around 4 a.m. Dawn was breaking early, or so it seemed to me.

"Two other G.I.s were shivering and dressing, so we took a walk in the blackout of dawn — if that makes any sense. As we walked a light showed, then disappeared. We tried the door and it opened. The shocked waiter couldn't believe his eyes. 'B....y Yanks in Liverpool!' Sorry, no coffee, we had tea. He reluctantly accepted our American money since we had no British coins. The tea warmed our interiors even though we'd rather have had coffee."

Later, back in the Fraser Street barracks Francis and his colleagues found the British mess hall and breakfasted there, but again they were told: "Sorry, no coffee." As Francis ate his breakfast he met another sign of British hostility from an English soldier who murmured under his breath:
"B....y Yankee bacon, they kept the lean and sent us the fat."

Leonard McDermott also remembers that first meal in England. He remembers that each soldier was given a boiled egg. One of the men gobbled up his meal quickly and went back to the 'chow line' looking for 'seconds'. When the British army chef saw this he exploded with:

"Seconds? What do you mean seconds? Don't you know that we only get one egg a week? We are giving you guys a special treat as a welcome to this country!"

4

Holland Road Barracks. This part of the building was first used as a dormitory.
(L. McDermott)

Slit trench at Holland Road Barracks.
(H. Brown)

No. 3. Barracks, Holland Road Camp 1943.
(H. Brown)

The G.I. walked quietly away and needless to say none of the others went back for seconds.

After breakfast the unit left the barracks for Lime Street Station and then travelled by rail, arriving at Whittington Barracks, Lichfield, Staffordshire at 4:10 p.m. There the men were billetted in one of the Victorian red brick barracks and were delighted to find a detatchment of A.T.S. in another! For the next two weeks the unit travelled daily by truck from Whittington Barracks to Sutton Park Railway Station for the purpose of setting up the Post Office.

Some of the British cooks at the Holland Road Barracks.
(L. McDermott)

On the 30th of June the enlisted men were moved to Sutton Coldfield and billetted in the uncompleted buildings of Upper Holland Road (now Plantsbrook) school. The building had been started in 1939 but had been halted by the outbreak of war. Upon the men's arrival the school was just an empty shell with wings but no rooms or partitions for classrooms. It was necessary to convert the interior into sleeping quarters, offices and a mess hall. Leonard McDermott wrote in his diary for that day:

"It should be very nice when they are finished with it."

On the 4th of August nineteen additional men arrived at the school. This party was a group of soldiers who had also had civillian postal experience. This group had left New York on June the 30th in the first military convoy to make the trip from America to England. They had sailed on the Argentina, which had been a peacetime cruise ship. Henry Brown remembers that conditions were very crowded aboard the Argentina. A hundred men slept in a relatively small space, the bunks were stacked five high to get the maximum number of men in each dormitory.

The convoy followed the usual zigzag course. One U-boat did attempt to attack but was sunk with a depth charge from one of the escorting destroyers. The convoy arrived safely at Greenock, Scotland, in mid July and from there the men travelled to Glasgow and then by rail to Cheltenham where they were billetted at the race track. After a few days they were transported by military trucks to the Holland Road Barracks.

On the arrival of the second group the school was still far from completed and the men had to put up with a number of inconveniences. Francis Sullivan remembers a particular double door in the school that no-one could open,

"– until the night we had an air raid and they dropped butterfly bombs near the school barracks. One of the men, Monette Gunby, jumped out of his cot with fright and smashed into the double door. It opened!"

During the first few months that the men spent in Sutton several hundred incendiary bombs and high explosive bombs landed in the immediate vicinity of the barracks but were dealt with by the local fire department. During the air raids the men were required to scatter to slit trenches in the school grounds.

Central heating and lighting were not yet installed in the barracks and the only heat available was from small, inadequate stoves. Phil Tillar remembers that many a cold evening would be spent huddled around these stoves eating fish and chips. He recalls that:

"somehow they tasted better at that time than on other occasions."

The shower block was also a very cold place due to the shortage of hot water. Henry Brown remembers that the first person in would get a warm shower but everybody else would spend a very short time in that particular room of the building.

At night the barracks were no warmer and Henry found that he needed to use his overcoat as an extra blanket. Jimmy Brands and his colleague also found that the three blankets that each G.I. was allotted was not enough to keep them warm. As the two men were working on different shifts they were both able to use the two sets of blankets. After a while they decided that this arrangement was rather unsanitary so they gave the six blankets a good shake, the barracks disappeared in a cloud of dust.

The officers were very strict about the 'lights out' rule at the Holland Road Barracks. Once, after lights out, the G.I. in the neighbouring bed to Ken Sell stood up, posed with his cigarette lighter and said:

"Look, I'm the Statue of Liberty."

Unfortunately an officer saw him and the G.I. and Ken, who had been caught in the flash of the lighter, were put on a charge. Ken was most annoyed about this as he had not actually done anything wrong.

More men were punished when Captain Jordan caught them gambling in the barracks after hours. Leonard McDermott's diary for April 2nd 1943 reads:

"Just after I got into bed Capt. Jordan stormed into the barracks and found about 20 of the fellows playing dice and card games. He took their names and sent them to their respective barracks. He was pretty mad but I think he'll cool off."

7

G.I. cooks: Neilson, Mitcham, Osgood, Scheessele and Ryan on K.P. 1943.
(H. Brown) ·

Mess hall 1943
(H. Brown)

Group shot outside barracks.
(L. McDermott)

8

Before he did cool off he removed the light bulbs so that the men would be unable to see to carry out their clandestine activities. Not to be outdone the gamblers decided to pay somebody to stand and strike matches to give them light to play by.

Roll call in the morning was also a time when the enlisted men at Holland Road tried to bend the rules. The G.I.s present at roll call would often answer for their colleagues who were aiming to snatch a few more minutes in bed. When the officers realised what was happening they would ask the man that they suspected was missing to step forward. This soon stopped the men from having lie-ins!

Already the G.I.s had been acquainted with English cooking and food and were not impressed so they were not pleased to find that English cooks were to feed them for the first few months. The men were also to eat British Army rations until there were sufficient American Army units in the area to obtain food and supplies from their own sources. Until this happened the men continually complained about the fish they had for breakfast and the smell of unrefrigerated mutton that would be their supper. Henry Brown felt that the cooks did not clean their pans properly as every meal seemed to taste of mutton.

"That's why we queued for fish and chips whenever we had the chance."

said Francis Sullivan.

The barracks included a P.X.*, where the men could obtain their monthly allowance of cigarettes and cigars and other items like shaving kits and soap. There was also a small inner courtyard where they could play a limited number of sports. Al Lucas remembers:

"There was a courtyard about 50 foot by 75 foot surrounded on all sides by buildings. It was much too small for good playing (touch football) but we had to use what we had.
On one particular day one chap glanced off a brick column (roof support) and broke his toe. We jeeped him up to Four Oaks to a British Forces Hospital as we had none.
"About an hour later another chap rushed down, cut sharply to the right and reached up for the pass while right on the perimeter of the playing surface. His momentum carried him right into a glass door. We stemmmed the flow of blood from head and arms and shipped him up to the hospital where the chief honcho# remarked: 'You Americans play rough.' Oddly enough, in the next 300 times we played, no-one got hurt."

The G.I.s had to contend with the basic living conditions for several months. In October of 1942 new cement floors were laid but central heating was not installed until February 1943. When the work was done it prompted Captain Jordan to write with a degree of clairvoyance:

"We shall soon have the best barracks in England."*

---

*— Post Exchange — equivalent to a British Naafi."
#— person in charge.
*— F.B.P.O. Historical Report 1943.

Chapter 2

Remember There's a War On

"Britain may look a little shop-worn and grimy to you. The British people are anxious to have you know that you are not seeing their country at its best. There's been a war on since 1939. The houses haven't been painted because factories are not making paint – they're making planes. The famous English gardens and parks are either unkept because there are no men to take care of them, or they are being used to grow needed vegetables . . . The British people are anxious for you to know that in normal times Britain looks much prettier,
   cleaner, neater."

The G.I.s were warned to 'remember there's a war on' in the small booklet 'A Short Guide to Great Britain' which they were given on their arrival in the United Kingdom.

The Americans were soon made aware of this fact as several bombs were dropped on Sutton Coldfield during their first few months here. Leonard McDermott recorded in his diary that he saw these attacks as

"the final dying gasps of the German Luftwaffe, which inflicted such a heavy toll on London and other British cities."

Betty Watts, nee Gardner, (a former Sutton resident) echoes the sentiments of 'The Guide to Great Britain':

"Wartime Sutton was a dreary place. Heavy blackout restrictions, not enough clothing coupons to be smartly dressed anymore, no petrol for pleasure trips, and severe rationing, while the food was not of the choicest quality. Even alcohol was in short supply. Then the Yanks arrived . . ."

The arrival of the 'Yanks' in Sutton Coldfield was something of a culture shock to both the Americans and the British. The British were not quite what the Americans had been led to expect. Arthur Johnson recalls that early motion pictures in America portrayed the English as titled aristocrats, Lords, Dukes, Earls etc., he says that:

"It was great to find out that the average people of Great Britain were no different from our own."

Don Whalen expected English people to be reserved and cool to strangers, but he was pleased to find out that he was treated with "universal friendliness, coutesy and openness" by everyone that he met. Leonard Nole remembers that all of the people he met in England "had a terrific sense of humor." He goes on to say:

"With all that the people of Britain had been through I was amazed at their attitude of 'grin and bear it.'"

One thing that the Americans did expect the British to hold in common with them was the language. When Phil Tillar found, after several days at sea, that his destination was England, his first reaction was of relief that he was going to a country of which he knew a little and could speak the language. He was made aware of his mistake on board the ship when he was given a British-American dictionary featuring Mark Twain's well-known quote:

"Britain and the United States are two countries divided by a single language."

The dictionary went on to give information on the meaning of a few English words that could be misunderstood.

The G.I.s were not the only ones to hold misconceptions. Many of the teenagers in the town were thrilled when they heard that American troops would be coming to Sutton (although the same could not be said of their parent's generation). These impressionable teenagers were convinced that the soldiers would all resemble their Hollywood heroes.

John Cox was away at boarding school when two G.I.s were first billetted at his parent's house. He and his friends discussed the G.I.s and the image they conjured up was of hard-drinking tough guys, swearing with every other word. When he got home he was quite disappointed to find that the two Americans, David Turney and Harry Tepe, were nothing like he had imagined!

Although both nationalities were prepared for some of the differences between the two cultures, the Americans were not prepared for the change in climate that they were to experience in England. One of the Californians, Charles Moore, went down with pneumonia twice and found it very hard to adjust to the damp weather.

Carl Berkowitz remembers that when he got up in the morning he had to take his overcoat out of the wardrobe and hold it up to the kitchen fire downstairs where he would watch the steam and damp rise out of it. He also remembers being astonished when his billetter remarked, after two sunny days in a row: "Wasn't that a lovely summer we had!"

Francis Sullivan also remembers the weather as always being rainy, damp, cloudy and foggy.

"A foggy night during blackout made you feel so blind that you had to grope your way along."

he recalls. On one such night he was out with his colleagues when Cowboy King walked into a telephone pole. "I'll never eat carrots again!" King exclaimed, "I still can't see in the dark."

A feature of England that impressed some of the Americans could be attributed to the damp weather, and this was the abundance of flowers that were growing in the gardens. Many of the Americans came from drier climes where flowers did not grow so well. Even though many of the gardens in Sutton were now used for growing vegetables the G.I.s were impressed with "the lovely lawns and flowers, especially roses" that they saw. Don Whalen considered at the time that the average Englishman took far better care of his home and grounds than the average American.

The single thing that the Americans probably found most difficult to come to terms with was the food situation in England. There was a shortage of many types of food and also there was a distinct difference between the way foods were prepared in England and the United States. The Americans did not enjoy the food cooked for them by the British

BRITISH – AMERICAN DICTIONARY

What did you say?

Mark Twain once said, "Britain and the United States are two countries divided by a single language". Most of us will agree with this, and in the interests of education, togetherness and whatever other things you have in mind, we hope you enjoy these few comparisons.

BRITISH	AMERICAN	BRITISH	AMERICAN
Beastly	Unpleasant	Plus fours	Men's golf knickers
Birds	Girls	Porridge	Oatmeal
Biscuits	Cookies	Postman	Mailman
Bloke	Man	Plimsoles	Gym shoes
Bonnet	Hood (of car)	Petrol	Gasoline
Boot	Trunk (of car)	Queue	Line
Blimey	Holy cow!	Rates	Property taxes
Brolly	Umbrella	Sacked	Fired from job
Caravan	Trailer	Savouries	Hors D'Oeuvres
Castor	Granulated sugar	Solicitor	Lawyer
Chemist	Pharmacist	Spanner	Wrench
Chips	French fries	Sponge bag	Cosmetic bag
Chuck	Throw	Subway	Underground walkway
Crisps	Potato chips	Surgery	Doctor's office
Daft	Silly	Sweets	Candy
Demerara	Brown sugar	Underground	Subway
Digs	Rented room	Torch	Flashlight
Dispensary	Clinic	Turf accountant	Bookie
Dripping	Rendered fat		
Dummy	Pacifier		
Dustman	Garbage collector	**SOME COCKNEY SLANG & OTHER EXPRESSIONS**	
Fags	Cigarettes	Apples and pears	Stairs
Flannel	Wash cloth	Bo Peep	Sleep
Flat	Apartment	Tit for tat	Hat
Frock	Dress	Uncle Ned	Head
Hire purchase	Time payment	Trouble and strife	Wife
Injection	Shot	Round the house	Spouse
Inquirey Agent	Private detective	Whistle and flute	Suit
Iron mongers	Hardware store	Butcher's hook	Look
Jelly	Gelatine	Proper toff	Gentleman
Jumble sale	Rummage sale	Billy Muggins	Sucker
Loo	Toilet	Cheeky	Smart Alec
Lift	Elevator	To flog	To sell
Lorry	Truck	Off the peg	Ready to wear
Macintosh	Raincoat	Gone for a Burton	Disappeared
Minced beef	Hamburger	Stone the crows	Good grief!
Nappy	Diaper	Half a tick	In a second
Nipper	Child	Belt up	Shut up
Pegs	Clothes pins	Linen draper	Newspaper
Pinchers	Pliers	To nip up	To run up
Pinny	Apron	Proper Charley	Fool
Plasticine	Modeling clay		

cooks at the barracks and even when they ate out they couldn't get the sort of food they were used to back home.

Jim Brady of the 17th B.P.O., who was billetted in Sutton for a short time said of the food:

"We appreciated the thought behind their restauranteurs trying to make hamburgers and hot dogs the way we had them at home. Although their hearts were in the right place, the meat was not from the right place or the right animal or sump'n. They deserved an E for effort, but for gastronomic achievement considerably less."*

Leonard Nole remembers that in the teashops in Sutton everything was served on toast:

Beans on toast, tomatoes on toast — whatever was available served on toast. That was because the bread had a dark color to it and it looked and tasted better toasted."

Francis Sullivan remembers a restaurant on the second floor of a shop in the Parade, where he and his colleagues asked:
"What's on the menu?" and received the answer,
"Beans or pilchards on toast." instead of the steak they were expecting. They opted for the pilchards (or, as they knew them, sardines) over which Cowboy King spread a liberal amount of mustard. After one bite he literally jumped out of his chair!

"Mustard back home was mild compared to the mustard they served us."

remembers Francis.

English beverages were also hard to adjust to. Tea was the usual drink in England instead of coffee, and when coffee was available it was a different drink to its milder American counterpart, as English coffee at the time had chickory blended with it.

To make matters worse beer was drunk at room temperature instead of being chilled. Phil Tillar remembers feeling ill after having his first glass of warm beer. This brought an abrupt end to any pub visiting that he might have felt inclined to do. However, only a small minority of the G.I.s were deterred by the warm British beer. Tom Morrissey admits that "We managed a few pints in our spare time." and Don Whalen declares:

"We did our best to help the English drink up beer as fast as the breweries could produce it."

One English meal the Americans did grow to enjoy was 'fish and chips'. There was always a queue of G.I.s at Carrie's Chip Shop' which was located at the bottom of Farthing Lane where it meets Holland Road. Two little old ladies had converted a house there into a chip shop. Carrie served while her friend cooked at the back of the house. A portion of chips could be bought for 3d a bag in those days.

Even at the chip shop the Americans encountered difficulties, this time with the English money, which was "based on an 'impossible' accounting system," according to the Guide to Great Britain. The Americans found it hard to understand that large coins

---

*17th B.P.O. The Invasion Outfit.

Upper Parade, Sutton Coldfield.
(H. Brown)

Sutton Parade, 1943.
(H. Brown)

The Odeon, 1943.
(H. Brown)

did not necessarily mean large amounts of money. Francis Sullivan remembers getting ten pennies change from his shilling when he bought tea and scones from the Naafi. "Each penny seemed as big as our silver dollars." (At the time the rate of exchange was $4.05 for a pound.)

Some less scrupulous individuals took advantage of the fact that the Americans had difficulties with the English currency. Pat Sinsheimer remembers that the G.I.s were often short changed at the cinemas in Sutton. An enterprising G.I. Abe Resnick took advantage of the fact that English money was so different from American currency. He was known as the 'junk dealer' and used to make brooches, bracelets and all kinds of jewellery out of British coins for the men to send home to wives and sweethearts.

Another difference the G.I.s encountered, especially when they were billetted in Sutton homes, was the lack of modern household appliances, items that had been taken for granted back home. Francis Sullivan relates:

> "When we Americans left our home most of us had central heating, refrigerators, indoor lavatories and abundant food."

However the G.I.s were warned not to boast about this in the Guide to Great Britain in a section entitled 'Don't be a Show Off.'*

The last major cultural difference that the G.I.s had to adapt to was driving on the other side of the road. Francis remembers that driving on the right side was a difficult habit to break, especially around roundabouts! Maybe fortunately for the Americans who might occasionally forget which side of the road their left hand drive vehicles were supposed to be on, petrol rationing had put many English motor vehicles off the road for the duration.

Bicycles were a common sight in Sutton. William Walters remembers a time when his group was marching to the Post Office from Wylde Green. He tells the story:

> "We were travelling along Eastern Road when a cyclist came up behind us, he was carrying his chimney sweep paraphenalia, some on his back and some strapped to his bicycle, he was also reading a book. Naturally he ploughed into us. No harm done."

In spite of all the differences that the G.I.s had to adapt to the Guide assured them that:

> "Once you get used to things like [these] you will realise that they belong to England just as baseball and jazz and coca cola belong to us."

It went on to advise that:

> "You defeat enemy propaganda, not by denying that these differences exist, but by admitting them openly and then trying to understand them."

A small number of the local residents did not try to understand the Americans and did not make them feel welcome. As G.I. Andrew Arden says:

---

*Appendix D.

15

There were a few who it seemed went out of their way to vent their anger at us by continuously remarking to us that we were 'overpaid, oversexed and over here.' I am happy to say that they were in the minority. In all fairness to the people some of their gripes were well founded as some of the men were not on their best behaviour. However by and large most of the people were very friendly and did their best to make us feel at home."

Al Lucas remembers the hospitality of the Little Aston Golf Club. When the first contingent of men had been in Sutton about a week a red sports car drove up to Holland Road School and an official from the golf club got out. He offered the use of the golf course to each one of the G.I.s and included the use of the member's personal golf clubs, as long as the men would provide their own golf balls. Those keen on golf soon started sending home for golf balls, which were at a premium in England, to help to keep the club members, aswell as themselves, well supplied.

Tom Morrissey found the people of Sutton more friendly and polite than he expected. He came from New York where "you could be trampled to death trying to board a public conveyance." He was amazed at that British tradition 'the queue' where everyone politely took their place and always waited their turn. He was suprised that everyone in Sutton bid each other good day or good evening even when they passed in the blackout with a torch.

Tom remembers that once he received a postal order from home and was unsure of how to cash it. He went into the bank in Four Oaks where the clerk dealt with the matter. Several days later Tom received a written invitation for himself and his colleague, Jack, to come to tea at the bank clerk's home. They both enjoyed the afternoon and as a token of their appreciation brought candy from the Post Exchange for the family.

Many residents would invite the newcomers around for 'tea'. Phil Tillar remembers receiving invitations from several families who made their homes available to the G.I.s for tea and biscuits and games of monopoly and darts. Kate Kendall (nee Gardiner) remembers that there always seemed to be a houseful of Americans when she arrived home from school.

Betty Watts recalls her youth group at Four Oaks Methodist Church inviting the G.I.s to join them. She remembers that by 1942 most of the group's members were female as the majority of the male element had been drafted into the various armed forces. The group decided to invite the young American soldiers to their meeting. She says:

"When the G.I.s arrived it was decided that this would be a nice way to 'do our bit' for the war effort."

An invitation was sent to the unit commander to invite those interested to come to the meeting. As Betty remembers:

"We offered tea, cookies, ping pong, dancing and friendship. The response was overwhelming."

While the Suttonians offered their friendship and hospitality, in return they received gifts of a more material nature. The G.I.s would often buy gifts from their P.X.s for their English friends. The most precious gift of all, remembers Betty:

"was nylons! Over here only the unattractive rayon stockings were available, and they cost three clothing points. Most girls bought and used leg make up so that points could be saved for more durable items."

The G.I.s also sent home for chocolates, canned goods and many other items virtually unobtainable in wartime England. Many families in Sutton benefitted from American generosity.

Chapter 3

Birmingham Z Calling

"Our Post Office was officially opened for business today."

So reads the entry for July the 1st 1942 in Leonard McDermott's diary. The First Base Post Office began operating on this date in a railway shed on a sidetrack of the L.M.S. Railway near Sutton Park Railway Station. The building still stands today and is little changed.

Remembering back to that date in 1942 Francis Sullivan describes the goods shed as:

"An abandoned building which was poorly lit with no toilet facilities."

The building contained approximately 2,500 square feet of floor space and incorporated a rail link through the one side. 'Johns', or temporary toilets, were erected outside the building. One of the less popular duties was emptying the five gallon 'honey' buckets by hand by carrying them down to the railway station. Some of the enlisted men found this easier to do while wearing a gas mask.

On the day that the Post Office was opened Mr C. A. Edginton was assigned by the G.P.O. as liason officer between the G.P.O. and the First Base Post Office. His main duty was to give advice on the quickest routing of mail between the Base and the various Army Post Offices around the country. Mr Edginton would also handle enquiries for the mail which would pass through both the American A.P.O.s and the British postal system and act as a liason officer between the railway companies and the Post Office.

The Post Office was located about a mile from the Holland Road School and the men were required to march to work at dawn and return at dusk. If they wanted a beer Francis Sullivan remembers that they had to sneak out of line to get to the pub.

"Our short day was ten hours long. Most days we worked twelve hours, not including the time we marched back and forth to work or training."

Francis recalls. The long hours were necessary because the postal workers had to carry out their own administration in addition to the actual post office work. This went on for a number of months until additional personnel were assigned to the Post Office.

The postal workers were told that they were soldiers first, mailmen second. But although they were military personnel Leonard McDermott felt that the unit experienced a minimum of military rules and regulations and once they were established at the Post Office it was simply a matter of 'going to work each day' as millions of other people did.

Tom Morrissey remembers differently and felt that sometimes the military rules were just made for the sake of it. He says:

"We were obedient but didn't always like what we were ordered to do."

He recalls a time when Private Stan Madsen made a face indicating his displeasure when a sergeant told him to do something. When the sergeant saw this he snapped, "What's the matter, don't you like it?" and Madsen replied, "No, I don't like it — you can make me do it but you can't make me like it."

Francis Sullivan worked in the C.O.'s office. He handled all the office work reports, morning reports and correspondence. He had the use of a phone so that he could phone the Post Office in Birmingham and let them know how much mail they were sending to the troops. "Birmingham Z calling" became a code for receipt and delivery of mail and parcels. (Birmingham Z was the name of the railway spur near the station where cars were shunted off for unloading.)

On the first of August 1942 the number 640 came into being as the A.P.O. number for the First Base Post Office, and, from this time on, all mail addressed to American personnel in Sutton featured this number.

The men's job as mailmen was to sort and dispatch all mail received from the United States destined for the American troops who were based in the European Theatre of Operations and North Africa. In the beginning all the mail from the United States to troops in the British Isles was gathered together in New York City, then sent by ship to ports in England and then sent by rail to Sutton Coldfield where it was sorted and directed to the Army Post Offices which had been set up in England, North Africa and Southern Europe.

The function of the First Base Post Office was originally intended to be merely a transfer point for the re-dispatch of sacks and pouches to the location of the Army Post Offices served. Regimental or Battallion mail clerks would pick up the mail from their local A.P.O. and deliver it to their companies. Each company mail clerk would make direct distribution to the soldiers at mail call. The same system worked in reverse, mail from soldiers was collected by personnel in the various A.P.O.s and sent to the First Base Post Office from where it would be sent back to the U.S.A.

Each A.P.O. had a number. Mail to all American military personnel was meant to feature an A.P.O. number in its address. Four digit numbers were used for Stateside ports like New York City or San Francisco., three digit A.P.O. numbers were used for destinations within the overseas areas.

After operations had begun it became evident that 80% of the mail received required distribution by units rather than by A.P.O. designation. The units often moved within the United Kingdom and therefore it was necessary to periodically change their A.P.O. designations. It was essential to maintain a scheme of mail distribution which could be changed daily as necessary.

The scheme locater system, which was supervised by Henry Brown, was responsible for plotting the movement of troops and directing the mail to them. A new scheme would come in every week with the up to date location of the troops. This, of course, was classified information.

Sacks labelled directly for other units were checked on the railway platform against the confidential list of unit locations. Francis Sullivan remembers that Sergeant Jerome Deutschberger worked on this and that he had a phenomenal ability to memorise and recall the unit locations that he directed.

Eventually direct unit pouches of mail became so abundant that port A.P.O.s were set up in England to send them directly to their destinations instead of going via Sutton, thus saving delivery time.

A problem that the postal workers encountered was that most of the soldiers failed to

Railway Goods Shed used as the first Post Office building
(K. Osgood)

Other side of building. (P. Tillar)

Carl Berkowitz of the Guard Detachment on duty at the rear of the Holland Road Barracks.

Original Post Office building seen here in January 1945. New building is in background.
(H.Brown)

advise their correspondents of change of address from the temporary A.P.O. number that they were given on leaving the States. The temporary number was given for security reasons so that soldiers would not know their exact destination. The A.P.O. number for the area was given the men on arrival at their base. The soldier then needed to inform friends and family of the new number. But even if correspondents were notified straight away it took six to eight weeks before mail was coming through correctly addressed.

Often the letter writers would be totally unfamiliar with military terms, titles and units, and in some instances were only barely literate. Frequently they would confuse the soldier's serial number with his company number, regiment number, division number or A.P.O. number. Because of this a lot of the work had to be turned over to specialists in the Directory Service.

The Directory Sevice began on a small scale to handle the mail of the small number of troops in Britain at the time, but during the three and a half years it was in operation it was to expand to assume gigantic proportions.

Each American soldier had a card in the file which gave his name, serial number and unit affiliation. These were filed alphabetically. Every time a division of Americans and their support troops arrived in Britain it was necessary for approximately 20,000 new cards to be filed in the directory. Just prior to D-Day convoys carrying thousands of Americans arrived every week which meant thousands of new cards had to be filed. (One of the enlisted men was so efficient at filing by this time that he could manage 100 cards a minute.)

The directory service was not infallible. Sometimes there would be more than one soldier with a certain name. Francis Sullivan remembers processing a letter bearing the name 'Edmund Wroblewski' that had been returned with two notations 'opened by mistake' stamped on it. Francis couldn't believe that there could be more than one person with that particular name, but when he looked it up he found three, all with different unit assignments.

The mail was censored and the postal workers were not even allowed to mention Sutton Coldfield in their personal correspondence. However the Germans managed to find out the Post Office's location and Lord Haw Haw announced on the radio that Berlin knew that the installation was there and promised it a visit. True to his word on the 28th of July at 2:15 a.m. the G.I.s experienced the worst air raid since they had arrived in Britain. Many homes in Sutton were damaged, but fortunately only four people were slightly hurt. On July the 30th there was another small air raid around 2:00 a.m. when a number of bombs were dropped on Sutton.

During the month of July the personnel were trained in air raid precautions which included fire fighting and the extermination of incendiary bombs. This training had to be carried out outside of the regular eleven or twelve hours per day of postal work.

In his report for the year Major Hartigan commended the men for distinguishing themselves by working such long hours while living and working under adverse conditions. He said that they did this because they desired to play a more active part in the prosecution of the war, rather than just carry out the routine work required in a non-combatant organisation of this type.*

The men were also detailed to carry out fire watching and guard duty. The perimeter fencing around the Post Office and barracks was not completed until February 1943 so it

---

*F.B.P.O. Historical Report 1942.

Registered mail being sorted in the registry section. The bars on the window and a large built in vault were used for the protection of valuable mail. (U.S. Army)

L – R Phil Tillar, Henry Brown, Gene Rothert on guard duty.
(A. Andrews)

23

was necessary for the security to be particularly high until that date. Later a group of G.I.s were selected to form a guard detachment so that the other postal workers did not have to perform, in Phil Tillar's words, "this undesirable duty".

The guards had their base in a requisitioned house in Holland Road. An efficient guard detachment was essential as one of the guards, Carl Berkowitz states:

> "The First Base Post Office was an extremely high security installation because it held the exact whereabouts of every soldier and unit in the American Army."

However Tom Morrissey's opinion of the security at the Post Office was that it was not always as tight as it should have been. He remembers coming in late one day because he had been to sick call. He entered the gates at about 10:00 a.m. without being challenged, he also remembers others coming and going in the same way. Ernie Stoeckal backs him up on this point as he remembers that the outside gates were often left unguarded although the guards were vigilant against theft and misconduct inside the Post Office and would often conduct spot searches of the G.I.s who were sorting mail.

When caught the men were harshly punished for violation of the sanctity of the mail. Tom Morrissey remembers two soldiers being court martialled for this crime. The first he remembers was intentionally stealing from the mail and in his opinion deserved the punishment of a year's hard labour and the loss of two thirds of his pay. Previous to the war he had been a postal employee in a small town in New York State so he was well aware of the severity of his crime.

In the second case the G.I. unknowingly committed the offence. While sorting, this youth of about 20, came across a postcard from a friend of his at home addressed to another soldier based 'somewhere in England'. The youth put the postcard in his pocket to show another friend who worked at the Post Office and knew both parties. Bearing in mind the fact that this G.I. had not had previous experience of postal regulations Tom thought that the man's sentence of six months hard labour in a military prison and the forfeiture of two thirds of his pay was unnecessarily harsh.

The men were all outraged with the guard who had made the arrest, presuming that he did it purely to gain promotion (he was a corporal at the time). A poem was written and printed on the bullettin board at the Post Office for all to see:

> "There was a little guard
> Who saw a picture card
> In the pocket of a coat of a soldier's ware.
> He murmured that's a sin,
> And turned that soldier in
> And now he's bound to make T4."*

Later in the war when the 17th B.P.O. were working alongside the 1st B.P.O. and there were 1680 men working at the Post Office there was evidence of petty thieving. Al Lucas remembers that when the day crew came on duty empty watch and camera cartons were found although armed guards had been patrolling the shift. Al continues:

> "In order to apprehend the criminal, the story goes that Colonel Hartigan had his own gorgeous heirloom watch planted on the work floor. A guard was assigned to do nothing

---

*T4 — Sergeant's grade.

but walk that particular area. Now in true Agatha Christie form the next morning the watch was gone and, I understand, never recovered!"

In August 1942, with the arrival of the new men from Cheltenham operations in the railway shed became quite congested and loading and unloading had to be carried out outside the building, along the railway tracks. The Directory Section also had to be moved into the barracks at the school.

On August the 15th Leonard McDermott recorded in his diary that:

"Rumors are flying thick and fast that we are to be moved from Sutton Coldfield to, of all places, Liverpool."

Several civillians and a colonel came to visit the Post Office and discuss its efficiency and whether it should be moved. Major Hartigan was against the move, and, whether his word held any weight or not, the move did not take place.

Leonard's diary entry for September the 10th notes that the Post Office was:

"Getting new men in all the time now . . . outfit now numbers about 60 . . . Yesterday we got three new vehicles . . . two big trucks and a sedan for the Major."

By the first of October the unit had 62 assigned enlisted men with four assigned officers and one attached officer.

On the sixth of October 1942 the operations were moved fifty yards to a new building being completed especially for that purpose.

Chapter 4

Mail is Piled up in Mountains

Extracts from Leonard McDermott's diary 1942:

"October 3rd — Worked pretty hard all day. Colonel Hahn was here on a visit from Cheltenham. We are now in the process of moving into our new building. It is very large and will be much better to work in. There are rumors that we shall have about 70 more men in soon. I sure hope so. October 5th — The process of moving into the new Post Office building began this morning."

The new building, which was located along the main line of the L.M.S. railway, contained approximately 52,000 square feet of floor space and included a 380 foot long platform adjacent to the railway siding. The loading dock accomodated fifty four railway cars on the siding and seventeen at the platform.

The building was divided into three sections. The southerly portion (about 150 foot long) was the mail processing area, the middle part was the Index or I.D. Room and the remainder housed the administration offices. There was a mess hall at the rear of the Post Office which served a lunchtime meal for the G.I.s Often the men had to work late and they would be served an evening meal there too. The men would always carry their mess gear with them as they would never know where they were going to eat that day.

The unit was by now accustomed to moving into unfinished buildings. A month after the initial move (November the 4th) Leonard McDermott's diary entry reads:

"The whole place here is [still] in a mess, muddy and littered with debris."

The heating and lighting was not completed, so temporary lights were used and small eighteen inch combustion stoves were provided by the British Ministry of Works and Planning.

The central heating was not installed and switched on until the 3rd of December and in the meantime the men had to wear overcoats over their cotton fatigues. The brick building and cement floors contributed to the cold and the small stoves only served to permit the men to warm their hands at intervals. This, coupled with the inadequate heating in the uncompleted Holland Road Barracks, led to the sick rate being exceedingly high during this period. As soon as more efficient heating had been installed both in the Post Office and the barracks there was a general increase in the efficiency of the unit.

When the building was completed the lighting was found to fall below the standard specified in the contract. The men had to wait until March 1943 for the installation of case lighting which improved the lighting facilities and also effected a considerable saving in the consumption of electricity.

As more mail started coming in the unit continued to expand. In October 1942, as Leonard McDermott had hoped, more men began to arrive. Some had docked at

Liverpool on the H.M.S. Hillary and travelled down from there. Others had further to travel when their ships docked at Greenock in Scotland. Phil Tillar, one of these men, remembers the welcome he and his colleagues received as the Argentina arrived in Britain.

The Argentina was one of the ships in a twelve troop ship convoy protected by twelve destroyers, a cruiser and a battleship. The convoy followed the usual zig zag course that was meant to confound U-boats. As they neared the British Isles Royal Navy destroyers and Royal Air Force 'planes joined the protective force. Once within sight of land the convoy dispersed to dock at various ports in the United Kingdom.

All the way up the Firth to Greenock the G.I.s were welcomed by people on the shore waving handkerchiefs. Once they had disembarked girls from the local church served them with tea and biscuits. Later Phil learnt that Lord Haw-Haw had falsely announced on his broadcast that the Argentina was one of a number of troop ships that had been sunk by U-boats.

On October the 12th Leonard McDermott noted that in spite of the recent increase in transport for the unit:

> "Our outfit is so large now that we don't have enough trucks to transport them [the men] back and forth to work so we sometimes have to walk over to the Post Office."

The amount of work was also growing. The work of the Directory Service grew to such proportions during the month of October that additional personnel were urgently needed. Arrangements were made to employ British civillian women part-time on the 'reverse lend-lease plan'. By the end of October 51 women were employed in the Directory Service, thus releasing the postal men for other duties. There were now 130 assigned enlisted men, 6 assigned officers, 4 attached enlisted men and 51 civillians working at the Post Office.

Francis Sullivan remembers the characters of two of the officers he was working under. Captain Jess Poffenbarger placed the importance of mail in a soldier's life high on the list. Francis Sullivan remembers him assembling the men at odd times for a 'pep talk':

> "When you get back home after the war, no one will ask you how many hours you worked or how much blood you sweat. Oh no they'll ask you one thing: 'Did you get the mail out?'"

Fifty years on and Francis is still waiting for someone to ask him that question.

Major Robert E. Hartigan (later to become Lieutenant Colonel) was the Commanding Officer at the Post Office. Unlike the rest of the men he wore dress uniform all the time. Eventually the men learnt to recognise the sound of his Oxfords and would know when he was around.

Major Hartigan was strict and believed in keeping the sanctity of the mail inviolate. He made it clear that this was a binding obligation for all with regard to all types of mail. Francis and his colleagues thought that giving directory service to newspapers coming through the mail with headlines three or four months old was senseless but Major Hartigan insisted that it was done.

Later, when the G.I.s were finding it difficult to handle the amount of mail that was going through the Post Office, letters and parcels were given priority and sacks of magazines and newspapers were laid aside. They were put outside and covered with

The new Post Office building built to the specifications of the U.S. Army for Postal purposes. (U.S. Army)

Loading and unloading mail from the goods vans on the loading dock. (Illustrated)

F.B.P.O. September 1945 Then . . .
(P. Tillar)

. . . and now. F.B.P.O. 1991. (M. Collins)

29

Birds eye view of the main buildings.
(U.S. Army)

Lt. Col. Robert E. Hartigan in his office.
(Illustrated)

Capt. Poffenbarger at his desk 1944. (H. Brown)

tarpaulin until there was a lull. Often there would be quite a glut so the sacks containing the most out of date magazines were discarded.

Magazines were not the only items to be discarded at the Post Office. Alcoholic substances were prohibited in the mail so any found in the earlier part of the war had to be disposed of. Francis Sullivan remembers having to pour whisky down the drain while First Lieutenant Lloyd Arthur (adjutant) supervised the procedure. (Ironically the evenings would find Francis and his colleagues queuing up for a 'shot' of scotch at the local pub.)

Spirits were not always available at the pubs and were often quite hard to come by. Ken Sell recalls that on one occasion the Mayor of Sutton had to be approached to secure some for Lt. Col. Hartigan and his officers. When the spirits were acquired it was considered quite an achievement on the officer's behalf.

Francis remembers another time when a colleague of his was dealing with the damaged packages and came across some tins of pineapple juice. His colleague called him across to see if he would like one, otherwise it would be 'dumped'. Francis opened the tin and took a large drink, nearly choking as he found that it was whisky he was drinking! Somebody had tried to get whisky through the post by putting it in soft drinks cans. Later, to prevent wastage, it was decided that whisky confiscated at the Post Office should be turned over to hospitals for 'medicinal purposes'.

Damaged parcels was the final category of mail that had to be disposed of at the Post Office. Any unsalvageable or damaged items that had come adrift from their packaging and had no means of finding the sender or recipient were dumped then burned. Francis Sullivan remembers an occasion when fifty pouches of mail that had been recovered from the sea months after a shipwreck arrived at the Post Office. These had to be dumped as they were completely ruined and any writing that had been on them had been obliterated.

All incoming bags of parcel post would be opened out onto a 'dumping table' then any objects that had become separated from their wrapping would fall out loose on the table. In the situations where the items could not be matched to their packaging and could not be identified to sender or recipient they would either be termed salvageable or 'trash'. The same would apply to parcels with no return address that were not received because the recipient could not be found or was deceased. Webb Armstrong remembers separating the packages that had no forwarding address on them. He recalls:

"They did not want us to waste too much time looking for an address. It was taken out and burned, I just could not believe what they were doing."

The damaged packages were piled up outside the Post Office at first. Janis Leonard (nee Anderson), who was a W.A.C., remembers that at one point the piles were as high as the Post Office itself.

All undamaged items were meant to be salvaged from the parcels. It was the responsibility of Master Sergeant John Dooley, who headed the parcel post section, to make sure that salvageable items found loose or in parcels with no means of identification were sent to the Salvage Section where they could be processed. Foodstuffs that were unclaimed and in wholesome condition were handed to charitable institutions or military hospitals in Britain. Valuable items were placed under lock and key and kept until claimed by the rightful owner. If the items remained unclaimed they were sent to the Lost and Found Department in New York City for disposal.

The 'trash', or unsalvageable items, were taken by truck, dumped and burned at

Parcel post being sorted in Section C of the main building.
(Illustrated)

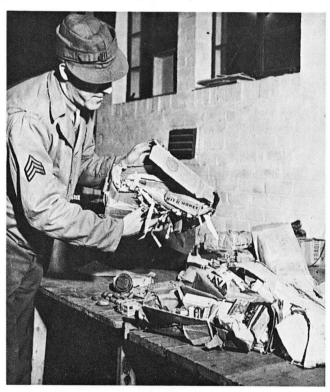

John Dooley sorting out undeliverable parcels for salvageable items.

Minworth, a village on the outskirts of Sutton Coldfield. The local residents found out what was happening when some housewives living nearby spied some broken packages containing, as it was reported in the Sutton News:

"delicious rich cakes, tins of meat and dainties mouthwatering to people still on meagre rations."

Some were bold enough to take the provisions while others, "seething with indignation at the wanton waste", complained to the authorities.

In mid 1945 the Inspector General came down to Sutton to see the situation for himself, and to see if salvageable items were being dumped. He checked the sacks that were waiting at the Post Office to be dumped. These were the sacks of supposedly out of date magazines and unsalvageable items. The Inspector asked one of the men in William Walter's group to bring him a sack and open it. He then fished around inside and pulled out a thin package (not a newspaper or magazine) that was addressed to himself. "Well that did it!" William said, "We all worked overtime for about two weeks reducing the backlog." Major Jernigin, the Commanding Officer at the time, was relieved of his command because of the incident.

Some time prior to this incident, on October the 22nd 1942, the Post Office had been visited by a group of high ranking officers. Included in this party was Major General Lee, second in command in the European Theatre of Operations. After a day of contradictory rumours the men learnt that the General had been instrumental in putting through a 'one day off in seven plan' for them. This was welcome news to the G.I.s who had been working long hours with no days off.

Their relief was short lived as the amount of mail increased with the Christmas rush which started in November. On the 8th of November 2,200 sacks of mail arrived at the Post Office. This meant that even more men were needed for the Christmas period, so postal men were temporarily loaned fom where they could be spared at various A.P.O.s in the United Kingdom. The increase in numbers at the Post Office meant that more construction work was necessary and huts and latrines were built for the new arrivals.

In spite of the increase in the work force on November the 14th Leonard McDermott noted that:

"Conditions over at the Post Office are in a terrible shape. Mail is piled up in mountains and is going out very slowly."

The size of the building restricted the use of any more staff on the day shift so it was decided to bring in a night shift so that a 24 hour day could be worked.

Soldiers from the replacement depots at Whittington and Pheasey Farm (Great Barr) were detailed to work as casuals on the night shift. (Some of the soldiers at the replacement depots awaiting relocation were Americans who had just transferred into the American Army after having served in the British Army and the R.A.F. for the early part of the war.) The regular postal men were assigned as cadres to instruct the casuals as to their duties. The extra manpower in the Post Office meant that it was able to dispatch efficiently to the 38 A.P.O.s it served at this time.

After the Christmas mail had subsided a little light relief for the postal workers was provided on January the 14th when the Duke and Duchess of Gloucester visited the Post Office. Leonard McDermott records in his diary:

MINWORTH DUMP

NEGLECT OF DUTY BY U.S. OFFICER

RELIEVED OF HIS COMMAND

Major D. C. Jernigin, Commanding Officer of the U.S. Army First Base Post Office at Sutton Coldfield, has been relieved of his command for neglect of duty, Brigadier General F. F. Koenig, Commanding General of the United Kingdom Base U.S. Army, announced to-day.

"An investigation by U.S. Army officials disclosed," a statement adds, "that Major Jernigin had failed to follow in every detail army regulations governing the disposal of parcels that have lost their identifying wrappers or are badly damaged in transit.

"Through lack of proper supervision, a very small number of un-damaged items was burned along with articles damaged beyond any possible use or value.

"U.S. Army regulations do not permit, in any circumstances, the destruction of goods that can be consumed or salvaged. Action has been taken by United Kingdom base headquarters to eliminate the conditions disclosed in the investigation."

Villagers at Minworth complained bitterly at the burning of quantities of food and other articles after being dumped in a bomb crater. This state of affairs was first disclosed in the " Birmingham Mail," and a reporter found that tinned food, cakes, whisky, cigars, cigarettes and even watches and lighters were unloaded and set on fire by German prisoners of war working under an armed guard.

Some of the goods were believed to have been sent by the wives, mothers and sweethearts of American soldiers who have been killed in action or are missing.

Sutton Council Not Responsible

The question of the dumping and burning at Minworth of parcels sent to American soldiers, was raised at Sutton Coldfield Town Council meeting last night.

The Mayor said the Council was asked by the authorities to provide a dumping place for refuse, and that what was dumped there was not a matter for the Council, but for the United States Army.

Sir,—I read with horror and disgust of the destruction at Minworth of American parcels containing food and other articles, which are so needed in this country and elsewhere.

In view of recent cuts in food and points, which make it very hard to manage, and the knowledge that German prisoners have been fed so well, this destruction of luxuries seems terrible. Surely the American women who sent the parcels to their dear. ones, would rather they were put to good use, than know they were burnt or tipped into water?—Yours, etc.,

INDIGNANT OLD SOLDIER'S WIFE. Solihull.

Sutton News 1945.

Postal Officer Gets Bounced

For neglect of duty, Maj. D. C. Jernigin, CO of the U.S. 1st Base Post Office at Sutton Coldfield, Warwickshire, has been relieved of his command, Brig. Gen. E. F. Koenig, U.K. Base CG, announced yesterday.

Jernigin failed to follow Army regulations governing disposal of parcels that had been damaged in transit or had lost identifying wrappers, Koenig said. Army regulations, he pointed out, do not permit destruction of goods that can be consumed or salvaged.

An official investigation was made after reports had appeared in British papers that valuable material, including edible foodstuffs, had been burned by APO personnel. Koenig's announcement made clear that only "a very small number of undamaged items" had been destroyed.

Stars and Stripes 1945.

Duke and Duchess of Gloucester (L. McDermott)

"There was quite a party in attendance, including some of our officers. The royal party was making a tour of inspection throughout the Midlands. At about four o'clock they entered the building and everyone was ready for them, the mail started flying as pre-arranged. Colonel Hirzy was escorting the Duchess and as they approached the parcel post section where I was working he asked me to answer a few questions for Her Highness. This I did to the best of my ability. She was very pleasant and charming. But — was my face red! I needed a shave! Everything happens to me!"

Phil Tillar, who was also present on that occasion, was most surprised to find that the Duke was not wearing some kind of regal attire but a military uniform, as were all the members of his entourage. The Duke was not aloof, as Philip thought he would be, but interested in the work and observed closely asking questions about several aspects of it.

Al (third from left) and his crew with G.P.O. Inspectors at New Street Station. (A. Lucas)

By February 1943 the volume of transfer mail had increased to such an extent at New Street Station in Birmingham that the British G.P.O. employees could not handle it and it was necessary to assign some men from Sutton to aid the G.P.O. in that operation. Al Lucas supervised this. There were four crews consisting of a staff sergeant and three enlisted men who worked eight hour shifts day and night in rotation.

Late 1943 saw the peak of operations at the Post Office. The men were dispatching 800 pouches and 5,000 sacks of parcels to the 175 A.P.O.s daily. The dispatches were carried out twice daily at 1 p.m. and 6 p.m. Al was responsible for making up the two complete trains of parcel vans each day, the earlier one consisting of about 15 vans and the later one 20 to 30 vans. These trains were run up to New Street Station where the American personnel, with the assistance of the British Inspectors at New Street, broke up the trains

Post Office buildings seen from Sutton Park Railway Station. September 1944.
(P. Pillar)

The view today. The station buildings were demolished in the 1960s.
(M. Collins)

Night shift sorting first class mail. (Illustrated)

and switched them (using a locomotive which was attached to the Post Office), to various of the six tracks to destinations all over the British Isles.

As regards incoming mail Don Whalen recalls that during the winter of 1943 there were over 100 goods vans loaded with mail awaiting processing at the Sutton Park Railway Station end. He remembers that the British railway authorities were putting pressure on the Post Office to return the vans which were needed for other purposes.

Meanwhile in October 1943 another group of men arrived at the Post Office. Roy Streib was amongst this party and remembers his ship, the Queen Mary, docking in Glasgow. He and his colleagues were honoured to be greeted by Winston Churchill himself who was giving his famous V sign and smoking his cigar. He gave a speech of welcome to the men, shook hands with each of them and then handed out small newspapers which were filled with current events and information on England.

At the end of 1943 yet another party of about 250 soldiers was assigned to the Post Office. On arrival a quarantine period of 72 hours was in order but at the end of this the men were welcomed by Sutton's Mayor at a children's Christmas party hosted by the Americans. Tom Morrissey remembers it as "a pleasant introduction to our new home and friends."

37

Although the men were welcomed by the people of Sutton Tom felt that the new group was not well received by the G.I.s already working at the Post Office. On the whole the existing postal workers outranked the new ones and Tom found them to be distant and aloof for the whole time he spent in Sutton.

Tom and his colleagues started work at a time when the volume of mail was yet again increasing, this was due to the heavy influx of American troops to the United Kingdom in preparation for D-Day. He remembers there being a staggering amount of unprocessed mail and I.D. cards. At this time there were two twelve hour shifts working seven days a week to clear the back log.

Andrew Arden found the work on the night shift tiring. He relates:

> "After a while we would look forward to the air raid sirens for then the lights would be turned off until the 'all clear' sounded and in this way we just sat at the sorting tables and tried to get a few winks of sleep."

Julia Goble (one of the W.A.C.s) remembers constantly falling asleep while on the nightshift, usually while standing up sorting, although once she fell off her stool after falling asleep while sitting down. She was often in trouble with the sergeant who had a good view of Julia's position at the end of the aisle.

Tom Morrissey found the work on the day shift hard, carrying bags around weighing about a hundred pounds each, while he only weighed a hundred and thirty pounds himself. On a 12 hour shift he and another G.I. would manage to process about 30,000 pounds of mail and clear every sack. He felt that his hard work was appreciated as the supervisor, Lieutenant Roszkowski, ensured that he gained a promotion to the rank of corporal. After this he was moved into the Control Section where he had a less manual task working with redirected mail.

Chapter 5

"It's Your War aswell as ours."

Requests for civillian workers were made from October 1942 onwards. This was necessary to relieve the pressure of the long hours worked by the enlisted men and also to give more time for training and recretational programmes. Advertisements were placed in the local newspaper, The Sutton News, to encourage housewives to apply for this 'real war job' and the response was good.

In December 1941 the National Service Act (No. 2) had made unmarried women and childless widows liable for drafting into military service or war work for the first time in British history. The women were required to join the armed services, the land army or take a job in munitions or other war work. Given the choice between these and working at the American Base Post Office many preferred the latter.

When Betty Watts met her future husband she was working at a small munitions factory in Belwell Lane. She had to use a drill press to make ammunition caps but had a hard time making up her quota on 'piecework'. She admits to not being very handy with machinery so when an opportunity arose to work at the Post Office she eagerly accepted the offer.

Many Sutton women were keen to work alongside the 'glamorous' Americans. Maybe they hoped to earn a pay comparable with the U.S. Army pay. The lowest ranks earnt $30 (about £8) a month which was approximately twice what the British lads received. Unfortunately, although the Americans were prepared to pay well the pay agreement came under the Lease Lend Act and was subject to the British Government. The wages decided on were much lower and comparable with the wages of other British war work. Weekend pay was at a higher rate. Frances Lines, who worked 12 hour shifts in the week (8 a.m until 8 p.m.), remembers earning treble time on Sundays.

Hundreds of local ladies were hired to help in the Directory Section where they were employed to search the files to ascertain the correct destination of misdirected letters. The women had to search machine record cards for the correct address of insufficiently addressed mail, incorrectly addressed mail and casualty mail.

Thousands of pieces of mail were mis-addressed or addressed to units that the men had been in previously. Some men had been hospitalised or sent home, so therefore their mail needed readdressing. It was necessary to cross out the original address on a letter or parcel and enter the correct address and A.P.O. number so that the item could be redispatched.

Some women were employed to carry out the sometimes morbid task of working in the 'Deceased Section' where it was necessary to put letters into pigeon holes ready to be sent back to the senders as the intended recipients had died, usually in action. Betty Watts worked in this 'section and found it rather depressing as did Violet Nicholls who got upset when she had to put the 'deceased' stamp on a letter. Although the sensitive did not like to work in this department others preferred it as the work was carried out in the main building which was warmer than the quonset huts where the directory section was now located.

Contrary to expectation the work was not easy and pressure was put on the girls to work

Sutton News 29 July, 1944.

AMERICAN ARMY NEEDS SUTTON WOMEN'S HELP

An appeal is being made to women to take either full or part-time employment at the American Army Post Office in the Sutton Coldfield area.

This post office distributes mail, parcels and telegrams to American troops in a great portion of Great Britain and in France. The tremendous influx of American troops into Great Britain has increased the volume of mail, and the army and civilian personnel of the post office has been unable to keep up with the work involved.

Until the present emergency arose, mail was sorted and moving to the correct Army organisations in less than two days. Now, however, there is danger of letters being left far longer. The value of mail and parcels to American troops, most of whom have been away from their homes for many months, cannot be over-emphasised. Indeed, U.S. Army postal units have moved into France to cut down the time involved in delivery of mail to fighting units.

Meanwhile, it is hoped to increase the staff at Sutton. There are many advantages about the job. The post office buildings are new and well lighted and ventilated. The job for which help is needed is the re-addressing of envelopes. Workers sit at tables with letter-files before them, and supervisors are there to answer queries and facilitate the job. Part-time workers will be welcomed. Allowances are made for domestic circumstances, and women may to some extent select their working periods. The atmosphere is quiet and the salary good, and a generous amount of leave is offered.

Women interested are requested to enquire immediately at the Employment Exchange, Railway Approach, Sutton Coldfield. It is a war job of immense importance to the fighting man.

Sutton News 22 July, 1944.

THEFT FROM U.S. ARMY PARCEL

At Sutton Coldfield Police Court on Tuesday, Mrs. McWatts (23), of Dean Road, Erdington, pleaded guilty to stealing two packets of razor blades (10d.) from postal packages in course of transmission by post, the property of the U.S.A. Army. She was bound over for 12 months, with supervision.

Superintendent Huggard said defendant commenced employment at a U.S.A. Base Post Office on August 8th. A parcel arrived which had burst open; and it should have been placed in a bag for re-wrapping and checking up. Mrs. McWatts did not follow that procedure, but tied up the parcel with string and passed it along to its destination. When the contents of that parcel were checked, two packets of cigarettes were missing.

Detective-Sergt. Morgan and P.C. Terry saw defendant who confessed that she had the two packets of cigarettes in her handbag. The officers also found two packets of razor-blades which the woman also admitted she had taken from another parcel. When charged with theft, she replied " It was a temptation."

The superintendent mentioned that defendant's husband is serving with the Army in France.

Mrs. McWatts said she had received a card that morning that her husband had been slightly injured.

Sutton News 26 August, 1944.

WOMAN'S THEFT FROM U.S. POST OFFICE

Mrs. Ellen Maud Parry, aged 23 years, of 35, Stone-house Road, Boldmere, pleaded guilty in Sutton Coldfield Police Court on Tuesday to stealing two postal-packets (total value, £4 10s.) from the U.S. authorities.

Superintendent Huggard stated that defendant was employed as a sorting-clerk at First Base Post Office of the U.S. Army. On the afternoon of June 21st, Detective Constable Ward was behind the Empress Cinema with P.C. Day. They found some postal - package wrappings bearing American addresses and postal markings behind a blast-wall; and also a photograph torn in halves and a case which had obviously contained the picture.

It was ascertained that at 12.45 p.m. the same day the accused woman and her husband had been seen acting in a suspicious manner behind the cinema.

It was learnt from the U.S. Post Office that defendant had had her meal-break between 12.30 and 1.30 p.m. The same day—at 3.15 p.m.—Mrs. Parry admitted to the police officers that she had stolen two packets during the morning. When charged at the Police Station she said " I have had a lot of worry lately. I don't know what made me take them."

In a statement to a police officer, Mrs. Parry said she met her husband by the Empress Cinema and asked him to come to the back, as she wanted to show him something. When she got there, she pulled two parcels from her bag and opened them. In one there was fountain pen and in the other a picture. Her husband told her to take them back, but she said she could not very well do that as someone might see her. She gave him the pen and threw away the photograph.

Supt. Huggard added that the pen was recovered from the house.

Mr. W. E. Warder (barrister) told the magistrates that Mrs. Parry could not account for the impulse which made her take the postal packets. She could have returned them as suggested by her husband, but she was too frightened.

Supt. Huggard mentioned that Mrs. Parry came into this district from South Wales to undertake work of national importance. She had worked at the American Post Office in Sutton for 12 months, her wages being £3 2s. 9d. a week. In October, 1942, she was bound over at Birmingham for stealing shoes from a shop.

The Mayor (Councillor F. W. Terry) said that the magistrates looked upon this theft at the U.S. Army Post Office as a serious offence. Defendant was fined £5.

Sutton News 7 July, 1945.

Civilian worker asking the advice of Armand Levesque.
(Illustrated)

MOTHER OF FIGHTING SONS CHARGED WITH THEFT

THEFT of a packet (containing articles to the value of 7s. 4d.), the property of the U.S.A. Army Post Office, was admitted in Sutton Coldfield Police Court on Tuesday by Mrs. Charlotte Teresa Farrell (48) of Shortheath Road. Erdington; and she was placed on probation for three years, one of the conditions being that she must not take up any employment except with the consent of the Probation Officer—so that she may not be exposed " to any avoidable temptation."

Supt. Huggard stated that since August 8th defendant had been a part-time clerk at the American Post Office. On the morning of October 25th, she was seen by one of the other clerks, and the superviser—to place a packet in her handbag. The police were informed, and at 12.30 Mrs. Farrell was seen by Policewomen Lee-Dennis, and Det.-

constable Ward, who stopped her and said they had reason to believe she had in her possession a packet which had been taken from the American Post Office. The woman replied: " Yes, here it is." and took the packet from her hand-bag. When charged and cautioned, she said: " I am sorry; I don't know why I did it."

It was mentioned that Mrs. Farrell has four sons serving in the Forces.

The Mayor (Councillor W. E. Lawley) suggested to Mrs. Farrell that if she sent a parcel to one of her sons she would not like to think that there was such a person as herself robbing him of that parcel.

"The magistrates have dealt very leniently with you," the Mayor added. " They hope with a bit of supervision you will pull yourself round and go straight."

Sutton News

					£	s.	D.
No.	1659 (38)			1st B.P.O.			
NAME	Hackedeae, Mrs.						
WAGES WK. ENDG. SAT.	6.11.5						
		£	s.	d.	DAYS 20		
TAX HAS BEEN ASSESSED ON EARNINGS					HOURS	1	15	-
PRIOR TO THIS WEEK					HOURS			
PLUS EARNINGS FOR THIS WEEK					OVERTIME			
TOTAL					TOOL ALLOWANCE			
THE FOLLOWING DEDUCTIONS HAVE BEEN MADE FROM YOUR GROSS EARNINGS.		£				1	15	-
PAY AS YOU EARN TAX					WEEKLY RATE OF PAY INCLUDING ALL ALLOWANCES			
WAR SAVINGS								
HOSPITAL					£3:10:6			
SUPERANNUATION								
ASSISTED TRAVEL					TOTAL DEDUCTIONS			
HEALTH INSURANCE				10				
UNEMPLOYMENT								10
B.P. & E.O., MISC. INST., W.C.	NET AMOUNT PAID £					1	14	2

Mrs Hixon's payslip.

Letter readdressed by worker in Directory Section.

Readdressed letter featuring 'deceased' stamp.

41

at speed. Announcements over the P.A. system gave out the numbers of letters that had been handled that day and urged the girls to process more mail. At the beginning the women did not work as fast as the more experienced postal men had been doing. By January 1943 they managed to average out at 30 letters an hour each which was thought to be 'reasonable', but as time went on they became more proficient.

Doreen Andrew found a little light relief in jotting down any unusual names that the women came across. They were incredulous at the wide variety of names of the U.S. Army personnel. The names reflected the many ethnic groups that comprise the United States of America, including, of course, those of Red Indian origin.

Veronica Smith (nee Hands) remembers re-addressing a quantity of mail for 'Buggs Glendenning' and also coming across the name 'Shot With Two Arrows'. When working on the 'E' files she came across 'General Eisenhower' although she never saw any mail for him. Jeanne Lidgate also remembers being amused by the lip prints on some of the envelopes.

Aswell as the pressure to work at speed the women encountered other difficulties as they settled down to do their job. Those that worked in the quonset huts, outside the main building, got very cold in the wintertime. They would sit with their coats wrapped around their legs to try and keep warm. Alternately, in the Summer it would be unbearably hot in the huts. The women had to sit on hard wooden chairs so many of them would take their own cushions.

The discipline at the Post Office was strict and there were rules and regulations that the women had to adhere to. Cadres would stand over the women and supervise both their conduct and their work. Even the women's posture was under observation. Those who needed to stand all day to do their job would be reprimanded if they dared to lean against the pigeon holes no matter how efficiently they were carrying out their work.

Smoking was not allowed among the women for obvious reasons, although the G.I.s themselves would often annoy the girls by coming into the room smoking. (To be fair, some women did take unofficial breaks to have a crafty smoke in the lavatories.)

There was no canteen for the civilian workers at the Post Office. A trolley would come around mid-morning and mid-afternoon with, according to Veronica Smith, "some horrible tea served up in thick white cups." She remembers that civilians were allowed an hour for lunch so they would either eat sandwiches that they had brought with them or, if they had the money to spare, they would go to Pattisson's Cafe (on the Parade) to eat some kind of 'mince concoction' always served with carrots.

As the women became more skilled at the job supervisors were chosen from their number to maintain the discipline. Doreen Andrew remembers that one used to sit at the end of the long rows of tables watching the women at work although Doreen comments that "she did not seem to do any actual work!"

One particular supervisor that Lily Bagshaw remembers was nick-named 'Horseface'. She wouldn't allow talking but as soon as she left the room it would start up again. Veronica Smith remembers nick-naming another 'The Commandant'. Veronica and the girls on her table were always on the lookout for her as she was often 'on the warpath' and was very unapproachable. Veronica remembers that one day her husband turned up at the Post Office gates unexpectedly. He was in the R.A.F. and he was unable to give prior notice of when he would have leave. When Veronica requested some time off from 'the Commandant' she was severely rebuked although eventually she was allowed a few days off.

A more serious problem that involved the civillian workers was the petty thieving that took place at the Post Office. In a time of austerity in Britain it would upset the women to deal with parcels marked 'abandon if undeliverable', showing that the senders put little worth on the contents. Bearing in mind that the women knew that the contents of ripped packages were often dumped it is not surprising that some items found their way into their pockets.

The guards watched out for instances of theft. One would walk along the loading docks like a prison warder looking into the sorting areas through small windows which made a good vantage point as they were above the eye level of those working inside.

If caught stealing, even if it was just a case of pocketting a few packets of razor blades or cigarettes, the women were liable for a harsh punishment. Some women went further and took whole parcels home to see what treats would be held in them. The authorites were quick to condemn the ladies (or men) who were caught carrying out these 'crimes' although we might think they were understandable given the circumstances.

It should be noted here that, again due to wartime shortages, more serious crimes were committed by some Sutton residents against the U.S. Army. One example was stealing petrol from the American motor pool at Eastcroft Garage. in times of fuel rationing this was a big offence and merited a severe punishment.

Another problem for the authorities, as far as the civillian workers was concerned, was absenteeism. In 1944 this got so bad that the absenteeism rate among the civillian workers averaged between 250 and 300 a day. A campaign had to be initiated to solve this dilemna and a committee of employees and officers was formed to deal with it.

The officers, nick-named 'The Gestapo' by the girls decided that 'pep talks' were in order and reprimanded the women for their slackness telling them: "It's your war aswell as ours." This did not go down well with the employees and several anonymous letters were sent (many by the women's husbands) pouring out the resentment they felt at being treated as if they were being lazy.

In the letters it was pointed out that British women did not need to be told that it was 'their war' with the evidence all around them. Often their nights were disturbed by air raids and many streets in Birmingham had been the target of high explosive bombs. The letters related that the women had homes to keep and shopping to do on a ration card aswell as working long hours at the Post Office. The letters were usually concluded by pointing out that if all this was taken into account the women were doing a good job and they were usually signed from a United States Admirer.

Not all of the Americans were unappreciative of the women's work. Kenneth Osgood, the G.I. in charge of the Unit Directory Section of the Control Section, supervised 80 ladies who checked letters of units outside the E.T.O. This was known as the 'unknown letter' section. He remembers that: "These ladies were hard workers and all got along well" and he goes on to say that he enjoyed working with them.

For many of the English workers this feeling was mutual. The girls often used to dress up in their best clothes to go to work to attract the G.I.s. Even some of the married women would flirt with the Americans who were better off and seemed more attractive than their British husbands. One poor G.I., who had a girlfriend back home, had to ask the advice of his billetters on how to discourage a certain married woman who was pestering him.

Of course not all of the G.I.s wanted to discourage the attention of the 'English Roses'. There were many romances between the G.I.s and civillian workers. Betty Watts remembers that a fair number of the English girls were dating G.I.s and concludes that, "We were a happy bunch."

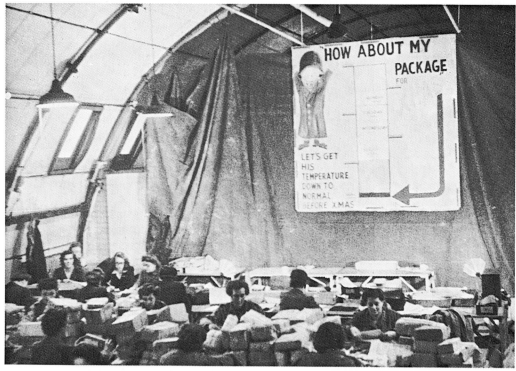

British civilian employees at work in one of the quonset huts. (U.S. Army)

Civilians working in the Directory Section. (Illustrated)

Civilian workers, Mrs Hansen and Rosemary Sewing on Henry Brown's 'Tec' Stripes in the office February 1944. (H. Brown)

G.I.s, W.A.C.s and Civilian workers from Troop Locator Section. (H. Brown)

Civilian employees supplying forwarding addresses to letter mail. (U.S. Army)

Betty got her job through a good word put in by her American boyfriend but Megan Lewis, another Sutton resident, found that this system worked to her disadvantage. She had put her name forward for the job of shorthand typist and was told that she could have the job and start on the Wednesday. The next day the job was handed to someone else. When Megan complained she found that the job had been given to one of the officer's girlfriends, even though Megan was better qualified.

Fair or unfair, the G.I.'s image was such that it attracted romance and this, of course, spread outside the Post Office boundaries and the hours spent working there. Although the postal workers worked long hours, especially at first, there were still some chances to encounter the residents of Sutton, and this was first and foremost achieved by billetting in private homes which commenced in 1943.

Rolling Ball	Harry Fell	Cliff Joneschild	Harlen Walkup
Arch Angel	William Kneebone	Urey Riddle	Francois Beeftink
Newborn Bates	David Medicine Bear	E. J. Peterschick	Tommy Trout
Memory French	Carl Drybread	Vasily Busygin	Manley Pow
Christian Klosset	Geary Gum	John Colliflower	William Prettyman
Bird Ole	Vile Gurganue	Joseph Sir	William Tallbull
Gum Jew	Bunkie Elzey	Dread Rhymes	Virgil Clingingsmith
Adam Two Two	Willie Holderbach	Roman Parent	F. G. Spooneybarger
High D. McBrayer	Christ Fritz	Richard Beenblossom	Devon Spaid
Twitty Mills	Tapley Golightly	Leroy Good Blanket	R. Shote to Pieces
Raymond Passwater	Love Erving	John Looney	Pony Rice
Gordy Foster	Henry Etter	Donal Dean Dunn	Erich Hellhammer
Real Comfort	Berry Eunice	Willie Twitty	Malcolm Greenleaf
Fish Narcisse Sharp	Lit Evres	Truman Well Off Man	Rochester Brickhouse
Grimm Death	Gentle Pride	Floyd Peede	Robert Gathercole
Easily P. Dupree	Grandberry Evans	Ritz Dirtyhole	Vincent Sawma
Wisie Pringle	Wee Fong	Siswof Glomp	John Kills-in-Water
Blonde Freshour	Yee Eye	Fate Dew	Harry Lammy
Olden Franklin	You Look	Lawyer Smith	Lulie Loving
J. O. Cabbagestalk	Alvin Howdyshell	Ken Yee	Cyril Cough
Ascencion Franco	Chariet Papapetrou	True Garrison	Grey Cotton
Stanley Wasmucky	Edward Prettyontop	Paul Loudermilk	Pleasant Young
Merry Frank	Kwong Kee Chin	Bee Postalwait	Daniel Doubleday
Fanniebelle Allen	John Silvertooth	Wash Nolan	Noy Wellbeloved'
Dries Franken	Royal Flagg	You Li	G. P. Whitemagpie
Loveless Babies	Golden Body	Loo Gen	Ivor Sod
Andrew Goodthunder	Reverend Brown	Carl Ruder	Jessie Swearengin
Felix Turnipseed	Park Fish	Vivian Lard	Other Ball
Hedwig Fritz	Raymond Ironteeth	Jesse Piggee	Joseph Two Bulls
Johnnie B. Free	Ramond Manygoats	Clarence Nicewander	Leif Lohne
Boris Friedkies	Albert Manychildren	Dock Mack	William Chattava
Gage Friek	Limberlagger Edwards	Sterling Hatt	How Wing
Carving Elliot	Muffmode Medlon	Fonda Pepper	Harry Risingsun
Jerry Izzy	Goodword Firm	Teddy Goldtooth	Guy Mooney Ham
Windfield Flanders	Shick Mun Su Chong	Norman Retching	Lung Ung
Fern Field	Levi Dreadfulwater	Mellow Pifher	Frank Pansy
Sanford Whiting Fish	Gum Sow Fong	Truly Hammock	Cock Hoyt
Welcome Footq	Chase Fitch	Teddy Poe	Randolph Tallbear
Good Frieday	Greenwood Breedlove	Wesley Unfried	Choice Scalf
Arthur Youngbear	Shuffie Wactor	Donal Moist	Heartiful Locklear
Eldon Toogood	Lucious Berry	Ink Chan	Thomas Nasti
Oliver Redeagle	Alex Stanke	C. B. Byrdsong	HainsfordeColdbath
Berry Birdie	Paul Yellowcloud	Haven Yoho	William Goodnight
Venerable Booker	Raymond Yellowhouse	Noble Capps	Warren Goodlad
Sampson P. One Skink	Earl Yellowhaie	Bong Chung	Ferman Sweetapple
Dinwiddie P. Fehrmeister	Norman Yellowthunder	Charles Under Baggage	
F. W. Muckenfuss	Vernon Looksbill	Sydney Two Foot	
George Roundtree	Erie Oree	Park Yee	
Wash Tapp	Nut Jun Yee	Man Yee	
Robert Goodbody	Sitting Bear	Thin Yee	
Joseph Seacat	Yook Yee	Donald Feelnaughty	
Australia Powell	Paul Finger	Asa Two Dogs	
Mar Chew	Harvard Freeborn	Ross Teehee	
Bing Wong	A. Stands on Island	Zeddie Teagarden	
Lincoln Ching	Noble Fox	Eugene Strawcutter	
Horace Holliday	Razza Fox	Progress Cordova	
Joseph Grandman	Malcolm Seashore	Brumpy Moonshine	

46

O'BRION. RUSSELL & CO.
108 WATER STREET
BOSTON 6

September 14, 1945

C O²-P Y

Levi Yellowboy
Arch Draper
Virgin Rainwater
Human B. Christ
William Bighead

Joe Thickneil
Clyde Muck
Carl Le Count
R. E. Knickerbocker

Curley Drejean

Daniel Elbowshield	Wiley Oke	Ferman Sweetapple	Frank Postma
Lovely Ritter	Earl Beerbower	Rush Gore	Lawrence Upthagrove
Lee Swan,	Sam Sugar	Jack Tripplehorn	Justin Groundwater
Earl Whitehair	Richard Seven Star	Horse Bird	William Bighorse
Mickey Poppin	R.A. Morningstar	Precious Stevens	Floyd Bear Savelife
William Clinkscales	Rollin Rideout	Seaborn Earden	Blue Stayathome
Woo Kew	Lorenzo Courtright	Oddest Beaver	Orvis Ogg
Gawn Chan	Glen Starkweather	S. N. Shoulderblade	Eang Tam
Either Nil	Artie Bledsoe	James Barefoot	Tester Sprinkles
Lum Jung	Albert Middlemiss	Greenland Side	Trinidad Morales
Fred Ax	Steady Painter	Bert Bluelegs	Swept Snow
D. E. Crempacker	Rush Petter	Donald Mumma	
Howard Goforth	Dick Chick	On Chow	
Osvel Godbehere	Gravy Bullock	Lark Allen	
Junior Blue Jacket	James Proudfit	Clair Allchin	
Pearcy Bible	Gee How	Bill Spankus	
Jim Whitecotton	John Lessaongang	William Murmery	
Samuel Battiest	Minus Parsley	William Mushrush	
Harold Fullride	Joseph Golove	Labert Barneycastle	
Alrich Grills	Edward Ruddy	Moon Gale New	
Fred Mantooth	Loren Nitkey	Kelly Gulley	
Charles Bloomingdale	Frank Wagonseller	Roy Pankake	
James La Fever	Frank Flinchaboy	Gordon Kavelpiece	
Woo Yee	Andrew Peed	Carnegie Hall	
Lim Yee	Plummer Underwood	Albert Hall	
Chuch Eye Yee	Calvin Younglove	Hatsuji Hadano	
Bow Yee	C. W. Wounginer	John Oldfather	
Carl Youngflesh	Look You	Ya-ha Aingell	
General Upshurch	Jim Mar You	Garden Ball	
Russell Longnecker	J. Youngdonald	Temple Bowling	
Russell Longnecker	Stephen Sneer	Christmas Arena	
Theophilus Tuttle	Hurley Linebackq	Bright Biggers	
Willie Lilly	Lonard Terrible	Nick Nicksick	
Leon Teal	Harold Rawbottom	Foret Nipple	
Ivory Vann	Guy Tarwater	William Clearwater	
John Youshock	Morgan Goodpasture	Please Polley	
Pink Downs	Looney Tete	Royal Green	
Pleasure Young	S. Nutbrown	Edward Grassmuck	
David Helps	Jack Trueblood	Harvey Greencoow	
Joseph Register	Saul Prick	Rogers Hellman	
Hans Klein	William Tallbird	Desire Heart Herbert	
Garland Sunday	Sunboy Swoop	Ben Teneye	
Douglas Beetlestone	Elwood Tallchief	Horse American	
Dorman Turnipseed	Wash Switch	Raymond Troutwine	
Green Cannon	Charles Mishmash	Bird Dog Harlan	
Orin Tootle	Fanny Wasserman	Crow Chasing	
Ceylon Carman	Jappie Messer	Clarence Spotted Wolf.	
James Yeerout	Dud Summers	Royal Witt	
De Witt Sprout	Lawrence Loves War	Bobo Scrubbs	
James Knuckles	Jerry Swims	Goodloe Stuck	

Chapter 6

Powdered Eggs, Spam and Griping G.I.s

As the number of American personnel at the Post Office increased so the amount of living space available at the Holland Road Barracks became more restricted. By August 1943 there were 10 assigned officers with 218 assigned enlisted men and four attached officers with 48 attached enlisted men.

At the beginning of August there was a request to construct a 600 man camp on the land adjoining the Holland Road Barracks. This would mean that 824 enlisted men could be accomodated there. These plans were waived in favour of billetting in private homes.

The officers were the first to 'move out' from the Holland Road Barracks. Wentworth House, which was two miles from the Post Office, was requisitioned for officer's quarters on the 11th of August 1943. In September Glenfield House was taken over for additional officer's quarters and was available for occupation on the 17th of November. Later Greyfriars House and Richmond House were also requisitioned for the use of the officers.

Before the enlisted men could be billetted messing centers had to be constructed in the areas where the men would be living. These were each planned to serve 250 men, 150 at a sitting. They included a kitchen, mess hut and latrine facilities.

On November the 3rd the Four Oaks Messing Center, which also incorporated a Day Room, was opened. This was situated two miles from the Post Office on the corner of Cremorne Road and Mere Green Road. Private houses now stand on the spot. Francis Sullivan, who was billetted in Moor Hall Park, Four Oaks, relates

"I didn't have to go far for breakfast – powdered eggs, spam and griping G.I.s moaning about it."

He also remembers that after roll call and breakfast, which was at dawn (5:30 a.m.) the men trained in the streets around the messing centre, waking up the residents of Four Oaks with the loud commands, before they marched to work at 8:00 a.m.

The noon meal for the men was prepared at the messing centre, carried to the Post Office and served in the messing hut at the rear. Occasionally after breakfast the cooks would give out brown paper bags containing lunch. When a packed lunch was served Webb Armstrong remembers that "we always had a good supper."

On the 22nd of September 1943 a messing centre was opened in the Maney district on Maney Hill Road. Maisonettes and a car park now occupy the site. On the 2nd of March 1944 Wylde Green Messing Center, on Wylde Green Road near the golf course, was opened.

Andrew Arden spent some time assigned to Ration Detail. This group would organise the rations for the men based in Sutton. Every other day the detail had to go to Stratford to get enough rations for all the mess halls. The ration trucks were then brought back to the Holland Road School yard where the supplies would be divided amongst the various detachments.

William Walter was in the detachment that used the Wylde Green Messing Centre. His detachment worked the swing shift so they never took breakfast but after the noon meal, taken at the messing center, the men would march to the Post Office along the Birmingham Road. Occasionally these men would start out earlier than usual from Wylde Green so that they could have a game of baseball in Sutton Park before work. After work William remembers that they had only 45 minutes to get to a pub before closing time.

To aid in the administration and control of the enlisted men the organisation was separated into detachments according to messing centre assignments. Detachment Commanders were appointed to function under a Headquarters Commander. Battallion Headquarters was a separate detachment and functioned with the usual officer and section assignments such as personnel, supply, plans and training and motor transportation.

Detachment A was based in Sutton, probably in Four Oaks, until 1944 when it was transferred to London to run the V-mail station. Detachment B was originally Maney District but in 1945 a new Detachment B was set up to run a V-mail station on the Continent and Maney became Detachment G. (Their orderly room was in Sandy Banks Road.) Detachments C, D, E and F covered Four Oaks, Penns Lane Camp, Wylde Green and Minworth Camp respectively. Detachment E's Orderly Room and Recreation Hall (Gunya House) was situated in Vesey Road, Wylde Green. The main W.A.C. Detachment was based at Holland Road School from 1944 onwards while the casual W.A.C. Detachment (6888th Postal Battallion), consisting of Negro W.A.C.s, was based at King Edwards School, Moseley, (Detachment H) for a few months in 1945.

Enlisted men having longest service with the unit were selected to move into billets in an area not exceeding one mile distance from the messing centre. The billets were located by the police force who ascertained where extra bedrooms were available for this purpose. Each householder had to list the number of unused bedrooms in their house and were assigned one soldier for each empty room. The exception to this was that houses with only female occupants did not have G.I.s billeted on them compulsorily. At this time British service personnel were already billetted on some of the householders in Sutton so this also made these households exempt from having to billet Americans.

The billetting system was not voluntary but enforced and was resented by some of the residents. To avoid the obligation of billetting some residents immediately called in relatives to occupy any vacant rooms. However most of the households in Sutton were resigned to do their duty as billetters. At one time households with empty rooms had the choice of billetting evacuees from London or G.I.s from the Post Office. Faced with this choice Sutton residents usually chose the G.I.s.

Instructions and information were given to the men to ensure that they did not cause undue nuisance to the householders. The hosts were required only to furnish a bedroom, the Americans brought their own bedding and sleeping bags. No meals were to be served although this rule was not always kept. Don Whalen remembers that his billetters, the Pecks from Cremorne Road, were always trying to feed him out of their limited rations.

David Turney was also offered meals by his hosts, the Coxs. Aswell as this in the Autumn time he would arrive home to find berries, sugar and milk left out for him. While the berries came from the Cox's garden the sugar and milk had been saved out of their rations.

Leonard Nole remembers that the Hall family, who he was billeted with in the Driffold, were marvellous to him. He was on the night shift at the Post Office so he would have breakfast with the family when he arrived home after his shift finished at 7 a.m. He slept all day and then had tea with them in the afternoon before he went back to work at

Four Oaks Messing Center. G.I.s awaiting to board the bus back to the Post Office. (K. Osgood)

The view today. Modern houses now stand on the site of the Center. (M. Collins)

Charles Watts and colleagues standing on the opposite side of the road. (C. Watts)

G.I.'s queueing for meal at Four Oaks Messing Center. (A. Andrews)

Maney Messing Center. The building in the foreground was the kitchen. Meals were prepared here and carried through to the barn beyond. (U.S. Army).

No trace today of the messing buildings at Maney. (M. Collins)

10 p.m. Like other G.I.s he tried to repay the Hall's hospitality by sending home for items for them that were not available in wartime England.

The householder was paid an allowance of one shilling a day for billetting each G.I. Some didn't think that this was adequate, others felt that they didn't need the money. After Ernie Stoeckal had been staying with his billetters, the Shillabeers of Tamworth Road, for a few weeks Mr Shillabeer gave him an envelope, in it there was a pound and a few shillings. When Ernie asked what was in the envelope he was told that it was the rent money that the couple had been given for billetting him. Mr Shillabeer said that they didn't need it and he wanted Ernie to have it. Ernie tried to refuse it but Mr Shillabeer insisted that Ernie keep it. Ernie says that he spent the money and enjoyed it!

Some trouble was expected in getting the men to report in the morning because of the lack of alarm clocks in some of the homes. The 'knocker-up system' was considered. This means that a man is appointed to awake the men in his section by throwing small pebbles or tapping a long stick against the window of a particular room. At the beginning it wasn't necessary to employ this method and for the main part the men reported to their messing centre on time.

David Turney and Harry Tepe encountered a problem when they found that the Cox's had only one alarm clock in the house. David and Harry had to rise at 6 a.m. while the Coxs did not get up until 7:30 so an arrangement had to be made. David had the clock and would wake Harry at six, then he would reset it and leave it outside the Cox's door.

Later, in October 1944 reveille formation (which had been phased out by this time) had to be resumed at some of the detachments because of late risers. At the time it was noted that:

"The majority of the enlisted men are billetted in private homes without alarm clocks. The people of this community are not early risers and the men are not being awakened by the householder resulting in many of them being late."*

Extra duty was given as a punishment for being late and this brought results. Colonel Hartigan noted that:

"For a few days many of the men spent the last hours of the night in a fitful sleep periodically consulting their watches until rising time."*

When it came to finding billets for the men Al Lucas was to find that there was initial suspicion amongst the Sutton householders to the 'horrid Americans'. He tells the story of when he turned up at the Clayton's house in Cremorne Road:

"The assignment of billets, I think, was hysterically funny — especially in my case. On November 3rd 1943 our 60 men were picked up by a fleet of lorries and driven to Four Oaks. It had been decreed by the British War Department that any vacant room in any house was to be available to house American troops. So up one side of the street and down the other this fleet of trucks deposited us and our personal goods at the house to which we were assigned. We were supposed to be restricted to our 'A' and 'B' barracks bags which contained all our clothes and personal items. We were additionally allowed a carrying piece and by now all of us had bicycles. Well, as I deposited my bags, bicycle, record

---

*F.B.P.O. Historical Report 1944.

53

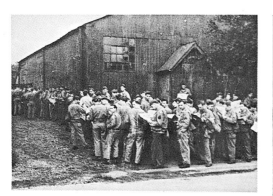

Night crew line up for chow. (U.S. Army)

"WE LIKE HAVING AMERICANS BUT BILLETING PAYMENT IS INADEQUATE"!

We have received the following letter from a housewife:—

Sir.—I think it is time some protest was made against the inadequate ratt pay payment that householders receve for billeting American soldiers, and in particular, the injustice of the discrepancy between the rate paid for officers and that paid for N.C.O.s and privates.

The sum of 7s. per week is nothing like sufficient to compensate for wear and tear caused by their heavy boots up and down stairs and about the house, to say nothing of the hot baths and lights they use.

It is a mystery to many of us why those who are housing officers are paid three times the amount of those who have privates and N.C.O.s. Surely the wear and tear, cost of heating, lighting, etc., is not different.

It is clearly understood that we welcome most cordially these men who are here in this country and so far from their homes, and though we are not expected to feed them, we do so on very many occasions, and are happy to offer them this hospitality.

The point I wish to make is, that the payment is totally inadequate, and now this week there has been a petty reduction of 2d. per day even in the small amount that has been paid hitherto. I believe this is on the score that no lighting or heating is required until after September 30th, even though double summer time ends early in August when it is dark soon after 9 p.m. and it gets dark progressively earlier. Are we supposed to take the bulbs off the electric lights in the bedrooms, and should the weather turn could during our British summer, are these men to sit in unheated rooms?

It is in no spirit of criticism of the men themselves that this letter is written—it is a criticism of our own authorities who pay for the billeting.

Sutton News 17th June 1944.

Gene Rothert outside the Four Oaks messing Center.
(A. Andrews)

Members of the H.Q. Detachment, relaxing.

5 October 1944

AG 620

SUBJECT: US Army Personnel Billeted in British Homes.

TO: Enlisted Personnel, 1st Base Post Office.

1. The following instructions and information are published for the guidance of enlisted personnel of this organization billeted in British homes.

2. Military personnel are entitled to lodging with separate householder's bed, or War Department single or double bunk, with use of toilet facilities, water and lighting, to a reasonable degree.

3. Billeting carries with it only the right to use the room allotted for sleeping purposes, and you are not to expect to have the use of any other room in the house except by express invitation of the householder. Military personnel will not take other people into their billets as only those billeted on the house-holder are entitled to access. Billets shall be kept neat and clean, and making of beds will be the individual responsibility of the soldier concerned, and made in the prescribed manner. All payment for billets is under the control of the British Officer. Moderate use of bathing facilities may be made by agreement between the enlisted man and the billetor. Should private arrangements be made for extra baths, additional service or space, it will be made subject to private payment by the individual. Dim-out regulations will be adhered to, and it is the responsibility of the individual to see that billet is dimmed out properly. In the event that provision for dim-out has not been made, you will report this fact to the billeting Officer.

4. Military personnel will make no undue noise in their rooms, or in coming in or going out. The householders may be war workers and deserve every consideration. Arrangement for the key of the house must be made, as the house must be kept locked. If there is only one key, individuals will lock the door on leaving, and replace the key where the householder wishes. Individuals will be responsible for the safe return of keys given them by householders. Military personnel are reminded that billets are to be treated as their own homes, and that walls, furniture and floor of the room must be kept clean, and not mistreated in any way. All enlisted men will be in billets by 2400 hours each night. Inspections will be made to insure these instructions are being followed, and individuals will be held personally responsible for any mistreatment of quarters.

By order of Lieutenant Colonel HARTIGAN:

WILLIAM R. BROGAN,
1st Lt., AGD,
Personnel Officer.

player, carton of books and violin (picked up for 3 guineas) on the porch I rang the bell. Being a bit of an Anglophile I anticipated a pleasant reception.

"Herewith a good attempt at recreating the reaction and conversation that ensued: Door opens 4″ on the chain. A tiny white haired framed face in the 4″ slot says:

'Oh! So you're one of those horrid Americans.'

A bit taken aback I answer in a slow deliberate tone:

'No, I'm not one of the horrid Americans — I'm one of the nice ones.'

She retorts:

'We know all about you from the newspapers. You smash our pubs, you seduce our girls, you're loud and inclined to be braggarts.'

Finally I answer:

'Ma'am, except for the loudness I think you're exagerating the situation. One pub fight in London or Glasgow doesn't mean it's happening every day in Glastonbury, Liverpool and Tidworth.'

The little lady:

'Well however small a percentage I just wouldn't feel safe.'

The G.I., beginning to lose his composure,

'Lady as regards your safety there are hundreds, perhaps thousands of A.T.S., W.A.A.F.s, Wrens and W.A.C.s in the area and, I would think about 40 years younger than you, who would attract me first. This thing is bigger than us both. Your War Department and my War Department have decided that I will occupy your empty room for the duration. Furthermore, though I have been an Anglophile since Beowolf, 1066 and all that and Robin Hood, I must say that I don't like you any more than you like me . Also there's a war on and, as allies, we ought to get along — so open the damn door.'

Five seconds of complete silence, then the bolts and chains clattered and a wee voice said: 'Come in and have a cup of tea.'

"After this preliminary encounter we got along very well. She introduced me to the hot water bottle, without which I would surely have perished before the year was out. In the ensuing year we lived like parents and son. Her husband, Mr Clayton, was a schoolmaster. I went to the Methodist Church with them on Sundays and on Sunday night we had a hymn singing fest — Mrs C. at the piano, Mr C. with a tenor voice and I on the violin. They were lovely people and we kept in touch with them for years."

Chapter 7

Our Home Away from Home

Mrs Irene Hurley, who lived in Holland Road at the time, also had reservations about having G.I.s billetted on her. In December 1943 when a sergeant and two G.I.s knocked at the door and asked if she could billet some soldiers her first reaction was to say 'no'. She was not obligated to billet as her husband was working away during the week.

Eventually she decided to take in the two G.I.s. The one soldier did not fit into the household and was removed to another billet, but the other one, Carl Berkowitz, got on well with the family. His own son, back home in America, was just a little older than Mrs Hurley's son, Barry, so Carl enjoyed being in a family situation similar to his own.

The Hurley's home was an 'open house' to Carl, he and his friends could come and go as they wished. Carl regarded himself to be 'the luckiest American in Sutton' when he was assigned to the Hurleys. They made him feel welcome and at ease and he found that his year in England, away from his family was made bearable by them.

Carl had a great affection for Barry and would smile to himself as he heard Barry creep into his room each morning, stand on tiptoes and search in his dressing table drawer. Barry would then take out a piece of candy and run giggling out of the room. Carl remembers that he did this every day that Carl was at home although he never took more than one piece.

Mrs Hurley came to think of Carl as a godsend, as his wife back home in America would often send parcels for the family. Carl remembers that when he received a package from home his buddies would crowd around to see what goodies he would get. They would be disappointed to find that the parcel was full of his son's outgrown clothes for Barry and nylon stockings for Mrs Hurley.

Another commodity that Carl could provide was food. Carl knew one of the cooks from the Holland Road Barracks and would often come home with tins of fruit and offcuts of fresh meat. When Carl brought home the latter Mrs Hurley had to get on her bicycle and pedal round to her friends to distribute what couldn't be eaten that day, as this was a time when very few had refrigerators.

On the whole the men preferred living in private homes to the impersonal barracks and would vie with each other as to who had the best deal. David Turney remembers that some got carried away and told of maid service and beautiful daughters which, in most cases, was considerably exagerated.

Francis Sullivan was billetted with the Savekers, whose family are well known for their good works in Sutton Coldfield. Francis was pleased with his room in the spacious house situated by Moor Hall Golf Course in Four Oaks. It had a gas fire in the fireplace and he found this much cosier than the school barracks. Phil Tillar found that there was not much difference between living at the Gees and living in his own home in America with the exception that the taps were the opposite way round to the way they were in his house and there was no central heating. (At this time most Sutton homes were heated with a coal fire in each room.)

Tom Morrissey was with a group of six soldiers who got much more than they were

Carl Berkowitz with his host's son, Barry Hurley.
(I. Hurley)

Gene Rothert with Angela and Clare Supple and their father. (A. Andrews)

David Turney with his billetters the Cox's.
(D. Turney)

Gene with the Supple girls. (A. Andrews)

expecting when they were billeted into the servant's quarters of a large house in Four Oaks. The house, which belonged to the Cheatles, was set in a large estate with well maintained grounds. (Although the family were not allowed servants because of the war, they did have an elderly gent who attended to the gardens.)

The men's rooms were small but comfortable, they had their own bathroom and a separate stairway to the main entrance. They were invited to use a spacious drawing room in the house which was well-furnished. It had a big hearth and glass panel doors which opened out onto the garden. At nine o'clock each evening Thelma Cheatle, the daughter of the house, would serve tea in the drawing room as the men listened to 'Ambrose and his Orchestra' on the record player.

This style of living was a big contrast to that which the men were used to, and probably none of them lived in such opulence again. Tom found it a respite from army regimentation although the men were still bound by strict rules and had to report at the mess hall on time in the morning or face punishment. When Tom's parents heard about the 'gracious outpouring of hospitality' shown to their son they sent packages of tea, sugar cubes and a mixed variety of goodies for his hosts.

Many of the G.I.s repaid the generosity of their billeters in this way. The Griegs would often find a bag of sugar or some other scarce food in their larder, deposited by one of the G.I.s who was billeted on them. When Joe Gardiner asked his billeters, the Beardshaws, what they would like from America they told him that they hadn't had grapefruit since the beginning of the war. He wrote home and after a month four grapefruits arrived at the house. When Mrs Beardshaw cut the first one open she was horrified to find that it was red. She had never seen a pink grapefruit before and refused to eat any before she had watched Joe eat some.

Other G.I.s were grateful for the hospitality they were shown. Arthur Johnson describes his home with Mr and Mrs Roland Kimberley and their daughter, Joan, as 'our home away from home', and he goes on to say, "I'll never forget the many kindnesses they (the Kimberleys) showed me." Joan and her parents enjoyed the company of Arthur and his companion, Charles Moore. She remembers that they were both pleasant, polite and friendly. They treated the Kimberley's home with respect and kept the bedroom they shared clean and tidy. The two G.I.s appreciated the rationing situation and brought home gifts of chocolate and other luxuries from time to time.

Andrew Arden was billetted with several families who all made him feel at home. The first family, the Coxs, (who had earlier billetted David Turney and Harry Tepe) agreed to take in Andrew's brother, who also worked at the Post Office, so that they could stay together. Andrew remembers spending Sunday dinners as one large family. He also remembers with fondness Grandma Cox who, although elderly, had an ambition to go lion hunting in Africa.

Colonel Hartigan, in his official report for the year noted that:

". . . generally speaking . . . the men were made welcome and generously treated . . . and often times (the hosts) treated them as part of the family."[*]

Betty Watts states that:

"Many a local American wound up being treated as a son of his host family and many lasting friendships were formed."

---

[*]F.B.P.O. Historical Report 1943/44.

Her husband, Charles Watts, was billeted in Lichfield Road, Four Oaks with a middle aged childless couple. He remembers that they were wonderful to him going far beyond the call of duty, in fact they treated him as their favourite son, rather than a stranger forced on them. Rose, the lady of the house, put a hot water bottle in his bed each evening which, as in Al Lucas's case, was much appreciated on a cold English winters night. A cup of tea was brought up for him each morning and Rose's husband, Stan, was always pleased to share his precious whisky with his 'adopted American son'.

After Charles' marriage he requested to have his billet changed so that he could move in with his new wife's family. Stan and Rose were most upset to lose him but Charles assured them that he would handpick his replacement. Charles and his wife were to correspond with this couple right up until the mid '80s.

Ken Sell writes of the family ties between the English billetters and their G.I.s. He recently found a letter written to his mother at the time about the close family relationships that had grown between the G.I.s and their adopted English families:

"The letter stated that the G.I.s finally realized that it was no longer prudent to complain about an unhappy or unsatisfactory situation with officers at the 1st B.P.O. because the 'English mothers' had a very protective attitude toward unhappy 'G.I. sons'. These ladies did not hesitate to phone the base and vent their anger on any officer they considered guilty. One matron walked up to an officer on the street and threatened to wrap her umbrella over his head. Beware of the 'English mother' when her offspring was unhappy."

Ken remembers being introduced to his 'British parents':

"On the morning of Good Friday 1944 I was told to get off a U.S. Army truck and a British policeman escorted me to the door of 28, Hill Village Road, Four Oaks. When the door opened the policeman said to the lady: 'Here's your Yank.' I was most embarrassed to be forced onto a stranger's home without first being invited and expressed my apologies. "It was the home of Mr Charles Edmonds and his wife, Rose. I was quickly made to feel welcome and to feel as one of their own. I loved this home and never forgot it. Living with the Edmonds was one of the glowing experiences of my life. They told me that they were my 'British parents' and I truly knew that I was their boy. We corresponded regularly for forty years until they passed away in their 90s."

Ernie Stoeckel was also treated like a son by his billetters, the Shillabeers. He had been billeted with the couple for some weeks when he was told that there had been a mistake in his billeting arrangements because the couple had originally asked for a Catholic to be billeted with them. When the sergeant returned to the house to change the arrangements Hugette Shillabeer told him: "If you move out Ernie you won't be bringing anybody else into this billet", so Ernie stayed.

The couple would always invite Ernie to eat with them when he was at home. Jim Shillabeer even told Ernie to help himself to his beer supply. Ernie took part in their social life and whenever they went out they would invite him along. They would often take him to see a show in Birmingham. Every so often Ernie would borrow Jim's clothes and go out with him as a civilian. (If he had been caught he would have incurred a harsh punishment.) Sometimes Jim would even let him drive his car.

Ernie was always included in family gatherings. One time several members of the

Chuck Moore and Arthur Johnson with their billeters, the Kimberleys. (J. Bashford)

Eddie Sprava with the Hudson brothers, Derek (right) and Maurice. (D. Hudson)

61

family were invited round for a meal and get together. One of the elderly relations enjoyed cooking so he was given the turkey to prepare. Halfway through the meal the relative excused himself and left the table, when he came back he looked worried. When Ernie asked what the problem was the relative explained that he couldn't find his false teeth. Eventually one of the guests found the missing item — as he went to eat the stuffing that had been inside the turkey!

Towards the end of the war Ernie was sent to Tidworth Barracks for combat training and was then assigned to the 376th Military Police Escort Guard as he had been in the Military Police while training at Camp Upton in America. This unit was attached to the Seventh Army. It policed German Prisoners of War and escorted them to P.O.W. camps. This involved travelling all over Europe.

Like most of the postal workers Ernie had not had a furlough while stationed in England. During the time he was in Belgium his Commanding Officer told him that he was due a seven day pass. He decide to spend the time with his 'second family', so he started to make his way back to England. Unfortunately, whilst he was taking a shower at the port of Le Havre, his wallet was taken so he cabled his mother to send some money to the Shillabeer's address. When he arrived at Tamworth Road he gave the family quite a surprise as they were not expecting him, although they were wondering why they had received a letter addressed to him from his mother. They gave Ernie a furlough that he wouldn't forget. He was always grateful to the couple for all that they had done for him.

While Ernie filled the gap in his billeter's family by being a 'son figure' Gene Rothert, billetted in Cremorne Road with the Supples, filled a 'father figure' role. Angela and Claire's father was away for much of the war and Gene helped to make up for this fact. It was Gene who bought Claire a toy horse to help her to learn to walk. In the photo of Gene with his billetters it is Gene who takes the fatherly stance with a hand on Angela's shoulder while Angela's actual father looks the stranger in the picture.

Eddie Sprava fulfilled a similar role in the Hudson family, whose home was in Sunnybank Road, Wylde Green. Eddie was a musician before the war and played with the Sammy Kaye Band whose slogan was 'Swing and sway with Sammy Kaye'. He also played the guitar with the 1st Base Post Office Band during his time in Sutton. Derek Hudson, who was about 15 at the time, was already learning to play the trumpet and he used to practise on an old British one. Eddie told him, "You'll never learn to play on that trumpet!" and he borrowed a brand new American 'Olds' trumpet from the stores for him, which Derek used until Eddie left.

Unfortunately, not all of the G.I.s made good lodgers. Some didn't appreciate the strict rationing that Sutton householders had to cope with. They would arrange to stay in for a meal then, after the householder had saved up the extra coupons to make something special they would change their minds and go to lunch at the local messing centre. Others would wait until the householders had gone away for a few days and then invite all their friends, including girlfriends around. They would make a mess and take advantage of the hospitality extended to them.

This sort of behaviour happened infrequently and most of the Sutton billetters were proud of their G.I.s and sad to see them go at the end of the war. Many Sutton householders found that their opinion of Americans had risen because they had G.I.s living in their homes. Al Lucas remembers that many of the billetters came to wave the soldiers off with tearful faces, although he does go on to say that they didn't earn all this love on their personalities alone — packages from home bringing sugar, lingerie and nylons helped a great deal!

Speaking for the Americans David Turney says:

"I am grateful for having had this opportunity of living with an English family and my only regret is that many more G.I.s did not have the same opprotunity of participating in real 'People to People' diplomacy. From this I learnt that only by mutual exchange are real friendships forged. No proud person is ever satisfied being continually on the receiving end. Because each G.I. and his English host contributed what he could what appeared to be an awkward situation turned out to be a pleasant experience for all, and, in a small way, contributed to better relations between our countries."

Chapter 8

Expansion

By the end of 1943 the Americans needed to find yet more accommodation in Sutton, particularly for those G.I.s working at the Post Office on a casual basis. By the 4th of December Penns Lane Camp, built for 250 men, was ready for occupation. This camp was located on the edge of Wylde Green Golf Course, approximately four miles from the Post Office. The men had to be transported to and from the camp, morning and evening, in buses. As was the case with the other detachments noon meals were cooked at the camp kitchens then transported to and served at the Post Office Mess Hall.

Penns Lane Camp took the nature of a staging camp where new outfits were accomodated. If it was determined that the men were to remain in Sutton for an extended time they were assigned to billetting in private homes with English families.

Andrew Arden spent some time at Penns Lane Camp before being billetted with the Coxs. He remembers being out on coal detail one day and getting particularly dirty. He hurried off for a shower at the end of the shift (about 3 p.m.). Just as he and his colleagues got all lathered up the water slowed down to a trickle and then stopped. They found out later that there was no water pressure at this time of day because Wylde Green Golf Course was watered then. After this incident Andrew ensured that he took his showers a little later in the day.

In April 1944 the 17th Base Post Office (or the Invasion Outfit as they were known) arrived at the Post Office in Sutton with plans to move to the Continent shortly after D-Day. The unit had been activated at Fort Dix, New Jersey and sailed to Greenock on the former French luxury liner, the Ille de France, which was one of the largest converted troopships afloat at the time. From Greenock they travelled by rail to the 10th Replacement Depot in Lichfield where they lived in tents for a short time before moving into the houses at Pheasey Farm Replacement Depot. After another short stay the 17th B.P.O. found, much to their dismay, that they were once more to be billetted in tents at Penns Lane Camp.

Upon their arrival at Penns Lane they found pyramidal tents symmetrically placed in the centre of a large field. Around the perimeter were a series of small nissen huts. Facilities at the camp had to be expanded to accomodate these men. More tents had to be erected and, as the kitchen became overloaded, field ranges were pressed into service. On the 4th of June a detachment from the 347th U.S. Engineer Regiment started to construct a central 500 man kitchen, some winterized mess huts and a branch dispensary. Unfortunately after 5 days work they were assigned to do a job elsewhere.

By this time only the foundations of the kitchen had been completed so the post Utility Officer and his staff had to undertake the task of obtaining the materials and completing the project. Although the men assigned to do this were not skilled craftsmen the work performed under the direction of First Lieutenant Barkholz was efficient and of a professional standard.

The 17th B.P.O. had many 'fond' memories of their time at Penns Lane Camp. Amongst these were: dodging the cow pats; cow rides in the pasture; chasing sheep

FIRST BASE POST OFFICE
AND ALL INSTALLATIONS

FOUR OAKS MESSING
DET. C. REC. HALL &
ORDERLY R.M.
2 Mi. from BPO.

GREEN GABLES
ORGANIZATION SUPPLY R.M.
" MAIL ".
PX. HQ. & SPECIAL SERVICE

EAST CROFT GARAGE
MOTOR TRANSPORTATION
PETROL STATION
1 Mi. from BPO

FIRST BASE POST OFFICE

58 HOLLAND R.D.
E.M. SICK BAY.
HOLLAND R.D. GUARD R.M.

EMPRESS THEATRE
POSTAL SUPPLY STORAGE
3/4 Mi. from BPO

HOLLAND R.D.
BARRACKS WAC DET.
1 Mi. from BPO.

BICKNELL
HOUSE
OFFICERS
QTRS.

GREY FRAIRS HOUSE
OFFICERS MESS
RE-GRADE: OFFICERS QTRS.
ORDER SEC ARMY BY TAG/SC 163
DECLASSIFIED

GLENFIELD
HOUSE OFFICERS
QTRS.

MANEY HALL MESSING CENTER
DET. G. 1 Mi. from BPO.

SECRET

SANDY BANKS HOUSE
DET. G. ORDERLY ROOM.
2 MESS HALLS

WYLDE GREEN MESSING.
DET. E
2 Mi. from BPO.

GUNYA HOUSE
DET. E. ORDERLY RM.
& REC. HALL.

LEGEND
RAILWAY TRACKS +++++++
MAIN ROADS ——
TENTS ◿
HUTS ■

REMARKS
TOTAL NO. BLDG. 121 SQ. FT. 203.481
DISPENSARY AT HOLLAND R.D.
BARRACKS SERVES OTHER UNITS
IN VICINITY
PETROL STA. SERVES AMERICAN
AND BRITISH MILITARY VEHICLES
MESS RATION VEHICLES SERVES
3 UNITS ON 27 MI. RETURN TRIP 3
TIMES PER WEEK

PENNS LANE
CAMP DET. D.
4 Mi. from BPO.

CAMP MINWORTH
DET. F.
6½ Mi. from BPO.

SCALE 3 IN. = 1 MI.

MOSLEY CAMP
12 Mi. from BPO.

65

around the camp; and cows munching alongside tents in the middle of the night and tripping over tent ropes.*

In bad weather this camp got very muddy and in 1944 prisoners had to be employed in laying a brick pavement through the camp. This was made from bricks salvaged from demolished buildings, the result of enemy bombings.

In May of this year a unit guardhouse had been established at Penns Lane Camp for the confinement of prisoners tried by Special Court Martials at the 1st B.P.O. Private H. Monk was the first prisoner, being charged with being A.W.O.L. (Absent without leave). In July Private Monk and another prisoner, Private Prill, escaped by attacking the guard. A disinfectant being used by the prisoners in cleaning the grease trap in the camp was thrown into the guard's eyes, blinding him temporarily and allowing the prisoners to take the carbine with which the guard was armed. Using the butt of the carbine the prisoners beat the guard to the ground and fled the camp carrying the loaded weapon.

An immediate search was instituted by a heavily armed detail and the prisoners were apprehended after several shots had been fired by the guard. Carl Berkowitz was one of the guards to apprehend the men and he remembers that when the guards caught up with them one of the prisoners was threatening to shoot a Sutton policeman. The policeman was calmly trying to talk him into surrendering the weapon. As the man was taken away Carl was amazed to hear the policeman saying: "Boys, mark the time, I'm working overtime." Charges were filed against the two prisoners and they were removed to the stockade of the 10th Replacement Depot at Whittington Barracks.

In November a new unit guardhouse and stockade to accomodate 20 prisoners was built. At the time it was thought to be big enough but even before the end of November the capacity was nearly reached. This was due to a large number of 'casuals' going A.W.O.L. The reason given for this was that they:

"were fed up of being shoved around replacement depots without benefit of leave."*

On the 18th of October 1944 the Post Office was able to take over a camp at Minworth which was six and a half miles from the Post Office. This camp eased the situation at Penns Lane by taking the attached personnel. These quarters consisted of huts and winterized tents as opposed to the summer tents of Penns Lane Camp. Around this time another camp was set up at Streetly. This camp was comprised of Nissen huts and was located in Sutton Park alongside Streetly Lane.

Other buildings in Sutton were taken over for the use of the G.I.s. 58, Holland Road, a house opposite the main entrance to the Holland Road Barracks which belonged to the Northwood-Bathams, was requisitioned by the Americans and served several different purposes. The Special Service Section used a rear ground floor room as their office prior to moving to Green Gables. The Guard Detachment also made use of the house as their base.

From around Easter time 1944 a medical detachment moved into the first floor of the house and established a sick quarters. (Although this was not a hospital as such it was probably the location of the unit known as the 77th Station Hospital.) G.I.s would report there for minor ailments, although 'gold bricking' (shirking) was not encouraged. Julia

---

*17th B.P.O. The Invasion Outfit.
*F.B.P.O. Historical Report. 1944.

Tent City. Penns Lane camp under canvas. (U.S. Army).

Penns Lane camp day room. (U.S. Army).

Goble (nee Lynch) remembers the morning that she had a severe stomach pain. Her colleagues tried to persuade her to go on sick call as she was doubled up with pain, but she wouldn't go (for fear of being labelled a 'Gold Brick',) until her C.O. personally escorted her there. When the doctor arrived at the building he had a look at her and ordered her to the hospital for emergency surgery for appendicitus.

Julia remembers:

> "Unfortunately the medics couldn't get me down the stairs on a stretcher from sick bay because the stairway was too narrow. I ended up going down the stairs backwards one step at a time because I was all bent over and it was much safer for me to go down those steps on my own. My C.O. didn't like it but she couldn't think of any way either."

Green Gables, a large mansion on the Lichfield Road, was taken over by the G.I.s as Battallion Headquarters. This building doesn't exist now but maisonettes with the same name occupy the site. Green Gables was described as large and spacious with beautiful interior decoration. Two unit censors (who originally occupied a small building in the grounds of the Holland Road Barracks), Captain Jordan (the Headquarters Commander), and three other officers were moved there on the 14th of April 1944.

The job of the censors was to remove anything from the men's letters that would give away their whereabouts. They would do this by cutting out any offending words with a razor. It was not possible for this small group of men (which later numbered 20 to 25) to censor every piece of mail that went through the Post Office so it was necessary for them to select certain batches, paying particular attention to units that were due to move.

Green Gables was able to supply storage space for unit supply and post exchange. It did not have messing facilities so the personnel who worked there would eat in the Holland Road Mess Hall. In July 1944 two huts were procured and erected on a site adjoining the main Post Office building. Battallion Headquarters moved into these huts from Green Gables providing additional expansion needed for Battallion Supply and Special Service Sections.

Ken Sell was in the Special Service Section. He remembers that Green Gables was owned by a wealthy family also who owned a department store in Birmingham. Once the owner's sister came to the house and asked to look around. Ken showed her over the place but thought it rather strange when she walked around the garden pulling off the flower heads. The next day he found that the owner was not on speaking terms with his sister and did not usually let her in the house. After her visit she left a note for him saying, "I got in the house thanks to Sergeant Sell." Needless to say, after that incident, Ken was not very popular with the owner.

Another incident at Green Gables that Ken remembers is the time when the three guards fell asleep at their post one evening. The next morning they awoke to find that a herd of cows had wandered into the grounds and were enjoying eating the grass, flowers and vegetables. The men had to report to Lieutenant Kooyman. Fortunately he could see the funny side of the matter and let them off with a minor ticking off.

Opposite Green Gables is 'Leasowes'. This house was occupied by a few officers, who had their bedrooms on the first floor, and a number of N.C.O.s. To the rear of the building there were several quonset huts. The American unit that occupied the building was not connected with the Post Office and was probably some sort of high security counter intelligence unit, although to this day the work of the organisation remains

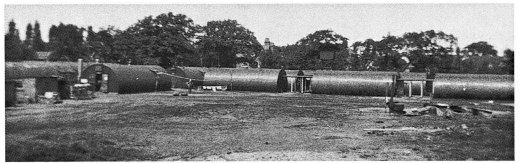

Temporary buildings at Streetly camp in Sutton Park. (P. Tillar).

Rear of Green Gables. (K. Sell).

Front of Green Gables. (H. Brown).

69

Vehicles at Eastcroft Garage. (R. Streib).

Vehicle undergoing maintenance at Eastcroft Garage. (U.S. Army).

As above. (R. Streib).

Buses used by the 1st B.P.O. behind the Empress Theatre Summer 1945. (H. Brown).

TWELVE THOUSAND "DONUTS" A WEEK
DUGOUT "A SWELL PLACE"

By A " NEWS " CORRESPONDENT

The American Red Cross in this country are doing a fine job and the " Donut Dug-out " at Sutton provides no exception to the standard of service. Miss Lorraine Adams, in conjunction with Captain Marjorie Jung, organises the Dug-out, which is the only section of the Red Cross in Sutton. In view of the number of G.I.s there this seems most surprising. So also is the fact that something like twelve thousand doughnuts are sold each week as well as five thousand cups of coffee and bottles of pepsi-cola, a favourite American drink. Four to five thousand American soldiers and W.A.C.S. attend there to "dunk" doughnuts, write letters, read books, and listen to the radio.

The "dug-out" itself is staffed entirely by British voluntary workers from the W.V.S., National Union of Teachers, the Women's Guild, the British Legion, the British Red Cross, the P.O.W. Relatives' Association, and the Electrical Association. Miss Rita Marshall, a voluntary worker from Aston, said that she attended for three nights a week and was only too pleased to do all she could to help the boys, her only reward being their appreciation. These workers do not confine themselves to serving coffee, however: they make themselves responsible for the darning of the boy's socks and clothes.

The dugout makes its own doughnuts with a special machine worked by a full-time cook who is certainly kept busy.

Private Joe A. Menendez and Private First Class Janice Anderson, a W.A.C., both agree that "The dugout is a swell place and the ladies who work here give very good service." There is, however, one big grumble with the "boys." In the words of Private Anthony Gioe, who comes from Brooklyn, New York, it is this: "This place is fine, but we sure could do with a recreation room large enough to house a billiards table, dart board, table tennis, and if possible a dance floor where we could bring in girls to dance." Incidentally, the dugout is barred to civilians and officers; but girls in the Services escorted by G.I.s are allowed in. In fact, the British girls are very popular.

Sutton News 5 May 1945

Example of censoring in 'Mail Sack'.

Motor Pool behind the Post Office building. (R. Streib).   *Eastcroft Garage.* (U.S. Army).

cloaked in secrecy. At the time the men were instructed not to talk about their duties therefore information about the unit is not easily accessible.

The unit was definitely involved in counter intelligence for Operation Overlord and also in sorting and classifying captured Nazi documents and films. It was necessary for members of the unit to read the documents and watch the films before they could file them appropriately and send them to the Army Archives in Washington D.C. As some of the films were rather riske this proved highly entertaining for those who had to view them.

Another building to be used by the Americans was Eastcroft Garage. Although the original building has now gone a garage of the same name stands on the site in Coleshill Road. Eastcroft Garage was requisitoned early in 1944 for use as a motor pool as the original motor pool behind the Post Office was too small by then. By the end of 1944 the Motor Transportation Section had 22 army vehicles, 31 civilian buses, 5 civilian vans, 4 civilian dump trucks and 1 civilian flat truck, so in addition to the area lying to the rear of the garage a parking lot at the rear of the Empress Cinema had to be requisitioned. The Motor Transportation Section was the responsibility of Captain Herbert Bisig and was run by Sergeant Toner. The unit were commended for doing outstanding work providing transport for the entire installation, which by this time was spread out all over Sutton. Roy Streib, who was transferred to the motor pool when he did a good job of repairing Colonel Hartigan's car, did a variety of jobs. In his words he:

"worked as a truck driver, mechanic, drove postal workers back and forth from school to Post Office, till buses took over. At times drove to London to pick up mail, made frequent trips to U.S. support depot at Ashchurch to pick up parts for vehicles, went out on maintenance calls if vehicles disabled on the road."

Practically all the necessary motor repairs were carried out at the garage and only body repair work needing welding had to be taken to the Ordnance Repair Depot. Inspecting officers from higher headquarters were impressed with the quality of work carried out there. The motor pool at Eastcroft Garage was disbanded in July 1945 when the bulk of the men left for France.

In 1945 the old King Edwards School in Moseley was acquired for the purpose of working directory mail and the quartering of various units temporarily assigned to the

Post Office. Seven rooms and a large auditorium were measured and wired to give proper lighting for the working of directory mail.

Another American institution in Sutton was the 'Donut dugout'. It was run by the American Red Cross and was officially opened on the 21st of September 1944. Major Benjamin F. Hartl represented the Post Office at the opening and the house committee consisted of representatives from all detachments. The Donut Dugout (to become The Rendezvous after the war) was located on the Birmingham Road opposite the Cottage Hospital and it was intended to be a place where American enlisted personnel could gather for coffee and doughnuts and relax. It was a popular spot and twelve thousand doughnuts a week were sold there."

Chapter 9

G.I. Jane

In April 1944 the remainder of the enlisted men were removed from the barracks at the Holland Road School to billets in the community. This transition was made to provide a camp for the imminent arrival of a detachment of W.A.C.s.

The Women's Army Corps had become a branch of the U.S. Army in September 1943. (It had existed 15 months previous to this as an auxillary army organisation). It was the policy both in the British and American services to use the women's forces to release as many men as possible for combat duty. This was the case at the 1st B.P.O. where there were plans to transfer some of the postal workers into combat units. The women's arrival meant that there could be a third shift of duty at the base and a 24 hour operation could be carried out as in November 1943.

A certain amount of alteration was necessary at the Holland Road Barracks so that the building would be suitable to accomodate 'lady soldiers'. Nineteen men of the 347th U.S. Engineers Regiment were brought in for the necessary construction. Obviously alterations had to be made to the latrine and ablution facilities. Other less essential changes were made as the women, being the fairer sex, would need more comfortable surroundings than the men. Elaborate post exchange space and a private reading and writing room were a couple of the projects ordered by higher headquarters for the comfort of the W.A.C.s.

Once completed the school was inspected by several high ranking officers of the U.S.Army to ensure that the W.A.C. Detachment would have every convenience and comfort to make their duties overseas as pleasant as possible. The officers were pleased with the work and it was said at the time that the quarters comprised the finest W.A.C. camp in the world.* Janis Leonard describes the barracks:

> "I was in a large room, double bunks − 80 women, long blackout curtains at the windows. Radiators at each end,not much heat. There were 4 bathtubs in a separate building − about 10 or 12 showers in a separate building, a mess hall, our own dispensary . . . The whole area was surrounded by high board fence with guards patrolling all the time (24 on, 24 off). Everything was spic and span. We washed the windows with vinegar water and dried them with newspapers. We cleaned our mess gear with dirt and gravel. We always ate out of mess gear and wore fatigues to work in."

Janis also remembers that it was so cold at night that the girls slept in G.I. underwear, pyjamas and hats.

At the beginning of April 21 women were attached unassigned to the Post Office as the advance detail of the W.A.C. Detachment. Later in the month 79 more women were assigned to the unit. Colonel Hartigan gave a party to welcome this group of women. He

---

*F.B.P.O. Historical Report 1944.

L-R. Verna Crowe, Margaret Malloy, Julia Lynch in front of Holland Road Barracks. (J. Goble).

Ina Anderson and Janis Anderson on cleaning detail. (J. Leonard).

'The finest W.A.C. camp in the world' from the air. (U.S. Army).

L-R. Bernice Beech, Ina Anderson, Janis Anderson and Sgt. Helen Carmody with mess gear. Shower room in background. (J. Leonard).

Margaret Malloy and Julia Lynch outside shower rooms. (J. Goble).

Vera Frome, Amy Rutledge, Betty Luty. (E. Buck).

Holland Road 1945. (H. Brown).

W.A.Cs. at Holland Road Barracks. (H. Brown).

gave a speech of welcome which included a historical sketch of the Post Office unit. 425 enlisted men and women were present at the party.

Andrew Arden relates:
"The arrival of the W.A.C.s brought a little of home back to us, however there was some resentment between the W.A.C.s and the girls of Sutton. Some of the W.A.C.s resented the fact that some of the G.I.s preferred the English girls and vice versa. In time this condition corrected itself without any confrontation on either side."

Julia Goble (nee Lynch) remembers that it wasn't only the teenage girls of Sutton that felt resentment to the W.A.C.s. She relates:

". . . it was very difficult trying to make friends with the English people. The G.I.s didn't seem to have too much trouble but they [Sutton people] didn't seem friendly to the W.A.C.s. We tried very hard but they just seemed to be so distant, as far as us women were concerned.
"I remember walking home to camp one Sunday afternoon, and I came to this house that had the most beautiful big roses I had ever seen. I stopped to admire them and bent over to smell them. (They had no scent.) I couldn't get over how big they were. I just stood there for a few minutes " 'admiring them when a lady came out of the house to see what I was doing. I told her how much I admired her roses and asked if I could have one. 'No.'she said. Then I offered to pay her for just one. No, she wouldn't even sell me one. 'You Americans and your money!' is what she said. I wanted to buy one for my Commanding Officer but she wouldn't sell one to me."

Ken Sell was one of the G.I.s who was grateful at the arrival of the W.A.C.s. As he was in the Special Service Section he ate at the Holland Road Mess Hall. Before the W.A.C.s came he remembers that:

"The regular G.I. cooks served us miserably prepared food. The powdered eggs were the worst of all. They had a terrible stench. No cakes were ever baked because the ovens were supposed to be defective.
"When the W.A.C.s arrived they immediately set about to vigrously clean the kitchen. The scrambled eggs served the first morning were excellent and had no bad odor.
Lovely cake was served in the evening. We quickly went into the kitchen to meet our new W.A.C. friends. We asked, 'How did you do it?' They replied, 'Nothing to it, just stir smaller batches of powdered eggs and beat the devil out of it until the sulphur is removed, then they were edible.
"As for the ovens they suddenly were in operation and producing lovely cakes for us. Hurrah for the W.A.C. cooks we loved them."

Upon the arrival of the W.A.C. Detachment a suitable training schedule was planned. It was decided that the W.A.C.s would be trained by their own officers and N.C.O.s who, in turn, would receive the necessary instruction from members of the Plans and Training Office. The first training course was an intensive course in chemical warfare.
The W.A.C.s did a variety of jobs whilst in Sutton. Some were attached to the motor pool and drove jeeps for the officers, and on occasions trucks. Several had jobs in the Post Office as clerks and typists. The majority of the W.A.C.s were assigned similar duties to

the men and spent most of their time handling mail.

On one occasion, while sorting mail, Julia Goble came across a letter addressed to 'The Standard', a newspaper from her home town in Virgil. She couldn't resist pencilling a brief message to her friend who worked in 'The Standard'office. Her friend, Mrs Fred Lathrop, got the message.

Janis Leonard says of the work she did:

"We worked very hard, hauling heavy mail sacks around, sorting mail and packages. I remember the mountains of packages that seemed to grow and grow — packages sent to soldiers that could not be found."

Julia Goble remembers the work as being strenuous, unloading trucks piled high with full bags of mail. She says:

"We were not supposed to be doing this kind of work, that's what the men were there for . . . [but] we were getting short of men at the Post Office because they were sending a lot of them into combat . . . so we were left with a lot of heavy work. But we never complained."

In July 1944 50 enlisted women were assigned to the First Class Section to work at mail distribution cases. This group was commended for being alert and interested in the work. The unit historian wrote of the W.A.C.s generally that their work was,

"excellent and no matter how difficult the task they always showed a hearty spirit of cooperation."*

When the W.A.C.s had settled into their new living quarters they made several adaptations to the school themselves. In August 1944 a pitchmastic floor was laid over the concrete slabs in the W.A.C. Day Room making an ideal dancing surface. Using the skill of Private First Class Loretta Fretwell (the W.A.C. carpenter) the W.A.C.s constructed a bar in the P.X. It was named G.I. Jane's Bar and it dispensed drinks to W.A.C.s only. The enlisted women were able to relax and enjoy themselves in this atmosphere of 'No-man's land'. The P.X. was later to be rated as the 'most attractive P.X. in the E.T.O.'*

The W.A.C.s eventually made themselves at home in the town of Sutton and got to know some of the locals. Kate Kendall remembers that her grandmother used to do their laundry in return for scarce food such as oranges, bananas or cakes.

On the 25th of November 1944 tragedy struck the W.A.C. Detachment when 32 year old Technician 5th Grade Mary F.Schuyler died of meningitus. Ken Sell remembers seeing Mary several days before she fell ill. She had been working with the cleaning detail at the Holland Road Barracks and complained that she felt very tired. Ken remembers that she looked ill then. The next time Ken went to see how she was she was dead.

Mary was buried on the 1st of December at the American Military Cemetary, Madingley, Cambridge, escorted by her colleagues Tec.5 Bessie Fell and P.f.c. Mary McGuire. Captain Jordan represented the 1st B.P.O. while 2nd Lieutenant Esther Lamprecht represented the W.A.C. Detachment.

The 79 other girls in Mary's dormitory were declared in quarantine for a six day period.

---

* F.B.P.O. Historical Report 1944.

Holland Road Mess Hall. (U.S. Army).

Motor Pool Drivers: ? Yuke, Ilene Hall, Janet Kinney, Cathelene Riggio. (R. Streib).

PENCILS NOTE HOME ON ENVELOPE FROM ENGLAND

When one is far from home there, is always an impulse to maintain contact. This is the story of a WAC in an Army post-office, in England who obeyed that impulse.

A pencil note, "Please say hello, Mrs. Fred Lathrop, Judy" appeared in one corner of an envelope from an Army base in England, addressed to the Cortland Standard.

It is easy to realize how PFC Julia V. Lynch of the WAC felt when she picked up a letter addressed to The Standard. She is a former resident of Virgil and knew Mrs. Lathrop, also of Virgil, employed in the Standard office. And so "Judy" added her note which has been delivered.

Members of W.A.C. Detachment in Directory processing Christmas parcels addressed to temporary A.P.O.s or insufficiently addressed mail. (U.S. Army).

W.A.C. Day Room. P.X. at one end of the room. Room also contains ping pong table, card and writing tables, easy chairs and a sign at the door station: "No beer beyond here". (U.S. Army).

Easy chairs, tables, a radio and phonograph were supplied to make the quarters more comfortable for the isolated group, but at the end of the time the W.A.C.s were glad to be out of their confinement and back at work. Janis Leonard remembers it as "a very frightening time". The Post Office was glad to have the girls back as it was a time (just before Christmas) when they were extremely busy.

In January 1945 meningitus broke out again in the W.A.C. Detachment. Sulfadiazine treatments and daily inspections of throats and chests were instituted for all members of the detachment and 24 and 48 hour passes were cancelled until further notice. On the 9th of the month 28 year old Cecil Champagne died at the 33rd Station Hospital in Lichfield. This time all personnel were restricted to their camps or billets for the next two days.

Corporal Champagne was buried on the 12th of January. She was escorted by Tec.5 Georgia Norman and Pfc. Seraphine Pelegrin. Lieutenant Esther Lamprecht while three other members represented the W.A.C. Detachment. Flowers were sent by Lieutenant Colonel Anna Wilson (W.A.C. Staff Director E.T.O.), Major Mary Weems, captain Margaret Philpot (W.A.C. Staff Director U.K. Base) and the W.A.C. Detachment. Mary Schuyler's and Cecil Champagne's graves can be seen today at the American Military Cemetary at Madingley. Fortunately this fatal disease did not spread any further although many of the British civillian workers were concerned at the time about catching it.

On the 7th of February 1945 Major Charity E. Adams and Captain Abbe N. Campbell were assigned to the Post Office as the advance party of the casual Negro W.A.C. Battalion, the 6888th Postal Directory Battalion, which was due to arrive in Birmingham that week. At the time although there were 130,000 black G.I.s in Britain there were only 130 black American women assigned to this country as nurses and American Red Cross workers. The battallion due to arrive in Birmingham was the biggest group of black women to be seen in Britain up to that time.

On the 12th of February 686 enlisted women and 24 officers were attached unassigned to the 1st Base Post Office. They were welcomed to the E.T.O. by Brigadier Davis, representing General Lee (Commanding Officer of the Commnication Zone), Major Mary Weems (representing Lieutenant Anna Wilson who was in the States at the time) and Major Margaret Philpot. On the 13th they were welcomed to the 1st Base Post Office by Major Jernigin (who had now taken over from Colonel Hartigan as Commanding Officer).

The detachment started work on the 19th of February. They worked the Directory Section at the King Edwards School in Moseley. Seven rooms were set aside for this purpose. The detachment also had their billets in the school. On the whole the black W.A.C.s did not come into contact with the white W.A.C.s as they resided and worked in Moseley. The British Women' Voluntary Service opened the 'Silver Birch Club' as a club exclusively for the use of the negro W.A.C.s.

While they were in Sutton the W.A.C.s organised and attended many social events and functions. On Sunday the 14th of May they commemorated the second anniversary of the Women's Army Corps. This involved several speeches including the main address (given by the Commanding Officer) entitled 'The Importance of the women's work in the war effort toward the defeat of the Axis forces'. In the afternoon an 'Open House' was held at the W.A.C. Barracks. Several distinguished guests were entertained including Lady Coventry (District Director of A.T.S.) and staff, the mayor and Mayoress of Sutton, Brigadier General A. M. Ramsden O.B.E., T.D., A.D.C. (British Army), Wing Commander Kenna (R.A.F.) and Colonel W. Bigwood M.C. (British Home Guard).

The W.A.C. Detachment had several visits from dignitaries. Lieutenant Anna Wilson

DECLARATION

We, the President of the United States of America, the Prime Minister of Great Britain and the Premier of the Soviet Union, have met in these four days past in this the capital of our ally, Teheran, and have shaped and confirmed our common policy.

We express our determination that our nations shall work together. in war and in peace that will follow.

As to the war, our military staffs have joined in our round table discussions and we have concerted our plans for the destruction of the German forces. We have reached complete agreement as to the scope and timing of operations which will be undertaken from the east, west and south. The common understanding which we have here reached. guarantees that victory will be ours.

And as to the peace, we are sure that our concord will make it an enduring peace. We recognize fully the supreme responsibility resting upon us and all nations to make a peace which will command good will from the overwhelming masses of the peoples of the world and banish the scourge and terror of war for many generations. With our diplomatic advisers we have surveyed the problems of the future. We seek the cooperation ...   cont. pg. 2

WAC SECOND BIRTHDAY

On Sunday, May 14th the olive-coated counterpart of the American Army celebrated its second birthday in a colorful round of events. Coming as a climax to the "Salute the Soldier" parade of Saturday, May 13th, which opened the week-end splash of activity, it is chalked up as a complete success.

From 1p.m. until 2 p.m. on Sunday, a message was read by Lieut. Adams, of Public Relations, from the Commander of WBS, Col. Fenton S. Jacobs. A high point of this hour was a short, significant speech by Colonel Robert E. Hartigan on " The Importance of Women in this Global Conflict". Lastly, was the birthday speech delivered WAC Commanding Officer, Lieut. Elizabeth Branch.

At two o'clock -- the doors of HR were flung wide open to the guests of the day-- Lady Coventry and Staff; the Mayor and Mayoress of this borough; Brig. Ramsden, British Army; Wind Comdr. McKinna, RAF; representatives of ATS and WAAF; and other leading citizens of the community.

Last but not least, an evening of dancing, given by the EM of this organization -- reported a huge success!!

Mail Sack Declaration & Second Birthday. No Cap.

6888th Postal Battallion on parade, Colmore Row, Birmingham.

visited the detachment in 1944 and 1945. In 1944 she was accompanied by Captain Margaret Philpot and Major Galloway, who was the personal representative of Colonel Hobby (the overall Director of the W.A.C.).

The officers of the W.A.C. Detachment were also called upon to do their part in official visits. Lieutenant Esther Lamprecht, the Commanding Officer, had to represent the unit in November 1944 at a conference of senior W.A.C. officers which was held in London. At this conference the unit was commended on the excellent record they had and on the fine job which was being carried out by them.

Another W.A.C., Sergeant Ina Anderson, went to London in November for quite a different reason. She was selected by the 'Stars and Stripes' (American forces newspaper) as one of the most beautiful W.A.C.s in the E.T.O. Ina's friend, Janis, who had the same surname, sent Ina's photo in to the 'Stars and Stripes', so it was she who accompanied her to London. Ina took part in the W.A.C. Beauty Contest there and became a runner-up in the final results. For this achievement the two W.A.C.s were able to attend the Army Navy football game at which the winner was crowned by General Doolittle, the Commanding General of the U.S. Eighth Army Air Force. They also attended several luncheons, dinners and dances while in London.

In 1945 Major Charity Adams, Commanding Officer of the 6888th Postal Directory

Battallion, and her executive officer did their part as ambassadors for their country when they lunched with the Lord Mayor, W. T. Wiggins-Davies and the American Consul in Birmingham, Mr Sokobin, at the Lord Mayor's Parlour in the Council House, Birmingham. On Sunday the 13th of May 1945 the battalion celebrated the third anniversary of the Women's Army Corps in a four mile victory parade in Birmingham.

The 6888th Postal Battallion remained at the Moseley School only until the 20th of May 1945 when the whole of the battallion was shipped to Rouen, France, where they were to undertake the operating of a section of the Directory. Meanwhile on the 23rd of January 1945 261 enlisted women of the main W.A.C. Detachment were transferred to the 23rd B.P.O. On the 31st of January the W.A.C. Detachment 1st B.P.O. was inactivated and the 23rd B.P.O. was activated. The majority of the personnel in this unit were sent to France in the Spring while others had gained enough points to be discharged from the service. In May the Holland Road Barracks was derequisitioned and the remaining 51 W.A.C.s were posted to London. At the end of 1945 the members of the 23rd B.P.O. received the Meritrous Unit Service Plaque for their efficient work.

Chapter 10

Off Duty

Because of the nature of the job it was very difficult for the post office workers to obtain any lengthy furloughs. Leonard McDermott remembers having only one 10 day furlough in the three years he was at the Post Office. he also remembers that the men became adept at making the most of what free time they could secure, be it a weekend, a Sunday or an occasional afternoon. Because there was very little time for travelling far afield most of the soldier's free time was spent in and around Warwickshire.

'Many of the G.I.s acquired bicycles and used them to get around Sutton. They were also keen to see the English countryside and would often cycle to Stratford, Warwick, Kenilworth or Coventry. It was necessary to obtain a pass from Captain Jordan for travel outside Sutton. For the part of the war prior to D-Day the G.I.s were restricted to travelling in the area that was within a three mile radius of Sutton. Those G.I.s who were getting married around this time found it necessary to cancel their honeymoons.

The Americans soon made themselves at home in Sutton Coldfield. On the whole they got on well with the people of the town and enjoyed meeting them and getting to know them. Art Johnson remembers that:

"meeting the people of Sutton was best accomplished by attending the various pubs."

Many of the pubs around Sutton became favourite relaxing places for the G.I.s.

The Wylde Green Hotel (Birmingham Road) was popular with the Americans in Detachment E. As reported in the Sutton News:

"Customers at the hotel are endeavouring to make the stay of the Americans in this country as pleasant as possible and have invited them to take part in bowling, table tennis and other games."

A group from the hotel organised several Anglo-American evenings. The main organisers were Mr Harry Parkes, Mr F. C. Dickinson and Captain and Mrs J. P. Brown (the latter two being the landlords of the house). The first event took place in 1944 and on this occasion Mr Dickinson pointed out that the evening (an old English evening) was to be just the forerunner of many they hoped to arrange.

The White Lion, on Hill Village Road, (an earlier pub than the one now standing on the site) was a favourite with the G.I.s of Detachment C. Perhaps the attraction was not just the beer as Margaret Clarke, the daughter of the proprieter, married one of the G.I.s, Staff Sergeant John I. Kallay.

Other pubs in Sutton that were patronised by the G.I.s were: The Kings Arms, The Horse and Jockey, The Crown Inn, The Three Tuns, The Cup, The White Horse, The Fox and Dogs, The Gate, The Duke, The Yenton, The Barley Mow (now Barleys at Mere Green Island), The Dog Inn (now the Knot Inn on The Parade), The Museum (formerly on The Parade) and The Royal. The latter pub was patronised by the officers.

```
                              HEADQUARTERS
                           1ST BASE POST OFFICE
                           SOS ETOUSA APO 640

                                              DEC 23 1943
                                                 (Date)

   McDermott, Leonard W.        ,  T/4  ,   31089082   , is authorized to be absent
        (Name)                    (Grade)    (ASN)
from his duties and station from   1600   ,  DEC 23 1943  to    2300      ,
                                 (Hours)        (Date)         (Hours)
  DEC 23 1943      for the purpose of visiting BIRMINGHAM.
     (Date)
This pass to be turned in to the Orderly Room at expiration.

                         For the Commanding Officer:

_____
 (Signature of Bearer)
                                          Fred W Jordan
Identification Card No._____   _____
                                          FRED W. JORDAN,
                                          Capt., A.G.D.,
         NOT TO BE SHOWN TO UNAUTHORIZED PERSONS   Adjutant.
```

Pass issued to Leonard McDermott.

The G.I.s also cycled out to outlying pubs like The Cock at Wishaw and The Blue Boar (now called The Highwayman) at Shenstone. After she heard a rumour that her Hollywood Screen Idol, Mickey Rooney, would be at The Blue Boar, Eva Cox and her friends cycled there one night. On arrival they were disappointed when they saw the man 'in the flesh'. Eva could not believe that the pimply youth she saw there was the movie star whom she had admired so much.

The Queens Head at Six Ways, Erdington, was also frequented by the G.I.s. Later in the war it became a regular meeting place for G.I.s on furlough from France and their friends in Sutton.

Unfortunately relationships between the English and the Americans sometimes became a little strained in the pub atmosphere. Sylvia Phillips (a Sutton resident) remembers that there were often fights at The Three Tuns, The Dog and The Museum.

Francis Sullivan remembers the time when Cowboy King had an argument with an Englishman over some trifle. They were threatening to come to blows so the Englishman said that they would settle it that evening at 8:00 in front of the Mitchells and Butlers. Cowboy King and Francis duly arrived at Mitchells and Butlers at the correct time, but although they waited the man didn't show up. Later they found that Mitchells and Butlers refers to the name of the brewery, so the Englishman could have been waiting outside any one of a number of Sutton pubs.

As a contrast another form of meeting place was the church. In 1944, when the W.A.C. Detachment was billetted at Holland Road Barracks a chaplain was appointed and held a non-denominational service every Sunday. Also services for three faiths were held at Penns Lane Camp, once that camp had been established. But, at the beginning the unit didn't have a chaplain so the G.I.s attended some of the local churches, in particular Holy Trinity Church, Trinity Hill; St. Peters Church, Maney; the Methodist Church on South Parade; the Congregational Church (now United Reformed) in Park Road; and Chester Road Baptist Church.

David Turney remembers his first visit to the Baptist Church. The Reverend Lawrence extended greetings to the G.I.s from the pulpit and at the end of the service most of the

David Turney and Harry Tepe. (D. Turney).

The Cup. (A. Andrews).

The Royal. L-R. Al and Pearl Lucas, Eddie and Margaret Pedlar, Leonard McDermott, Celia and Don Whalen. (L. McDermott).

Horse and Jockey. (H. Brown).

The Yenton. (E. Ward).

George Meinhausen, Joyce Fuller and Delbert Backhaus (later killed at St. Lo) outside South Parade Methodist Church. (H. Brown).

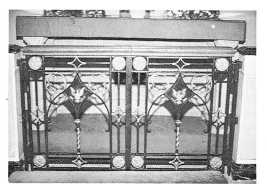

Altar rail in Holy Trinity Church, Lichfield Road.

C. D. Watts and colleague relaxing in Sutton Park.
(C. Watts).

Hugh Zuber, Roy Streib, Paul Decker, James Lamacchia. Kings Arms in background.

Wylde Green

CLUB'S AMERICAN GUESTS

Wylde Green Congregational Cricket Club had an enjoyable afternoon on Saturday. A U.S. Army baseball team visited Britwell Road ground, and played an innings of cricket, followed after tea by baseball.

At cricket the American guests, batting first, made a total of 75, and Wylde Green C.C.C. were able to knock up that score without loss. Tea was served, and the club's chairman, Councillor J. Busby, welcomed the visitors.

and wished them good luck in their future activities. Sergt. J. Pascarofa, for the visitors, thanked Mr. Busby for his good wishes and the club for the afternoon's happy association. Mr. Hadley, on behalf of the guests and friends, also thanked Mr. Busby, and referred to his generosity in defraying the cost of tea and refreshments. Thanks were expressed to Mrs. Hadley for so ably carrying out the catering.

The game of baseball after tea was a high-spirited affair, and concluded a friendly and happy afternoon's entertainment.

Sutton News 8th July 1944.

Weddings of the Week

S. SERGT. J. J. KALLAY AND MISS M. CLARKE.

SEVERAL United States Army officers attended the wedding at Holy Trinity Catholic Church, Sutton Coldfield, on Saturday, of Miss Margaret Clarke, daughter of Mr. and Mrs. Charles Clarke, of the White Lion Inn, Hill, Four Oaks; and a member of the U.S. Army, Staff-Sergt. John J. Kallay, of Detroit (Michigan) and Scranton (Pennsylvania).

Choral Nuptial Mass was celebrated by Canon de Capitan, and Mrs. Nash was at the organ, with Miss Woodward as soloist.

The bride was given away by her father, and wore a white satin gown, with a string of pearls and a head-dress of orange-blossom, holding in place a long net veil. She carried a sheaf of arum lilies.

Two bridesmaids were Miss Maureen White (bride's cousin) and Miss Rosemary Terney, both of whom were in cornflower blue georgette, with bouquets of deep rose-coloured tulips.

M./Sergt. Robert French, also of the U.S. Army, was best man.

A reception followed at the bride's home, when the guests included: Mr. and Mrs. F. G. Butcher, Mr. and Mrs. F. Carpenter, Mr. and Mrs. H. Rogerson, Miss P. Rogerson, Mr. and Mrs. S. Claret, Miss P. Claret, Mr. and Mrs. S. D. Hope, Mr. and Mrs. G. Terney and W./O. G. Terney (R.A.F.), Mr. and Mrs. Postle, Mr. and Mrs. L. C. Spencer, Mr. and Mrs. R. Wilkins, Mr. and Mrs. R. Cooke, Mr. and Mrs. John Lucas, Mr. and Mrs. R. A. Williams, Mr. and Mrs. R. Wilson, Mr. and Mrs. L. J. Iveson, Mr. and Mrs. Showell, Mr. and Mrs. Jacques Brown, Mr. and Mrs. W. Wallace, Mr. and Mrs. R. L. Collins, Mr. and Mrs. W. Askew, Mr. and Mrs. H. Nation, Lt. John Badger, Mr. J. Greensill, Mr. J. Smith, Mr. E. Turner, Mrs. H. Platt, Mrs. and Miss Godwin, Miss P. Saunders, Miss F. Adderley, Mr. J. Butcher, Miss B. Purdy, Miss H. Wakelam, Mr. P. Ruane, the Misses Ruane, Mrs. H. White, Madame Alexandra, Mrs. G. Upton, Miss R. Wheen, and 17 officers and N.C.O.s of the U.S. Army.

Sutton News.

TWENTY-ONE AND FAR FROM HOME BUT HE WAS NOT FORGOTTEN

THERE was an interesting ceremony at the Wylde Green Hotel, Sutton Coldfield, on Saturday.

An American soldier came of age on that day, and a few of the friends he has made at the hotel decided to present him with a memento of the occasion.

It was felt that, as tankards are not used in the U.S., the presentation should take the form of one of these useful articles, and it bears the following inscription:—" To Jim Barry, with good wishes

from his friends in Wylde Green, England on the occasion of his 21st birthday, June 17th, 1944, eleven days after D-Day, we present this typical English tankard to a typical American as a token of our friendship for him and his great country."

Customers at the hotel are endeavouring to make the stay of Americans, in this country as pleasant as possible, and have invited them to take part in bowling, table tennis and other games.

It is felt that arrangements such as these help to cement the growing effectiveness of Allied friendship and those responsible for these events at Wylde Green have expressed hope that other communities of people will organise programmes on similar lines.

congregation came and greeted him personally. The Reverend and Mrs Lawrence and others invited him to visit their homes.

The Catholics attended Mass and other services at Holy Trinity Catholic Church on the Lichfield Road. At that time the pastor was Canon Francis de Capitain, who made the G.I.s very welcome. He even arranged Masses to accomodate their busy working schedule. The G.I.s were very fond of him, after the war he used some of the money received from them to have special gates made for the altar rail with the United States seal and Sutton Coldfield's Tudor Rose include in the design.

Sport also played a part in the recreation time of the G.I.s. Several of them played golf at the Little Aston, Pipe Hayes and Moor Hall Courses. At Moor Hall the G.I.s were allowed to play whenever the members were not using the course. A golf professional there occasionally gave them tips on how to improve their game. Phil Tillar found this "a welcome diversion from the monotony of army life."

Those billetted at Penns Lane Camp played golf at the Wylde Green Course. Jim Brady remembes the time when Lieutenant George Lucas of the 17th B.P.O. had a memorable game there. He:

"eyed the hole a couple of hundred yards away, assumed a faultless stance, took aim, drew the driver back and WHAM, cracked the white spheroid with a whack that resounded for yards. The ball whizzed through the air, straight as a die, and came to an abrupt stop right on the head of a passing sheep. The animal was stunned, but survived. The Lieutenant also survived the ordeal and continued his game."*

The Americans taught the locals to play baseball and then challenged them to matches. For their part the local people taught the G.I.s to play English football and a sport that the postal workers found very strange at first: bowls. The residents also liked to challenge 'the visitors' to darts at the local pubs. The Post Office had teams in some of the pub dart leagues which acquitted themselves well.

Another place the G.I.s could meet the locals was Sutton Park. Don Whalen spent many happy hours walking there and met lots of people. For the first year or so that he was in Sutton there were not too many Americans around so he was somewhat of a novelty and people would often stop to chat.

The G.I.s also went to Trowes Milk Bar on The Parade and Joyce Terry remembers that many love affairs started at Gardeners Milk Bar on the High Street, Erdington. The cinema, of course, was also very popular. Sutton had two cinemas: The Empress (which was situated where the library now stands) and The Odeon at the top of The Parade. Both venues showed all the up to date Hollywood films. As Don says:

"Movies were big and we gave The Odeon and the Empress a lot of business."

Andrew Arden remembers that he enjoyed going to the movies as it helped him to forget about the war and about being far away from home.

A different form of entertainment was to be had at the many concerts that took place around Sutton during the war. Leonard McDermott attended several concerts in Sutton. Among these were 'La Vie Parisienne' put on by Sutton Coldfield Operatic Society and various Celebrity Concerts at the Town Hall. He also attended concerts in Birmingham

---

*The 17th B.P.O. The Invasion Outfit.

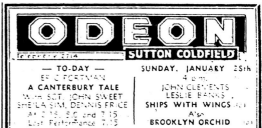

Local cinemas' adverts.

and collected some well-known autographs including Malcolm Sargent, Henry Holst, Yehudi Menuhin and Albert Coates.

Not everybody likes to just sit and listen to music. Many of the young G.I.s liked to dance, as did the young people of Sutton. There were numerous dances during the war years. Some were held at The Orange Grove (later to become Crystal Palace) in Sutton Park and some at the Guild hall (on Lichfield Road). Kate Kendall remembers that there used to be fights between the G.I.s and R.A.F. airman at The GuildHall. M.P.s would often have to step in to sort the trouble out.

Dances at Maney Dance Hall (the Parish Hall of St Peters) were popular before and during the war. Each Saturday there would be a lively band like The Ronnie Hancox or Ray Challenge Orchestras. Doris Hendley and her mother-in-law helped with the refreshments which were included in the admission price. She remembers that the Americans were always sticking their gum on the bottom of the cups and saucers, which would end up as a sticky mess in the washing up bowl. In the end an announcement had to be made to stop the men from doing this.

Betty Watts remembers that Maney Dance Hall was 'the' popular gathering place for groups of boys and girls. She recalls:

"You rarely took a partner with you, it was 'the done thing' to go with a group of friends of your own sex and hopefully meet someone there."

As Maney Hall was a parish hall no alcohol was allowed so if you wanted to pop out to the 'local' (Horse and Jockey) you had your hand stamped so that you could get back in. Although the G.I.s thought it strange that girls would attend a dance unescorted (a thing apparently 'not done' in the U.S.) they did approve of the 'pass out' idea and Betty recalls that many literally did 'pass out' at The Horse and Jockey.

The night shift from the Post Office also enjoyed attending dances. A dance hall called 'The Casino' in Corporation Street, Birmingham, held a dance with a 'big band' every Monday afternoon. This was convenient for the men as they could be back from the dance in plenty of time to start their shift at 10 p.m.

Sutton Town Hall was another popular venue for dances. On the 23rd of September 1943 the enlisted personnel at the Post Office held a 'Yanks Ball' where Bebe Daniels, stage and screen star, attended with some of the cast of her current show 'Panama Hattie'. She gave a short performance during the course of the evening.

As temporary inhabitants of Sutton the Americans were welcomed at most, if not all, the social events in the town. In their turn the G.I.s were glad to involve themselves in the community outside their long work hours. As Leonard McDermott says:

"I think it is fair to say that we entered fully into the activites of the community as time and circumstances allowed."

Chapter 11

An American Son-in-Law

"The Americans were passionately fond of children, even those that hadn't got families of their own. They liked nothing better than to be allowed to 'walk the buggy' if they met any of us walking babies. I met and made many friends when walking my God-daughter. No-one took offence at being approached by the Americans in this way."

remembers Joyce Terry.

The G.I.s were very popular with the children of Sutton. Youngsters used to stand at the gates of Holland Road Barracks and also sit on the fence surrounding the waste ground opposite the barracks (now a car park) and ask for gum and candy. Kate Kendall (then Gardiner) remembers being given 'Hershey bars' and 'Lifesavers' by the G.I.s. Don Whalen remembers giving so much chewing gum to the children that every time he went out he was greeted with the well-known phrase: 'Got any gum, chum?' In fact one G.I. used to ride around Sutton with a sign on his bike that said: 'Sorry, no gum, chum.'

Tom Morrissey used to give the children the apples and oranges he was given at the mess hall for dessert with his meal. He felt that it was just a small thing to share although it obviously meant a lot to them. Andrew Arden remembers saving his orange for six year old Jennifer Law. He realised the far reaching impact of the war when Jennifer's mother said that she would not know what it was as they had had no fresh fruit since the outbreak of the war.

In 1943 the men organised a Christmas party at the Holland Road Barracks for the children who lived nearby aged 5 to 16. Music, food, gifts and entertainment were donated by the men of the Post Office. The older children provided some of the entertainment themselves. Tom Morrissey remembers a very talented 16 year old playing the piano.

At Town School (formerly in the building used by Sutton Baptist Church) some of the Americans came to introduce themselves and talk to the children. This gave the teachers the opportunity to teach subjects such as American History. Miss Davies, one of the teachers, taught her pupils to sing 'The Star Spangled Banner'. The lesson was taught well as Kate Kendall can still remember the hymn word for word.

Not all of the G.I.'s encounters with Sutton's children were entirely friendly. Henry Czerniak light-heartedly tells of one incident in the G.I.'s newsletter, 'Mail Sack':

"If you have seen snowmen walking about camp recently you might wonder how such a miracle came into being. As I was one of these many white miracles I can assure you that it was not a condition of one's choosing.

"It was after the recent snowfall that could be called 'the white Christmas we've been singing of', that a trio of us decided to go to town. Brother, did we go! The moment we set foot outside the gates of our post we were targets for all the snowballs in England, it seemed. Since we are soldiers, we couldn't let a little affair like this , cooked up by 50 to 60 kids flanking either side of the street, stop us, so we did the least soldierly thing – run.

AMERICAN SOLDIERS' CHILDREN'S PARTY.

American soldiers gave a party to nearly 200 children at Sutton Coldfield on Christmas Eve. After a concert by an American troupe, each child received a huge plate of ice-cream and a parcel containing American candy, which had been given up by the troops for the benefit of the children.

The Mayor and Mayoress (Councillor and Mrs. W. E. Lawley) visited the party with Colonel Hartigan and Capt. Jordan.

Sutton News 1st January, 1944.

Pat Sinsheimer, (left) and her cousin, Jean Hassell outside the Empress where she worked and met Bob. (P. Sinsheimer).

London orphan, Janet adopted by F.B.P.O. 1943. (P. Tillar).

```
                    HEADQUARTERS
              1ST BASE POST OFFICE
              APO 350, U.S. ARMY
                                        3 October 1945

            C E R T I F I C A T E

      This is to certify that the following named EM, a member
of my command has made application for leave to the United
Kingdom on or about 11 October 1945. His application for marriage
on or after 21 September 1945 has been approved.

      Sinsheimer, Samuel, Sgt. 32351913
```

THOMAS J. BELL, Jr.
Major, AGD.,
Commanding.

Once we had run the pelting line we thought we would be safe, as the kids would wait for other gullible Americans. But −

"After we had brushed off the snow and had a hearty laugh about the incident, two girls, about 15 I suppose, allowing us to pass with the most angelic smile on their faces, suddenly sneaked behind us and bathed the face of the fellow on my right with a generous portion of snow. Before we had awakened to our predicament they were gone. Immediately, we decided these happenings would never include us again. But are we masters of our destiny?

"On our way back to the post we prepared some snowballs ourselves to use only as mollifiers, and as a further precaution we walked in the middle of the street right back to the scene of our infamy, our faces split in the widest of grins, relieved grins mind you. The street was deserted save for three youngsters who were standing directly in front of a fence which was on the other side of the street. None of the kids had snowballs. We looked silly with ours. I noticed the other fellows let theirs drop rather unobtrusively, and so did I. We breathed easier, relieved.

"One of the kids asked, 'Got any gum, bub?' None of us had. He looked at us pityingly and smiled. Then, with a war whoop. yelled, 'The Yanks!' Fifty to sixty faces appeared over what had been a bare-faced wall a moment before. So −

"I put up the collar of my coat, removed my cap, picked up and laid down my shoes faster than I have ever done. All the snow did not hit me, but you couldn't prove it if you had seen me."

On the whole the G.I.s loved the children and did what they could for them, often providing an 'uncle' figure while many of their real uncles and fathers were away fighting. In 1943 the Post Office 'adopted' a little girl called Janet, who had been orphaned in the London Blitz and was being fostered by a family in Sutton. A collection was taken up among the G.I.s to help pay for her upkeep.

The G.I.s also 'adopted' fourteen year old Sutton boy, Ronald Orton, and financed his education at Lawrence College. He lived near the Holland Road Barracks and would often visit his American benefactors there where he would be given sweets and candies. In November 1944 Ronald was 'guest of honour' at one of Colonel Hartigan's official dinners.

The teenagers of the town looked up to the G.I.s as older brothers. The relationship between Bob Sinsheimer and Pat (his fiancee)'s brother, Des Fellows, was a special one. Des would often turn up at the Post Office where Bob worked to help him stamp papers, lend a hand in the P.X., or go for a jeep ride. The jeep was not Bob's only form of transport. He had a bike and would often give Des a ride on the back. On one occasion a local policeman stopped them but it was Des who got the reprimand as, being British, he should have known better. Obviously the policeman regarded this as the sort of behaviour that one would expect from a 'Yank'.

When Pat Fellows first met Bob her parents had already forbidden her to have anything to do with the Americans. Parents of teenage girls made up the one section of the community where the G.I.s were not popular at first. Most parents warned their girls off dating the Yanks as they were 'only after one thing'. Sylvia Phillips, Pat's cousin, was warned by her parents that they'd have her guts for garters if she got 'mixed up' with them. Betty Mason's mother threatened to cut her legs off at the knees if she had anything to do with them. On the whole this opinion was to change as the parents got to know the G.I.s better.

One night Pat arrived home with Staff Sergeant Bob (Samuel) Sinsheimer, a telephone

Photo: H. Chapman, New Oscott.

SGT. S. SINSHEIMER AND MISS P. FELLOWS

SERGEANT SAMUEL Sinsheimer, son of Mrs. and the late Mr. Samuel Sinsheimer, of Brooklyn, New York, and Miss Patricia Fellows, daughter of Mr. and Mrs. Thomas Fellows, of 9, Chavasse Road, Sutton Coldfield, were married last Saturday at St. Peter's Church, Maney. The Rev. F. S. Golden, vicar, conducted the service. The church was decorated with white and gold chrysanthemums.

The bride was given away by her father. She wore a gown of shell-pink satin with a silver cross, the gift of the bridegroom, and carried a bouquet of pink chrysanthemums.

Two of the bridesmaids— Miss Rita Fellows (sister of the bride) and Miss Jean Hassell (cousin of the bride)— wore dresses of lemon net over taffeta. The other two— Miss Maureen Fellows (sister of the bride) and Miss Gwen Ryder (cousin of the bride)— wore pink net over taffeta. All carried velvet muffs, and wore gold bracelets, presents from the bridegroom.

The bride's brother, Corporal Thomas Fellows, was best man. The bride's mother wore a dress of black georgette, with black accessories, a spray of pink chrysanthemums and a silver fox fur.

Fifty guests attended the reception at the bride's home. The honeymoon is being spent in London.

Sutton News 27th October, 1945.

Bob and Pat Sinsheimer (P. Sinsheimer).

Al and Edna Jennings. (E. Jennings).

94

Pat and Bob's wedding 20th October, 1945. (P. Sinsheimer).

Bob and his brother with the Fellows family.

95

operator at the Post Office. She had told her parents that she was going out with an English soldier so she said 'goodbye' to Bob at the garden gate as she didn't dare invite him in. Unfortunately her father arrived home while they were standing there. He was furious and strode straight past them, not giving Pat the chance to introduce her new boyfriend.

Pat had met Bob at The Empress where she worked as an usher. Bob had to bribe her friend, Cathy, with a dollar to take him to meet her. Later Bob took Pat to the pictures and wanted to pay for her but Pat's pride wouldn't allow her to accept this so she insisted on paying for herself. This led to an argument and, in the end, Pat said she would throw the money away if he wouldn't accept it, which is what happened. Needless to say next day, at the crack of dawn, Pat was to be found on hands and knees searching Holland Road for the money!

When Pat's parents could see that she was serious about Bob they agreed to meet him. They invited him in and offered him cheese on toast, then left the room to make it. While doing this the air raid siren sounded, so of course, the family disappeared into the shelter leaving poor Bob sitting there waiting a long time for his toast!

Once Pat's parents had met Bob they found that they all got on well. In fact Pat used to complain that Bob saw more of her dad than her as they often went to play snooker at the British Legion. One of the main things that endeared Bob to Pat's parents was his sense of humour. As Pat says, "He was always fooling around." Every Valentine's Day Bob would make up a card of Mother-in-law jokes that he had cut out of magazines and papers. After getting a friend to sign it he would post it to Pat's mother. She always knew who it was from.

Pat's mother was determined to get her own back, so, one day she waited until she could see Bob coming along the garden path and then placed a bowl of custard by the window, above the front door, ready to throw on his head. Unfortunately for her the insurance man came along at that moment and, being polite, Bob stepped back for the other man to go first. One can imagine the rest and suffice it to say that Pat's family did not open the door to the insurance man that day!

Bob was true to the reputation of the Americans as regards their generosity. Once, at the train station, Bob saw someone selling ration books on the black market. He paid a substantial amount of money for a set for Pat's mother only to find that they were out of date and of no use.

Bob often did a duty at the P.X. At the end of his shift he would sometimes creep up the road to Pat's house with a big tin of sugar or some other luxury item from the stores. Once he tried to sneak out with a large ham but was caught by the Adjutant who asked him where he was going.

"To the larder." was Bob's answer.

"Well, you're going the wrong way!" was the reply from the Adjutant.

Bob proposed to Pat one lunch hour while they were sitting on the churchyard steps at Trinity Hill. The following day he arrived at Pat's house with a ring and formally asked her parent's permission. They agreed, but Pat's mother remembered that she had seen a much nicer ring at the hock shop in Aston. Bob wasn't the sort to be offended so he took his ring back to the jewellers shop in Sutton with a tale of being jilted, fortunately they believed his story and refunded him so that he was able to go and buy the 22 carat sapphire and diamond ring that Pat's mother had seen.

The couple had an engagement party at a dance hall in Birmingham which the Post Office cooks made a cake for. Shortly after this Bob was posted to France. While he was

Ray and Jean Lasker (J. Lasker).

there he sold many of his possessions to the French so that he could send money home to Pat for the wedding.

Pat and Bob were married at 3 p.m. on the 20th of October 1945. Pat wore a borrowed wedding dress of pink silk and dyed her headdress and shoes with pink food colouring to match. Pat's older brother, who was in the British Army, went A.W.O.L. to attend the ceremony. (Unfortunately the next day he was arrested by the M.P.s) Many of Bob's colleagues from the Post Office attended and the civilian workers who worked under Bob at the Post Office clubbed together their clothing dockets to get the pair a set of twill sheets.

As Bob got to know Pat's family through meeting them Pat got to know Bob's family through letters. She became fond of Bob's mother, Charlotte (his father had died when he was young), and his two brothers (one she met while he was stationed over here). She received, in her words, "some lovely letters and presents" from them. The brothers sent jewellery and silk stockings, presents very much appreciated in the austerity of wartime Britain.

Towards the end of the war Bob's mother died and he was allowed to leave the army early on compassionate leave. He returned to the States to deal with the arrangements for the funeral. After this he set up a fish and chip shop in New York which he planned to invite Pat over to help him run. Before Pat could travel to the States a double tragedy struck her family. First her father, then her 24 year old sister died. Pat sent a telegram to ask Bob to come back to England for the funerals. He came and then stayed here until he sadly passed away in 1978. Bob enjoyed living in England and got on well with the people of Sutton. Coming from New York he found things quiet over here and he couldn't understand why everything was closed by nine or ten o'clock at night.

Sutton girl, Edna Sowter and her G.I. husband, Al Jennings, also settled down in England after their wedding. Al, who was originally from Pennsylvania, was living in England along with his sister and father at the outbreak of the war. The family had come overseas to manage a mill in Yorkshire. Al went to London to enlist into a combat unit but was sent to Sutton Coldfield to the 1st B.P.O. in 1944.

At the time Edna was living with her widowed mother and three sisters in Walmley. Her mother worked part time at the Post Office and when some vacancies arose she told 16 year old Edna, who applied for and got a job there. Edna was put to work in the quonset huts at the Post Office and this is where she met Al who was working in the First Class Section.

Shortly after she had started work at the Post Office Edna went to a dance at the Guild Hall with a friend. Al came in with two colleagues and when he saw Edna he came straight over. From this date they courted for twelve months and then Al proposed on the bridge on Wylde Green Road in a romantic moonlit setting. He was posted to France shortly after this but came back to England to get married. The couple were married when Edna was just eighteen at St. John's Church, Walmley and honeymooned in a farmhouse in Pwllheli.

Edna knew that she could not leave her mother and go back to the States with Al. Al, for his part, was not close to his own family, who were due to travel back to the States, and did not mind settling down over here. At first the Jennings lived in Walmley with Edna's family. They later moved to their own house in Penn's Lane.

Pfc. Ray Lasker was with the 30th U.S. infantry Division when he was injured fighting at St Lo shortly after D-Day. After a brief stay at the 22nd General Hospital he was assigned to the 1st B.P.O. and billetted with the Weavers of Britwell Road, Boldmere. He met Jean Butler on a blind date arranged by her sister, Megan. When Megan broke the news to her that she had arranged the date, Jean said that she would only be interested if her date was taller than her.

The four met up for the date and Jean found that although Ray was shorter than her they got on well together and walked arm in arm from The Yenton to the Odeon in Sutton. After only a week the couple realised that they were falling in love. Ray asked Jean's father's permission and they were engaged in May 1945. Ray was interviewed by an officer at the Post Office and given permission to marry Jean although, as was the usual practice, they had to wait 60 days for the wedding.

The couple were married at Erdington Parish Church on the 14th of July 1945. Jean had borrowed a wedding dress from her next door neighbour and painted a pair of her shoes silver. Megan Butler was bridesmaid and a friend of the family made her dress out of material that cost one shilling and eleven pence a yard. Megan trimmed her hat herself and also painted her navy blue shoes silver. After the wedding Ray and Jean enjoyed a week's honeymoon in Barmouth.

After the war Jean travelled to America to join Ray. The couple were unable to get their own house so at first they lived with Ray's parents. Later they lived in a trailer on a trailer park. After spending five years in America Jean' father fell ill so the Laskers both travelled to England to see him and ended up settling down over here.

98

Chapter 12

Sweetheart of the Forces

Another G.I. bride was Betty Gardner. She met her future husband on a most appropriate date, December the 7th 1943, the second anniversary of the attack on Pearl Harbor, and also the date that the United States of America joined its British allies in their fight against the Axis forces.

As mentioned earlier the Four Oaks Methodist Church invited the Americans along to its youth club. At this time the G.I.s were expected to work long hours at the Post Office, Sundays included. If they signed up for attending church they were allowed the time off so when the Methodist Church gave the G.I.s the opportunity to have some time off work, naturally a number took it.

On December the 7th the youth club was putting on a short play. Betty (a member of the club) was wearing an elegant black dress to play her part and felt that she looked 'fetching' in it. She continues her story:

"After the play was over we mingled with our guests, 'blue boys'*, 'G.I.s and a few English soldiers, serving them tea, cookies and entertaining conversation (we thought!). When it was time to close a nice looking blond G.I. came over to me and asked if he could 'carry me home' (meaning could he take me home). My mother had warned me against 'those fast Americans' so I was a little hesitant but decided I would let him push my bike for me. I reasoned that if we had the bike between us I would be safe! He told me later that he and his good buddy both wanted to 'carry' me home but he 'sicked' the buddy onto 'that good looking blonde' (my best friend). I invited him into the house to meet my mother and as we parted he said he would like to see me again and would be back the following Saturday night. Mamma thought he seemed a very nice young man but warned me not to be too disappointed if he did not come back.

"Saturday night it was pouring with rain and even darker than usual. All the houses were 'blacked out' on account of the air raids, cars and lorries were permitted only a small slit in their headlights, so a passing vehicle was not much help when you were trying to find a strange place in the dark. But he made it! Apparently he had gone to the next road over from us, had knocked on a door and was given the needed instructions to find me. He arrived wet and with a large box of chocolates, a rare treat in those days.

"Our first 'real' date (in the sense that we went out somewhere rather than being in my home) was to see 'This is the Army', the musical written by Irving Berlin for W.W.1, then redone for W.W.2. I believe it was playing at the Theatre Royal. It was a wonderful show and Irving Berlin himself played the same part as before. His great hit was 'Oh how I hate to get up in the morning'. He did not have much voice but it was a great thrill to see such a famous man in person.

"During our courting days we would go with my mother and some of her neighbourhood friends to the White Lion pub and also to the Blue Boar at Shenstone.

---

*British casualties.

Betty and Charles Watts. 'Sweetheart of the forces'. (E. Watts).

This involved rather a precarious bike ride, since there was no petrol available for pleasure purposes, and with the prevailing 'blackout' the roads were somewhat hazardous. I shall never forget one particular night on the way back from Shenstone. My generous husband to be had given one of mamma's friends a surplus G.I. overcoat. This garment was rather long and the man wearing it was rather short. We were all happily pedalling away when a convoy of army lorries came sweeping down the road. Everybody hastened over to the side to wait until the convoy had passed but the unfortunate man became entangled in the back wheel of his bike, What a to do! Next thing we knew we saw him scrambling along on his hands and knees, dragging his bike behind him. It seems very funny now, but at the time it could have been a tragedy since with the headlights so dim the lorry drivers probably would not have seen him until too late to avoid him. However, all's well that ends well, we untangled him from the bike and made it safely home.

"Our courtship lasted ten months and on my 20th birthday my American gave me a beautiful diamond solitaire ring purchased from my jeweller grandfather and made by my uncle."

Betty admits that ten months was considered very short by English standards. She remembers that at the time tongues wagged and people started 'counting' and wondering if she 'had' to get married, although this was not the case.

Betty and Charles were married at 12 noon on October the 7th 1944. She remembers her wedding day vividly:

Charles Watts (E. Watts).

Betty and Charles Watts. (E. Watts).

"We had a lovely wedding, white dress, long train and a bouquet of pink and white carnations with a matching headpiece. I had borrowed the outfit from a friend, a very common occurrence at that time with clothing coupons being so limited. I wanted a nice going away outfit and the points were not enough to cover both. My father's oldest brother gave the bride away and his daughter was my only attendant. My other girl cousin, who would have been there, was serving in the A.T.S. Chester Carter (a G.I. from the Post Office) was the best man.

"We had a traditional wedding ceremony, then my mother gave a wedding breakfast at the White Lion. It was a lovely meal, especially by wartime standards. There were 70 people for the seated dinner, quite a big group for wartime England. We had extended hours for the liquor that was served, drinks were on the house until the bride and groom left, then it was 'pay as you go'.

"A truck load of G.I.s from the base served as my husband's back up group. I felt like 'The Sweetheart of the Forces'. From what we heard later, after the bride and groom had left on honeymoon, the party became very lively. But the bride and groom were having their 'own' party at the Mitre Inn in Oxford, by way of the Red Lion at High Wycombe.

"We went by train to High Wycombe, headquarters of the U.S. 8th Army Air Force, trailing confetti all the way, and spent the first night at the Red Lion Inn. Then onto Oxford to stay at the Mitre, an old coaching inn with low ceilings and twisting hallways. The weather was good and we walked and talked and acted like young people in love always do. I had saved up enough coupons to buy a rust brown two piece outfit, some stylish shoes, a smart hat and borrowed my mother's squirrel coat. And I had my nylons!! I thought I looked really good. Maybe I did. Will never really know how good, everything is beautiful seen through the eyes of love.

"My husband moved into our house and lived there until he was transferred to Paris in the early part of 1945. He was able to get weekend passes about once a month, so he caught a ride, maybe a convoy to a port, rode a transport across the channel and caught another army vehicle up to Four Oaks. He spent those trips getting deadly sick in the rocky English Channel and recovering immediately his feet hit dry land and he was on his way to me."

In December 1945 Charles was shipped home and was followed by Betty in March 1946. Betty's one regret about her wedding was that, like everything else, film was in short supply, so that her wedding album is rather limited although she does have some photos. Later, when asked why there were so many romances, and subsequently weddings between the G.I.s and the Sutton girls Betty replied: "There were no British men around and we were at that age."

Another Betty, Betty Welsh, met her future husband, Francis Sullivan, at a fair in Sutton Park. The occasion is still fresh in Francis's mind:

"Betty had worked 60 hours during the week and had come with her cousin to see a 'flicks' in Sutton. Sgt. Hay and I had spent the day helping to set up our initial Base Post Office. This was the background that day prior to us all going to the park where they had a small carnival set up — a merry go round and a large arm with seats on each end that stopped momentarily when one end was 180' directly above the other end. It rotated on a fixed axle in the center like a ferris wheel.

"After the movie Betty and her cousin went to the park to do something different like we did. In uniform we were a 'curiosity' to the people there. Some even thought we were German P.O.W.s. As we walked along the side of the park Betty and her cousin were coming toward us trying to determine what uniform we were wearing. Sgt. Hay satisfied their curiosity: 'We're Yanks,' he told them as we walked by.

"Later we saw them again riding the merry go round and got around to talking to them. We dared them to get on this twirling arm. After some friendly kidding they joined us. During that momentary stop 180' overhead Betty became frightened and almost turned green. I never realised anyone could change so quickly from fear of heights.

"Later, as we walked along a path, I asked Betty,
'Do you like chicken?'
'Yes.' she said.
'Grab a wing.' I told her, bending my elbow toward her. Next thing I knew it was dark and Betty and her cousin were frightenend they'd miss the next bus home.
'Don't worry about it,' Sgt. Hay told them, 'I'm the motor sergeant, I'll get a jeep and drive you home.' (This was strictly forbidden by regulations but Sgt. Hay and the motor officer were good friends.)

"That's what happened. We drove them home in a jeep and they invited us in for tea. We thought we had it made but Betty woke up her mother and introduced us to her. Two G.I.s drove back to the school barracks with a promised date for next weekend."

This date led to another and still others until there was yet another G.I. wedding being planned. About the time that Francis was processing his papers to get married an

Francis and Betty Sullivan. (F. Sullivan).

The Sullivan's wedding reception at The White Lion, October 1944. (H. Brown).

elegant gold and diamond ring showed up in an envelope that he opened at the Post Office. There was no name, no forwarding address and no one else in the office seemed to know anything about it, it was a complete puzzle to Francis. He immediately took the envelope and ring to the Adjutant. He never heard any more about it and at the time he wondered whether it was a 'plant' put in the mail to test his honesty.

Miss Natalie Pike (Sutton's registrar) married Francis and Betty in October 1944. Betty managed to get a suit for her wedding by buying clothing coupons off a lady she knew who had several children and so received a fair number of coupons. As Betty said: "She needed the money and I needed the coupons." Like Charles and Betty they held their reception at the White Lion in Four Oaks. In lieu of Francis's family Mr Saveker (Francis's billetter) gave the main speech.

After the wedding reception Francis and Betty travelled by train to Scarborough and then went on to Edinburgh for their honeymoon. They went sight seeing around Edinburgh and visited the palace of Mary, Queen of Scots. They were musing at the smallness of her bed when they heard a loud explosion. At first they thought they were being bombed, but then found that it was only the cannon there that fired to indicate the hour!

On returning home Betty returned to her mother's house in Slade Road, Erdington. Francis was only able to stay overnight there occasionally as he had to report at the Messing Centre in Four Oaks for reveille at 6 a.m. As Francis says: "Remember, the army said that we were SOLDIERS first!"

Chapter 13

Lend Lease Weddings

Captain Jordan was the personnel officer for the first two years in Sutton. His duties in the unit covered the welfare and behaviour of the men. He was responsible for the condition and care of the billets, the rations, the supplies and the men's conduct in the town. He was the officer that the men had to approach if they wished to get married.

Jordan was a World War One veteran. On his arrival in Sutton his rank was First Lieutenant, although he was soon promoted to Captain. Later, near the end of the war, he was to become Major. In his dealings with the men he was always very stern, the type that followed army orders strictly to the letter.

In the official military report for the year 1944 Jordan was commended for his efficient work with the unit for the two and a half years he was assigned to the 1st B.P.O. in Sutton. It reads:

"Much credit is due his efforts in shaping the organisation to such a degree that inspections by higher headquarters resulted invariably in 'Excellent' and 'Superior' ratings."*

Captain Jordan was keen to see that his men remembered to write home as he believed that 'mail and morale go hand in hand'. If he found that one of his men wasn't writing home he would call the individual into his office for a 'heart to heart chat', then sit them down at a desk to write a letter there and then. Then he would censor the letter himself and see to it that it was mailed.

Ken Sell remembers that Captain Jordan kept a close watch on his men:

"Late one night he paid a surprise visit to the infirmary located in the present building of the resident caretaker. He found a pan of fudge made from the supplies reserved for patients. He sternly informed the two medics on duty that he would court-martial them. He took the fudge back to his office, placed it on his desk and gave orders to the Corporal in Charge of Quarters to guard it.

"The next morning the Captain's Staff Sgt. came on duty. While the Corporal went to breakfast the Staff Sgt. ate the fudge. Upon entering the office Captain Jordan demanded to know the location of the fudge. His Staff Sgt. blushed and meekly admitted that he had eaten it!"

Due to the lack of evidence Captain Jordan was unable to proceed with the court-martial.

As the men got to know him better they realised that although he liked to act tough he had a heart of gold and was genuinely interested in the men and concerned for their welfare. Don Whalen felt that he took a deep, personal interest in his troops and was a most generous, kind and caring officer.

---

*F.B.P.O. Historical Report 1944.

CAPT. F. W. CORDAN AND MISS N. M. PIKE.

CAPT FRED W. CORDAN, of Washington, son of Mrs. H. M. Gordan and the late Mr. Cordan, of Vincennes, Indiana, U.S.A., and Miss Natalie M. Pike, only daughter of Mrs. Pike and the late Mr. M. Pike, of Malvern House, Park Road, Sutton Coldfield, and niece of the late Col. H. G. Wheeler, were married last Saturday at the Parish Church, Sutton Coldfield. The bride is Superintendent Registrar of 'Sutton Coldfield—taking on the office in succession to her father who died recently. The Rev. J. M. Boggon officiated and Mr. A. W. Francis was at the organ. A peal of bells was rung after the ceremony.

Capt. L. Banks, British Army, British - American Liaison Officer at Sutton Coldfield, gave the bride away. She wore an oyster satin dress, with an orange-blossom headdress, an embroidered tulle veil and a double row of pearls. Her shower bouquet was of shaded pink carnations.

Miss Audrey Luckham and Miss Anne White (cousins of the bride) were the bridesmaids. They wore floral white organdie dresses, with pink taffeta sashes, pink hats and pink accessories, and carried bouquets of mauve and pink sweet peas.

Capt. Walter F. Siders, First Base Post Office, U.S. Army, Sutton Coldfield, a brother officer and close friend of the family, was best man. The bride's mother wore a two-piece suit of black and duck-egg blue, with black accessories, a fox fur and a spray of carnations. Her aunts wore costumes and floral dresses.

More than 100 guests attended the reception at the Royal Hotel. The three-tiered wedding-cake had been made by the bride's mother. Later the bride and bridegroom left for Edinburgh, the bride in a turquoise-blue two-piece suit with black accessories and a fox fur.

Sutton News, 4th August, 1945.

Pearl and Al Lucas. (A. Lucas).

Captain and Mrs Jordan (A. Lucas).

(A. Lucas).

It was the Captain's duty to advise and counsel the men before the army would grant permission for a marriage. At the same time a similar procedure would take place with English girls who wished to marry G.I.s. They would be questioned by the town registrar, Sutton Coldfield's registrar being Miss Natalie Pike.

In Al Lucas's opinion Captain Jordan was easy to get past, asking questions like:

"Do you realise the responsibility of getting your wife back to the U.S.A?"

On the other hand Miss Pike was pretty tough when questioning the Sutton girls asking questions like:

"Do you realise you will be just a plaything for the Americans until the war ends and then you will be left behind?"

"What if your husband to be was sent into combat and got killed?"

In some cases she with-held permission. This infuriated Captain Jordan who soon got on the telephone to talk to her. Al says that it was general knowledge that the two of them were destroying the Anglo-American relations which so many of the G.I.s had been devoting their time to strengthening!

It was necessary for the two to meet to sort out official forms. In Don Whalen's opinion it was because the Captain had to make so many trips to the registrar's office that he began dating Miss Pike. Up to this point Captain Jordan, who was in his late 40's at the time, had always given the men the idea that he was the 'typical confirmed bachelor'.

On July the 28th 1945 the 'confirmed bachelor' and the woman who had with-held permission for some of the would be G.I. brides to get married, were married. The original 32 enlisted men and other officer friends were invited to the wedding of Captain Fred W. Jordan and Miss Natalie Maud Pike at Holy Trinity Church and reception at the Royal Hotel in Sutton.

Earlier Al Lucas had sought permission for his own wedding to Pearl (Kathleen) Golding who was working at Sutton Library at the beginning of the war. Pearl commences the story of how she met Al:

"After matriculating from Sutton Coldfield Girls High School in 1936 I became the first library assistant to be hired in the then unfinished library (formerly a methodist church) on Sutton Parade. The Librarian, Assistant Librarian and young men assistants had all been called up for military duty. We were managing the library with a skeleton staff. (Because I was taking a man's place I was deferred from call up until 1944.)"

Al had decided to visit the library as a change from the nightly pub crawl where we endured the warm mild and bitter beer that was available. He takes up the story:

I decided to cut my nightly visits in favor of some serious reading. I had always been an avid reader but had never found the time to read 'War and Peace', so off to the local library I went. The librarian found me the Tolstoy epic, set me up with a library card and checked me out. All this activity gave me time to study her. I remember thinking she was a comely lass, shapely and attractive in her black dress with a white collar, but I hadn't the temerity to ask her for a date.

"That evening I went to the Jockey for a shandy (disguised mild) and then to a dance at Maney Hall with a couple of my G.I. friends. I danced with a girl I had met on a previous occasion. I asked her if I could see her home from the dance. She responded:

'Oh Al, I'm so sorry − Bill just asked me the dance before and I accepted.' (Bill was one of my friends.) 'However,' she said, 'I have a friend who is staying with me tonight. She's standing to the left of the doorway at the moment. Would you like to meet her?'

I turned to look and instantly replied,

'By all means.' − It was the lovely girl of the earlier part of the day in the library. We

SGT. D. L. WHALEN AND MISS C. L. PEARCE

AN American soldier-colleague of the bride-groom's was best man at the wedding on Thursday of last week of Miss Cecilia Lillian Pearce, daughter of Mr. and Mrs. Arthur J. Pearce, of 3, Newhall Drive, Sutton Coldfield, and Sergeant Donald Laverne Whalen, of the United States Forces, son of Mr. and Mrs. Emmett L. Webber, of Niles, Michigan, U.S.A.

The wedding took place at Sutton Coldfield Parish Church, a choral ceremony being conducted by the Rector, Rev. G. L. H. Harvey.

The bride, who wore a gown of white cloque and a halo head-dress supporting a long net veil, was given away by her father. She carried a bouquet of red roses.

Sgt. John W. Mulcahy, U.S.A., was best man, and there two bridesmaids, the Misses Margaret Hemming and Iris Pearce, in blue taffeta, with posies of primroses and violets.

Following a reception at the Church House, Coleshill Street, Sgt. and Mrs. Whalen left for a honeymoon in Wales.

Sutton News, 15th April, 1944.

David and Mary Stopher. (H. Brown).

Pearl and Al Lucas. (A. Lucas).

LOCAL WEDDINGS OF THE WEEK

CAPT. D. R. STOPHER AND MISS M. D. BENNINGTON

AN all-American wedding, probably the first in the district, took place at St. Michael's Church Boldmere on Saturday, when Capt. David Robertson Stopher, of the United States Army Air Force, was married to Miss Mary Doris Bennington, W.A.A.C. The bridegroom is the son of Dr. and Mrs. H. W. Stopher, 3,628, Park Drive, Southdown, Baton Rouge, and the bride is the daughter of Mr. Ernest Bennington, Blue Creek, Ohio.

The service was conducted by Canon E. W. Brown, who stated that is was the first all-American wedding to take place in the church. Mr. Beckett played the organ for the choral service. The church, which was decorated with daffodils, was filled to capacity.

Given away by her commanding officer, Lieut. Lamprecht, the bride wore a gown of French brocade, from Lyons, with a five yard long train, a wreath of orange blossom, and an opal and ruby brooch, a gift from the bridegroom. She carried a bouquet of pink and white carnations.

The bridesmaid, Miss Dora Barker, wore French blue taffeta with cyclamen velvet with a Russian ermine cape, and carried a solid silver compact, a gift from the bridegroom. Diane Anwyl, the

three-year-old granddaughter of the bride's hostess (Mrs. D. G. Beer) was train bearer.

Captain Wallace Stopher, the bridegroom's brother, was best man.

The reception was held at the Boldmere Hotel, when Mrs. D. G. Beer, of Redacre, Sutton Coldfield, who has been the "English mother" of Captain Stopher and Miss Bennington, was hostess. Music was provided by an American band and Miss Rosa Riley played piano solos and Miss Vera Wood sang. The honeymoon is being spent at Weston-super-Mare.

Captain Stopher holds the Air Medal with 14 Oak Leaves and is a well-known athlete. He is a Bachelor of Music from Louisiana State University and is a member of the Sigma Alpha Epsilon Fraternity. His father is a noted conductor and has appeared in many parts of Europe, including London. His mother studied at Oxford and Birmingham under the late Dr. de Selincourt and has had many poems published.

Included amongst the many guests were Mr. and Mrs. D. G. Beer (host and hostess), Major Jernigan (commanding officer), Major Hartt, Capt. Hutchison, Lieut. King, Lieut. Galvani Lieut. Lamprecht Lieut. Dwyer, Mr. and Mrs. A. Beer, Andre Beer, Mrs. Anwyl, S.-Sgt. R. Ryan (cousin of the bride), Mrs. E. Ward, Miss Peggy Sketchley, D. Hunter, Sgt. Levesque, E. Robeson, Sgt. Griffin, E. Downing, Miss Cooper, Sgt. Bartle, Pte. M. Malloy, Sgt. Dodson, A. Pobieki, Sgt. M. Samways, Pfc. F. Shope, Cpl. L. Schuster, Cpl. Sonka, Pte. L. Stiles, Sgt. C. Stopar, Sgt. Tonry, Col. S. Wadros Sgt. J. Wishner, Sgt. N. Bavek Pfc. M. Boudllion, Pfc. H. Chambers Pfc. Conlon, Pfc. V. Dehn, Cpl. D. Dempsey, Pfc. D. Ebertowski Pfc. Flanagan, Pfc. Finnerty, Cpl M. Gee Cpl. George, Pfc. D. Hall, Pte. A. Krajewski, Cpl. M. Krukar, Pfc. M. Larkin, Cpl. B. Luty, Pte. J. Lynch, Pfc. H. Mattson, Pte. M. Prybyla and Pfc. J. Reeve.

Doris and Marlin Collins. (D. Hendley).

were introduced, we danced and, at the conclusion of the dance she accepted my bid to walk her with Bill and Joan to Joan's home on Station Road."

"On the walk home I found her easier to talk with than most girls. There seemed to be less superficiality with her. When I probed her music interests I was enchanted to hear that she was a Gilbert and Sullivan officianado, a fan of musical comedy, and was developing a library of classical music. I immediately asked for a date the next night and also for a symphonic date at the Town Hall in Birmingham on the following Sunday. Thus began (February, 1943) a string of dates that had us meeting many of the greats of the British concert halls including Menuhin, Sargent, Boult, Barberolli, Hess, Catley etc."

Pearl continues:

"We became good friends but our time together was limited. Al was working long hours and I, of course, had my library work, plus many nights per week on duty at the Civil Defence Report Centre in the basement of the Town Hall. Our free periods did not always coincide. Also, at that early point in our relationship, we both had dates with others. Sutton Park, of course, was the Mecca for G.I.s and their dates and we were no exception. If we both had a free afternoon, we would cycle to surrounding areas – the little villages, Tamworth and Kenilworth Castles, Castle Bromwich, Coventry and Cannock Chase to name but a few.

"In between air raids, long hours for Al at New Street Station, where he was in charge of dispatching box cars full of mail to the correct destinations for the G.I.s in England, and my library work in the day and Report and Control work for Civil Defence at night, somehow we kept up our acquaintance and eventually romance blossommed.

"By Christmas 1943 when my parents invited Al for dinner I knew that our friendship had developed into something more. Realising all the ramifications of marrying someone from another country, giving up my career and leaving England, I was hesitant to commit myself. Three weeks later I received my calling up papers and two weeks later was doing my Basic Training at a castle on the banks of Loch Lomond. From there I was sent to Mill Meece in Staffordshire to be trained as an air mechanic in the Fleet Air Arm of the Royal Navy. We spent long hours studying all aspects of aircraft engines, with little free time. Al and I saw each other infrequently. On Easter Sunday however he said he was cycling to Stafford with two of his buddies . . . and would I meet him there and bring two Wrens for his friends. This I did and after lunch Al and I left the others and went to the movies during which Al put an engagement ring on my finger. I don't remember him asking me to marry him, but he evidently believed actions speak louder than words! I, taken completely by surprise, kept the ring on! We tentatively planned an August wedding.

"I had very little to do with the arrangements for our wedding – my main responsibility being to show up on time. By that time I was back in Scotland on a maintenance station at Abbotsinch. My family and Al, with the help of Len McDermott and other buddies got the whole thing together. A Mrs Clarke, hostess of the White Lion in Four Oaks with whom Al had become friends, supplied the cake. I think a little black marketting was involved in getting the marzipan and white icing for it! Al had managed to get 7 days furlough but I was having a tough time getting leave. My C.O. didn't approve of my marrying an American and tried to dissuade me – she was tougher than the registrar in Sutton (Miss Natalie). I finally got my 7 day leave pass signed on 6 p.m. the night before the wedding, leaving me time to get my hair done in Paisley, grab a bus to Glasgow, and catch the 11 p.m. train for Birmingham where I arrived at about 7 a.m. on

Roy and Joyce Streib (R. Streib).

S. SGT. R. F. STRIEB AND MISS J. H. BAKER

THE wedding took place at Sutton Coldfield Metho-dist Church last week of Mr. Roy Frederick Strieb, son of Mr. and Mrs. F. Strieb, of 3,002. Olympia Way, Lons-view Washington, U.S.A. and Miss Joyce Helen Baker, daughter of Mr. and Mrs. J. W. Baker, of 6, Kathleen Road. Sutton Coldfield. The choral service was conducted by the Rev. A. J. Treblico, and Mr. J. A. Horton was organist.

Given away by her father the bride wore a gown of ivory lace, and carried a bouquet of carnations and lilies - of - the - valley. Her matron-of-honour. Mrs. Molly Baker (sister-in-law), wor-dusty pink crepe, and carried pink and mauve tulips. Flying-Officer Roy Mobray was best man

After the reception at the Supper Room, Town Hall, Sutton Coldfield, the couple left for London, the bride travelling in a beige two-piece with an off-white coat.

Sutton News 23/3/46.

Reunion hope of real GI Joe

AN AMERICAN Army veteran is hoping to be reunited with the Sutton Coldfield woman who nursed him through a Second World War injury.

Former GI Joseph Gardiner spent several months of 1944 45 working at the First Base Post Office in Sutton after suffering an injury.

During his convales-cence he befriended Eva Cox and her broth-er David.

He believes they may have been con-nected to the Cox fami-ly who ran a butcher's shop in Mere Green Road, Four Oaks.

But GI Joe and Eva lost touch when he returned to France.

Now Mr Gardiner, a

■ **REPORT by EMMA WILLIAMS**

former member of the 29th Infantry Regiment, hopes to meet her again when he flies from his Bromley, Kentucky, home, to Sutton later this summer.

He decided to make contact after helping Great Barr authors Martin and Frances Collins.

They are writing a book centred around Sutton Coldfield as the home of the First Base Post Office to handle mail from the US for forces stationed in Europe.

After more than 12 months' research, they have completed a draft copy of *Letters For Victory*, and are look-ing for a publisher.

The self-confessed American enthusiasts have also arranged for a plaque to be unveiled at Plantsbrook School in the autumn to com-memorate its use as an American Army bar-racks during the war.

Anyone who can help trace Eva or knows of her whereabouts should contact the *Sutton Coldfield News* newsdesk on 354 7676.

Sutton News 5/6/92.

Eva Cox in her bus conductress uniform.

111

Joe and Eva reunited September 1992. (Sutton News).   *Joe Gardiner. (J. Gardiner).*

: 021 626 6604 Display : 021 626 6600 Distribution 021 626 6629   **12 JUNE 1992**

We find GI Joe's wartime pal Eva

A FORMER GI can look forward to a happy reunion with a wartime friend thanks to the *Sutton Coldfield News*.

Mrs Eva Attree, née Cox, from Falcon Lodge, read our story in last week's paper about the search for the friend of a former GI, only to realise it was her.

Eva befriended GI Joseph Gardiner when they together at the First Base Post Office in Sutton Coldfield, but they lost touch when he returned to France.

Now they are looking forward to seeing each other for the first time in 47 years.

Eva, now aged 68, was persuaded to contact the newspaper by her husband Norman.

She said: "It's come as a bit of a surprise but it's quite nice because we were great friends.

"I am looking forward to talking about old times."

Eva, who comes from a family of seven children, has always lived in Sutton Coldfield.

She said: "Our father died when we were quite young and Joe was great to us."

Her sister Theresa married a GI friend of Joe's and the couple live in California.

They returned to Sutton Coldfield for the first time in 38 years two years ago for a family reunion and Eva is hoping they will be able to make this special reunion too.

Authors

Joe decided to make contact with Eva after helping Great Barr authors Martin and Frances Collins.

They are writing a book centred around the First Base Post Office, which handled mail from the US for forces stationed in Europe.

Joe is planning to fly over in time for the unveiling of a plaque at Plantsbrook School in the autumn to commemorate its use as an American Army barracks during the war.

Sutton News 12/6/92.

Eva Attree – reunion plans

August 17th 1944, our wedding day. (A side note – I sat up all night with two British Merchant Marines who, on learning that I was geting married, presented me with an orange and a banana, the first I had seen in almost 5 years!)

"On arriving home in Wishaw I barely had time to change into a clean white shirt, dust off my shoes and head for St Chads, the 13th Century Wishaw Church. I was married in uniform. The procession to the church, we think, was unique to say the least. I was driven by my father in a Rolls Royce – courtesy of my father's employer. Al arrived in a jeep with Len McDermott (best man) and Captain Jordan. Down the winding country lanes came a procession of guests on bicycles – the library staff, about 50 G.I.s and dates, plus relatives and other guests. After the ceremony the same procession went to the Memorial Hall nearby for the reception. Afterwards my father drove us to Sutton, where we boarded a train en route for Stratford on Avon. Due to wartime restrictions Al was not allowed to travel beyond a 25 mile radius of his base. He had therefore booked for 3 days at the Black Swan (Dirty Duck).

"Al had also reserved front row seats for a performance of 'Hamlet' at the Shakespeare Theatre. By this time I had not had any sleep for about 30 or so hours. We both fell asleep in our seats! from Stratford we went on to Matlock where Al had managed to get accomodation for another 3 days. The last day saw us on the train back to Glasgow. We spent our last night at the Central Hotel. Early the next morning we parted as I returned to Abbotsinch and Al to Sutton.

"For the next year we saw each other about once a month. Al would come to Paisley for a few hours if he could get a day's pass and I would come to Sutton on the same premise. Otherwise we communicated via letters and perfectly timed phone calls between phone booths in Paisley and Four Oaks.

"On August the 15th 1945, as a married Wren, I received priority discharge. At the same time the 1st B.P.O. was transferred to Paris. Al however was sent to a London B.P.O. on Oxford Street. He found a room for me off Edgeware Road, behind Marble Arch. Higher ranking officers had gone home and Al, a technical sergeant, was in charge of the operation there. As in Sutton, civilians were employed there so, rather than sit in a room all day I joined their ranks and helped sort the mail. Al had volunteered to serve an extra six months until my passage to America could be assured."

Celia Pearce was another Sutton girl who had to weigh up the consequences of leaving her parents and all that she was familiar with to start a new life in America with her husband Don Whalen. Don remembers:

"Her parents at first took a very dim view of me. English parents were apprehensive, with considerable justification, that the invading Yanks – over paid, over sexed and over here – would seduce their daughters, leave them pregnant, take off for Europe or Africa and never be heard of again. However I bribed her father with American pipe tobacco, which he loved, and finally was accepted into their home, first as a guest and finally as a son in law. My wife was the youngest of 14 children, she was their baby, so they were reluctant to see their child marry a Yank and move to the U.S. in case they would never see each other again, which indeed was the case."

Don met Celia in the autumn of 1942 when she was working at the 7 Hour cleaners, a dry cleaning shop on The Parade where he had to take uniforms. He saw her later at a dance at Maney Hall and finally asked her out. They courted for 16 months before they got married. Don takes up the story:

"We were married on a beautiful Saturday afternoon (April the 6th 1944) at Holy Trinity Church with many members of my wife's family present along with several of my G.I. friends. My wife's mother had saved her scarce rations for some time to provide a beautiful and tasty wedding cake. I had managed to get a few days off and we were going to Llangollen in Wales, but a week before we were married the military stopped any such travelling of this distance so we took a bus into Birmingham and went to the cinema. Later, when I met my wife in new York City in May 1946 we drove down into some of the Southern States in the U.S. for a delayed honeymoon. We finally rented a car in 1987 and drove in Southern England and finally to Llangollen, Wales 43 years late."

There were many more G.I. weddings in Sutton, too numerous to mention them all. Some all-American weddings took place when W.A.C.s married G.I.s they had met over here. In many cases brides had to borrow dresses for themselves and their bridesmaids. Dorothy Anwyl's three year old daughter, Dianne, was bridesmaid at W.A.C. Mary Bennington's wedding to Captain David Stopher, which was the first all American wedding in Sutton. The bride borrowed Dorothy's own dress for the wedding.

When Doris Hendley's seven year old daughter, Angela, was a bridesmaid for Doris Lackey and Post Office G.I. Marlin Collins she wore a dress that she'd had when she was a bridesmaid on a previous occasion. This time she was given a hat to match which she didn't like, hence the pouting face in the photo!

Joyce Baker was one of the last Sutton G.I. brides. She was working as a volunteer at the Donut Dugout when she met her husband to be, Roy Streib. Even now she remembers the date that they met, which was May the 11th 1945. Once they became acquainted Roy started giving Joyce lifts home in the truck that he drove for the Post Office. Unfortunately in July he had to leave for France to take charge of the motor pool of the 17th B.P.O. in Paris.

The couple corresponded until Roy came back to England on leave in September and again in December when they got engaged. Then followed a rather traumatic time as Roy fell ill with yellow jaundice and Joyce didn't hear anything from him for a month. Finally they managed to make contact through the Red Cross. He recovered and in February 1946 he was transferred back to London.

As Roy's departure back to the States was imminent the couple decided to bring forward the date of their wedding from August to March the 12th. They were married at South Parade Methodist Church, Joyce in a borrowed wedding gown and Roy, of course, in uniform. As there were none of Roy's G.I. friends left in Sutton an R.A.F. friend, Flying Officer Roy Mobray, acted as best man for the couple. They held their wedding reception at the Town Hall and then travelled to London for a honeymoon. On the train Joyce opened her suitcase to look for something and was embarrassed to find that it had been filled with confetti, which flew out everywhere. The couple spent just two months in England before going to the States.

Not all the romances between G.I.s and English girls ended in marriage. Joe Gardiner met his sweetheart, Eva Cox, when he caught the bus outside the Dog Inn to go to Birmingham. She was the conductress on his bus on the journey there and, as luck would have it, she was also on the bus that Joe returned to Sutton on. Joe asked her where she usually went in the evenings and she told him she was going to the Guildhall that evening.

"I'll see you there," he said as a joke. Later in the evening, as he had nothing else to do he decided that he would go to the Guildhall. He met Eva there, danced with her and, at the end of the evening, walked her home.

After this Joe and Eva started dating but when Joe got sent to France with the Post Office they lost touch. Almost 50 years later they made contact again through an article in the Sutton News. Joe came back to Sutton for the 50th Anniversary Celebrations of the First Base Post Office and spent some time with Eva (now Attree) and her family.

Chapter 14

R and R*

As the American contingent in Sutton became larger activities were organised to fill the men's leisure time. For most of the men it was their first time out of the United States and they wanted to make the most of their time 'abroad'.

Conducted tours were organised so that the men could visit places of interest around Warwickshire, such as Stratford Upon Avon, Kenilworth and Warwick, much as American tourists do today. In 1945 a similar tour was arranged for the W.A.C.s of the 6888th Postal Battallion, but on this occasion the women were greeted by the respective mayors upon their arrival in each town.

Numerous theatre trips were made to Stratford in the evenings by members of the unit to see Shakespearean plays and on one occasion the 'Ballet Joos'. The transport usually left Four Oaks on Saturday evenings at about 5:30 p.m. and returned around 10:30 p.m. Phil Tillar remembers that these trips were very popular with the men, usually attracting enough G.I.s to fill a bus Trips were also arranged to Birmingham to hear the National Symphony Orchestra and see the Sadlers Wells Ballet.

A Special Service Section was set up to cater for the needs of the men, sort out complaints and provide entertainment and social activities. Lieutenant Andrew P. Zirpoli was the officer in charge and it was his responsibility to staff the department. Sgt. Kenneth M. Sell had been working at the Post Office for just two weeks when Lt. Zirpoli approached him while he was sorting letters to ask him if he knew of any qualified teachers working at the Post Office that he could enlist into the Special Service Section. As Ken was a teacher in civilian life he was delighted to volunteer his services. Lt. Zirpoli also requested Sgt. Robert E. Dayo and Sergeant Otis O. Pepper for his staff. Captain Jordan gave his approval and the men were duly transferred into the Special Service Section.

The main aim of the organisation was, in Lt. Zirpoli's words:

> "to strengthen the cooperation of the British and American people through a better understanding of their common heritage; and to successfully bring victory; and to continue this cooperation in the Post War World."

Each detachment had a representative on the Special Service Council who would voice the opinion of the personnel in that detachment. A newsletter called 'Mail Sack' was produced every Friday or Saturday (depending how busy editor Ken Sell was). Each detachment would be given ten to twenty copies which had been run off on a duplicator at Green Gables. This paper kept the men and women informed of any social activities that would be taking place aswell as keeping them abreast of all the latest gossip.

The Special Service Section of the 17th B.P.O. also produced a newsletter whilst in Sutton Coldfield which had the original title of 'No Name News'. A competition which

---

*Military term standing for Rest and Relaxation.

was run for the best name was won by Rowland Lomax with the title 'Invasion Courier' whose prize was £1.

In January 1945 the Special Service Section reviewed the 'entertainments situation' and found that although there was an increase in requests for concerts and musical shows, dances were by far the most popular of all the activities.

The 10th Replacement Depot had its own dance band and the Sutton G.I.s often attended their dances where they could hear the distinctive 'Big Band sound'. This band played at Sutton Town Hall in May 1944 for 'Salute the Soldier Week'. In January 1945 they changed their style somewhat to cater for the W.A.C.s Tea Dance at the American Red Cross Club.

The G.I.s from Sutton decided that they could do the same. Lieutenant Zirpoli secured musical instruments while Ken Sell had wooden music stands made. Auditions were held for the purpose of selecting musical talent to form a 1st Base Post Office dance orchestra. The band was organised and the talent was said to be 'beyond expectations'.* The musicians in the band were:

Ed Leamond (leader) – saxophone, trumpet, clarinet.
Harvey Arner and Wilburt Reinhardt – saxophone and clarinet.
Louis Lento – trumpet.
Raymond Sexton – string bass.
Ed Sprava – guitar.
Henry Hanneman – piano
Leonard Nole – drums.
Joe Shapiro – violin and vocalist.
Bill Winberger and Jack Power also sang with the band. Bill was a favourite with the audience as his style was very like the Inkspots. Jack, of New York City, was a singer with dance bands before the war and he sang with the Louie Prima Band in the 1950's. Doris Hendley (a Sutton resident) rated the band highly and remembers that they always played Glenn Miller's 'In The Mood'.

The band played at numerous venues, both for American and British audiences. They would play in the evening after spending the day working at the Post Office. They played for wounded soldiers at military hospitals within a 50 mile radius, for benefit dances and also for dances organised by the various Post Office detachments. On the 23rd of October 1944 there was a 'Battle of Music' between the 1st B.P.O. Band and the R.A.F. Orchestra at the Inter-Allied Dance which was held at Sutton Town Hall.

The band also played for an 'Anglo-American Dance' at the Town Hall in January 1945. This had been organised by members of Holy Trinity Catholic Church. In February they played at the Washington Birthday Ball which was also held at the Town Hall and was organised by the officers based at the Post Office. Both events were well attended by uniformed guests.

The band also played at concerts. On the 15th of July 1944 a show was staged, in which the band took part, for the entertainment of 200 wounded soldiers of the Allied Nations recently returned from Normandy. This took place at Britwell Hall in Boldmere.

The troops from the Post Office ran several concerts. Some of these were run for charity or towards the war effort, as was the piano recital by Edward Kilyeni in March

*F.B.P.O. Historical Report 1944.

MAIL SACK

1st BASE POST OFFICE   7 October 1944

WELCOME TO DETACHMENT "D"

The members of the 1st BPO wish to extend their heartiest greetings to the new members of Detachment "D". You are now one of us, and are all invited to participate in our activities. May your stay with us be a good one.

G.I. DANCE

Next Wednesday evening, October 11th, the 1st BPO Band will sing out with plenty of "Jive" at the Abbey Hall for the Benefit Dance. It will be a "stompin" big affair. Bring your dates or come stag, for the fairer sex will be well represented.

In benefit of whom? It is for all of you in our organization. Special Service needs funds with which to carry on the detachment activities. Consequently, the more you boost this scheme, the more you will receive in return. The price of admission will be 2/6.

Town Hall was not available, so the next best thing was to have two dances, each one with special consideration to the various detachments. The first one is primarily for Detachments "D" and "E", and the second dance at Maney Hall on December 9th will be for Detachments "D", "C" and Headquarters. The WAC Detachment is invited to attend both dances.

SALUTE TO AN ALLY

To Mrs. Diana Baker, assistant to Miss Shirley at the Red Cross Club, came the information that her husband, Pvt. George Baker, British Army, was killed in action. Originally he was wounded at Dunkirk, and was safely evacuated to England. He returned to fight the Nazi on the Anzio beachhead, where he gave his life for the cause of freedom.

The men and women of the 1st BPO, whose welfare she has zealously worked to promote at the "Doughnut Dugout," extend to her their sincere sympathy. To the condolences of the King and Queen, they add a salute in recognition of Pvt. Baker's sacrifice, and of Mrs. Baker's loss.

WEDDING BELLS

Sgt. Charles D. Watts of Detachment "C" was married today to Miss Elizabeth Gardner at 12:00 Noon in the Four Oaks Methodist Church. Sgt. Chester Carter of Detachment "C" acted as the best man. Capt. Fred W. Jordan, Lt. Roszkowski, and many friends in uniform attended the wedding and the reception which was held at the White Lion inn. With many wishes for a successful marriage, the bride and groom left for a honeymoon at Oxford.

At 2:30 P.M. today in St. Peter's Church, Maney, T/Sgt. Marlin G. Collins and Miss Doris V. Lackey were married. The best man was Sgt. David E. Mosley. Lt. Fisher and many other friends of the bride and groom attended the ceremony and the reception which followed at the bride's home. Blackpool will be the scene of their honeymoon. The personnel extend to Sgt. and Mrs. Collins its sincere congratulations.

118

WAC SNOOPS

Hi-ya all! seems like we always have a... lot of rumors...Let 'em fly gals as long as it keeps you happy. M/Sgt Land's appearance at the Holland Road Rec Hall! Nice going Dot.

Oh,.. yes---what happened to that nose of Docley's Does he need a pilot, or less brew?. . . Guess Dick and Dot really rate here; they got a "singing" Good Morning from the gals the other day . . . Congrats to T/Sgt Collins .e. hope he'll be v very happy.. . ... Then there's that little Pfc. "Tommy" who thinks a certain Sgt. is just about tops. Also see that Joe Saracin still goes for blondes- - - but good! Heard that some of the Wacs have been restricted lately. What's the trouble gals? - -Slow watches or fast love affairs?. . Somebody ask "Wrong Way" Dempsey how she got that name? Bet she'll learn her right from left in the future. Hey, Fannie, What's the idea of going "West" on us? . . . Well, I'll be seeing you when more rumors get to the Directory.

Snoopy Suzie

- - - - o O o - - - -

BRICKIBUS AUREATUS
by Scorchie

It's strange to me
Why it should be
I never get caught working
But it seems
That fate just schemes
To make the Serge think I'm shirking.

I strive all day
To earn my pay ... to
And work my fingers to the bone
I toil and sweat
But what do I get
I might as well be all alone.

His eagle stare
Is never there
The while I work like mortal sin
But let me slack
To ease my back
And that's the time the

"ONE OF THEM WACS HAS BEEN WEARING MY FATIGUES!"

MOVIES

	EMPRESS
Sun:	"Three Smart Girls Grow Up"
	"Jungle Siren"
Mon:	"Buffalo Bill"
	"Unknown Guest"

	ODEON
Mon:	"For Whom The Bells Toll"

	PAVILLION
Sun:	"Tarzon and the Green Goddess"
Mon:	"Andy Hardy's Blonde Troubles"

	PICTURE HOUSE
Sun:	"Rings on her Fingers"
Mon:	"His Butler's Sister"
Thurs:	"Texas to Tokio"

"King of the Cowboys"

THEATER

ALEXANDER
"The Doctor's Dilemma"

REPERTORY
"A WINTER'S TALE"

ROYAL
"ROOM FOR TWO"

—

Sarge walks in.

I'm branded now
Just like a cow
A Gold-Brick, slacker never-has-been
And just because
That one brief pause
Was just the time the
Sarge walked in!

NEWS AND VIEWS

With the closing of the dance season at the Crystal Palace Ball Room, the Grey Friars men have claimed the distinction of taking most of the prizes for contests there Phil Sadow was chosen as the smoothest waltzer "Scottie" Leckie won the crooning contest, and Si Pressman got the award of the best "Worst Dancer".

Did you say two pints Garfield? T/4 Gus Michael still hasn't explained his whereabouts on Sunday evenings. What's cooking, Gus? Say, who is this man Garfield? Anyhow?

An there is a certain Cpl who is still trying to discover who tucked him in the other night.

Odd discovery: Pvt Hall keeps the mirror of her jeep focused so that she can see whether her nose is shiney. Tch, tch, such vanity!. . .

"Tex" Blalock has a new hobby. Keep it up Tex, you may be a Rembrant some day. . . . . . .

Why is it T/5 Louis Jones always fills his cigaretslighter at the Red Cross? Doesn't he know that it can be had at the PX for a small fee?

It doesn't take a keen observer to notice that "Smitty" of Hqs. rushes to the "WAC Shack" for another reason than for chow. . . . .

Det "C" has been having so many marriages that it is hoped. T/4 Irv Schankein will soon make his announcement, and put an end to this suspence.

WANTED
Names for the two mascots of "The Doughnut Dugout" Place names in the suggestion box in the Club.

FREE SHOW
The play "Fresh Fields" will be given at the WAC Det. on Sat. Oct. 14 th 8:00PM, by the Borough Players. Everyone is invited.

119

Sightseeing at Kenilworth Castle. (E. Ward).

F.B.P.O. Band with Lt. Zirpoli. (L. Nole).

F.B.P.O. Band Aug. '44.
(H. Brown).

F.B.P.O. Band (L. Nole).

Les Devore and Barringer jitterbugging. (H. Sprava).

Les Devore and Miss Wood singing 'Ah, Sweet Mystery of Life'. (H. Sprava).

W.A.C. Jenny Baker singing 'Embraceable you'. (H. Sprava).

1944 where the proceeds went to the Red Cross. (Kilyeni was later to become Professor of Music at the University of Florida.)

The W.A.C.s staged several shows in the Recreation Room at the Holland Road Barracks. Ken Sell remembers one which involved Hula Hula girls wearing two mess tins as bras and ammunition belts strung with nylon stockings as skirts. Patients at the 77th Station Hospital in Sutton were also willing to play their part in entertaining the troops. Those who were not seriously ill or injured were able to put their spare time to good use. They presented a show at the Holland Road Barracks and invited enlisted personnel of the British Army. The much talented men of the 10th Replacement Depot also produced a show called 'Laugh Parade' which was shown to several of the detachments and was well acclaimed by all who saw it. When the British Forces staged shows for the G.I.s in Sutton the men and women of the Post Office would collect cigarettes as payment for them as military regulations prohibited them from paying cash.

There was always special excitement when U.S.O. concerts were held in Sutton, as these would usually be of a more 'professional nature'. Several U.S.O. shows were staged in Sutton at the Holland Road Barracks. In March 1945 a U.S.O. show starring Rudy Satrito and his 'All Girl Orchestra' played at the W.A.C. Day Room. This was enjoyed by over 300 of the personnel. U.S.O. shows would also be performed at the 10th Replacement Depot and the G.I.s could be trucked in from Sutton to Lichfield if they wished to see them. The comedian Bob Hope was a performer in one of these shows.

On the 1st of April 1945 a stage was completed at the Streetly camp so a series of variety shows were booked to perform there once a week. Plans were also made to bring a travelling theatre to detachments that did not have a stage.

Films were also a good form of entertainment for the postal workers. Aswell as having access to the two cinemas in Sutton the Post Office had its own film library, and from the 22nd of August 1944 this was kept at Green Gables. In March 1945 a movie projector (Victor Type 13), speaker and transformer were obtained from 3272 U.S. Signal Service Detachment. A.P.O. 515 (Chester). This helped the movie schedule as all detachmments with A.C. current could now be serviced. The officers were keen to bring as many films as possible to the posts where the men were working on the night shift as their working hours restricted access to some of the other forms of entertainment.

Movies were shown regularly at most of the detachments. Holland Road and Streetly Camp showed films Monday and Wednesday evenings, Penns Lane Camp showed them Tuesday, Thursday and Friday. Minworth Camp's showings were on Monday and Friday, and Swanhurst Camp had its turn on Mondays and Thursdays. The night force, located at Moseley, watched films once a week in the afternoons.

It was found that if a good film was to be shown men were likely to stay on the post in off-duty time and gain the necessary relaxation and rest there rather than go off the base and into the town. In the officer's eyes this lessened the fatigue seen in the men which was causing inefficiency in the work.

Films were generally well attended and the officers believed that they helped to maintain a good standard of morale. A film programme was arranged so as to achieve a good balance of education and entertainment. The list of morale building films included such titles as 'Rape of Czechoslovakia', 'March of Time − Post war jobs' and various newsreels. The more interesting entertainment type films included such titles as 'The Canterville Ghost', 'Here Come the WAVES' and 'Hollywood Canteen'.

As the various detachments within the Post Office Unit grew larger inter-detachment sports contests were held in the men and women's off duty time. The sports included

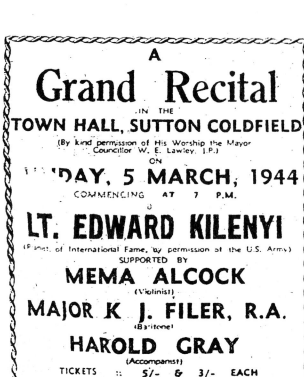
Sutton News 19/2/44

Sutton News 17/6/44.

U.S. ARMY PIANIST

Sunday evening's concert at Sutton Coldfield had a two-fold purpose: to benefit the Red Cross (which it must have done substantially, as the Town Hall was packed), and to introduce Lieut. Edward Kilenyi, of the U.S. Army, to the musical public of the Royal Town.

Lieut. Kilenyi was described on the programme as a pianist of international fame. He is certainly a pianist of more than average attainments: his technique is highly developed, and he plays with a vigour that at times becomes almost violent — this was very noticeable in the Bach Choral - Prelude, which was accorded a "hammer and tongs" style of treatment quite alien to its nature. Lieut. Kilenyi was at his best in the works of Chopin and Liszt that he played, all of which received thoughtful and impressive renderings. His Beethoven, somehow, left one rather cold.

Major K. J. Filer, the singer of the evening, had recently come out of hospital and was obviously suffering from catarrh, consequently it would be unfair to be too critical of his performance. It was clear, however, that he is the possessor of a fine voice, which, moreover, he knows how to use.

Mema Alcock joined forces with Harold Gray (who paid a welcome, though all too-fleeting, visit to Sutton Coldfield for the occasion) in a Handel sonata, which was tastefully played. Mr. Gray also accompanied Miss Alcock in some effective violin solos, and Major Filer in his songs, his playing at all times being alert and sympathetic.

G. A.

Sutton News 26/2/44.

F.B.P.O. Band. (H. Sprava).

F.B.P.O. Baseball team '43 in Rectory Park. (H. Brown).

Volleyball Court at Streetly Camp. (P. Tillar).

tennis, golf, swimming, ping pong, basketball, volleyball, badminton, baseball and softball. Courts for the latter five of these were set up at the Streetly and Penns Lane Camps. Baseball and Softball could also be played (with permission from the officers) in Sutton Park directly behind Grey Friars Mess. Contracts were taken out for the use of civillian tennis courts and golf courses.

In May 1945 Corporal Hughes was appointed Athletics N.C.O. and he brought out a newsheet called 'Sport Script' to keep the men informed of the sports activities and athletic events on the base. Corporal Hughes managed to secure Pvt. Donald Lunger, who was a swimming and diving champion, to be an aquatic coach for the men. He selected Erdington Swimming Baths as the best place to start beginner and advanced classes. Swimming parties were also given to stimulate interest in swimming. At Streetly Camp Hughes set up a gym where he himself took a body building course and exercise group and various weight lifting classes.

Corporal Hughes was also asked to make a survey of all the athletic organisations in a radius of fifty miles of the Post Office and arrange bookings for the Post Office Baseball teams. He managed to obtain permission from Mr Higgs, the Borough Surveyor, to use Rectory Park as 1st B.P.O. home field. The Post Office Team played the 10th Replacement Depot and various convalescent hospitals. Two players from the team, Pfc. Chopick and Pvt. Osbourne were selected to play with the All Star Professional U.K. Baseball Team and were placed with this team for an international tour.

Softball was another sport that was played against other units. The R.C.A.F. were challenged in May 1945 and won the game 4–0 against the Penns Lane Detachment.

The Minworth and Wylde Green Detachments were called to demonstrate this sport for the 2129 Squadron Air Training Corps at Beeches School at the end of May. Detachment A, which was based in London at the time, had a softball team that worked its way up the 'Grosvenor League' and got as far as the play off for the London Championship in September.

Also in 1945 there was a U.S. Army Sports Exhibition at the 825th Convalescent Hospital. 75 night tour men attended the afternoon's events and took part in some of the sports there. The feature event of the day was a sparring match between Sgt. Suska from Streetly Camp and the famous Billy Conn. According to official sources Sgt. Suska acqutted himself well.*

---

* F.B.P.O. Historical Report 1944.

Chapter 15

Salute the Soldier

"All available opportunities in orientation, information, and education activities were used to create and maintain in the personnel a feeling of their responsibility in this war, namely the importance of the mail, and to strengthen their efficiency by increasing their understanding as to why we fight, keeping them informed as to the course of the war and giving them the advantage of adding to their military effectiveness and individual competence through instruction and study."*

Training and studying were not quite as popular as the outside work activities mentioned in the previous chapter. Some lectures were compulsory for the men and women and would take the form of 'Army Talks', these would cover subjects of current interest and the extent and purpose of the war. The Special Service Section also instituted a 'Speakers forum' where English experts were called in to give talks with titles such as 'The British, are they human?' (16/5/44) and 'How we are governed.' (18/5/44).

Many G.I.s and W.A.C.s volunteered to do correspondence and self- teaching courses, some worked towards the completion of high school and college degrees that would stand them in good stead at the end of the war. Leonard McDermott, Dick Conlon and Bob Johnson joined the Sutton Coldfield University Extension Society at Sutton Library and attended lectures there.

Shortly before D-Day French classes were initiated with an excellent response, undoubtedly brought about by the desire to see France and to be able to converse with the French allies. On D-Day plus 2 a French club for enlisted men and women was organised and started to meet weekly. Mrs Gye, the Language Advisor to the Allied Forces, came to lecture to the members.

Essay contests took pace with such exciting subjects as 'The Conservation of Tires.' Each of the detachments had a winner. The lucky one in Detachment C was Leonard McDermott. The covetted prize was four days off. For the G.I. who had only had one furlough during his three years in England this was a prize worth winning. He used the time to play golf at Little Aston Golf Course, ice skate at a rink in Birmingham and attend the U.S. Army Air Force Band Concert at Birmingham Town Hall, but in his opinion the best thing about having this time off was being able to get up late.

The Americans were often asked to give lectures themselves. Lt. Zirpoli (Public Relations Officer) and Sgt. Sell were frequently called on to give talks to various local institutions. These included Sunday Schools, Youth Clubs and Churches and covered subjects such as 'American children', 'English and American youth' and 'A comparison of the election systems of the United States and Great Britain.'

In November 1944 a team of enlisted men were asked to speak at six local schools on 'The Meaning of Thanksgiving'. In 1945 Professor Jones, the Headmaster of Bishop

---

*F.B.P.O. Historical Report 1944.

Vesey Grammar School, requested that Lt. Zirpoli organise a series of lectures and dicussions on 'America, its People and its History' for the senior boys at the school. The aim was to provide first hand information concerning America so that a better understanding could be acquired by the boys. In February 1945, in cooperation with the 34th Brigade of the British Army, Lt. Zirpoli organised a day's course for members of the British Army, Home Guard and R.A.F.

On the 6th of June 1945 Corporal Hughes gave a lecture on 'The American Theatre' at The Highbury Little Theatre, Boldmere. After this he was contacted by Miss Bacon from the B.B.C. and asked to take part in a series of broadcasts she was arranging. On the 12th of June Cpl. Hughes made his first broadcast over the Home Service network, his topic being 'The English Theatre'. Following this performance he was asked to participate in an international broadcast and arrangements were made for a hook up on the 30th of June between the Dallas Little Theatre (Texas) and The Highbury Little Theatre. Unfortunately the shipping schedule of the personnel of the 1st B.P.O. to the Continent conflicted with the date of the broadcast so a recording with transcript was made so that Hughes's colleagues would be able to listen to him at a later date.

To compliment the lectures and talks a discussion group was set up where differing opinions could be listened to and questions asked. This was called 'The Anglo-American Forum'. and was set up in January 1945. Speakers were invited to speak on topics of mutual interest and concern to both the U.K. and the U.S.A. On the 10th of the month an English audience was able to ask three officers from the Post Office questions concerning America. The range of subjects varied from drugstores and politics to fireplaces and 'the colour bar'. On the 25th the subject was 'Women and the Post War World'. Members of the W.A.C., American Red Cross, A.T.S., W.A.A.F., and Wrens were able to give their opinions. The general conclusion to come from this forward looking discussion was that a woman, regardless of whether she remained in the home or in a profession, must have a better understanding of local and national affairs. This would be the only way for her to assume a well-balanced and more efficient way of life.

Each month there were Anglo-American Forum activities. In February there was a 'Religious Brains Trust' and a debate on the country of Russia. In March the volume of mail meant that the orientation hour or 'Army Talks' had to be suspended so the Forum took its place in attempting to create a better understanding of the nature of war. The titles for discussion in this month were 'The Mind of the Nazi' and 'China'. In April the title was 'Dunbarton Oaks, Yalta, San Francisco – what they mean to you.'

The last Anglo-American Forum was held at Pattisons Cafe on the 28th of June. 'The Press' was the subject and the speakers were Pfc. Mason for America and W. H. Bush Esq. for Great Britain. The audience consisted of British and American forces as well as civilians and therefore there was much interesting discussion on the freedom of the press in each country. Looking back at the success of the forums the Commanding Officer, Major Jernigin considered that:

"It was evident that a strong bond of friendship had been forged between the British and ourselves as a result of these forums. The speeches of goodbye were warm and heartfelt. The Anglo-American forum had achieved its purpose far beyond original expectations."*

---

* F.B.P.O. Historical Report 1945.

Ken Sell of the Special Service Section with 'Army Talks' poster.

"The American Way"

U.S. SERGEANT'S ADDRESS AT YOUTH CLUB

NO CHANCE OF MEETING "NICE TYPE OF GIRL"

THE American way of life was explained to members of Sutton Coldfield Methodist Church Youth Club by Sergt. K. C. Sell, of the United States Army on Friday. The Sutton club, he said, looked exactly the same as any youth club in America and their activities were also similar.

Co-Education ?

Speaking of co-education, Sergt. Sell said that the British appeared to look down on women and to consider them educationally inferior; whereas in many cases the woman of the house had the brains.

Speaking of the coloured members of the Women's Army Corps, Sergt. Sell said that they were "very nice girls." Although the coloured people in America in some districts outnumbered the white, "sparks began to fly" when a Southerner met a negro.

The fact that they were in a 'foreign' land, and that no one knew them in this country, was Sergt. Sell's explanation of the apparent low moral standard of some Americans over here. He thought that they never had the chance of meeting the "nice type" of girl.

In America prizes were given to the historian who wrote the truest acount of the war between America and Britain. There were various things that unfortunately reminded America of the war, and Sergt. Sell advocated that they should be forgotten.

Sutton News 24/2/'45.

"PSYCHOLOGY OF AMERICAN YOUTH"

A meeting of the Sutton Coldfield Youth Council was held in the Lecture Room, Sutton Library, on Thursday last, when Mr. Alan Hossell was in the chair and Miss Janet Chatwin read the minutes.

Lieut. Zirpoli, an education officer of the American Army, gave a most interesting talk on "The Psychology of American Youth." He said the way one is brought up and not one's race determines a person's behaviour. He outlined the differences in outlook of the young American and the young Briton, and the reason for the differences. He said that in America there had been such astounding all-round development in American life that the young American was taught to respect the new whereas Britons respected the past to a great extent. American development had encouraged a rugged individualism, whereas in Britain a community spirit had developed, and Britons respected people's privacy more than did the Americans. Experience in the development of America had stressed that all men were created equal, and to a large extent early Americans had little class distinctions.

In America there was a tendency in the pre-war years to stress extra-cogricula training, and as most young people in America stayed at school until they were 18 years it meant that British boys and girls, so many leaving school at 14 years, reached maturity earlier. He said he believed in co-educational schools such as they largely had in America.

Lady Bennett spoke briefly of a meeting to be held in the Supper Room, Town Hall, on May 1st, when young people will be invited to hear speakers on local government.

The business meeting of the Youth Council then followed. Mr. Alan Hossell gave brief reports on the football and netball leagues and on the table tennis tournament, which 200 young people have entered, and the first round of which has just concluded;

Miss Slarke gave details of the Youth Eisteddfod, and stressed that entries must reach her by March 10th.

The following were elected on the committee of summer sports: Mr. Hossell (Youth Council chairman), Mr. Cliff Dawson (Wylde Green Congregational Youth Club), and Mr. John Lester (Emmanuel Young Men's Club).

Mr. Hossell reported that £23 16s. was the profit of the youth dance held on February 3rd. Five guineas of this had been sent to the Guide Commissioner, Mrs. Sperryn, for the Guide International Service Fund, and the rest had been handed to Mr. A. Loach for the Youth Council Magazine Publication Fund.

Mr. Basil Casson (St. Peter's Maney Youth Fellowship) gave the report of the sub-committee on the Youth Council constitution.

It was decided to hold a games rally on June 7th, and further details will be sent to clubs.

Mr. Alan Hossell was thanked for the splendid lead he has given the Youth Council during his term of office.

"The part that the British Commonwealth has to play in the new world order is essential to the success of any new world order. We can make a contribution which nobody else can make, from our long history and experience," said Lord Cranborne, Secretary of State for the Dominions, in a recent speech.

AMERICAN'S TRIBUTE TO BRITISH WOMEN

Members of Sutton Coldfield Methodist Church Youth Club were recently addressed by Sergt. K. C. Sell, of the United States Army, who said that British women had not been accepted as man's equal in society to the degree enjoyed by American women. The important role played by British women in this war, however, he said, had proved to everyone their capabilities.

Sergt. Sell said that an antagonistic attitude to be found between blacks and whites was entirely erroneous.

In reply to a question by a member of the audience if there was any foundation to the impression that the American soldier had a low moral standard, the speaker gave a negative reply. A small percentage of any Army always attracted attention to its conduct and, gave a poor impression to some people. Britain, he said, had played the role of host in a most efficient and friendly manner. It was not the fault of the English people if some U.S. soldiers met the "street girls."

To continue to recall the unfortunate past between America and Great Britain, mainly the wars of 1776 and 1812, with a feeling of hatred that blinded all reasoning of present problems and the necessity of future co-operation between these two countries, was a grave mistake, he said.

A report of this meeting appeared in a recent issue of the "News," but parts of it have been said to be misleading.

Sutton News 10/3/45.

MAIL SACK

((("TIRES FOR VICTORY" CONTEST)))

Napoleon said that an army travels on its stomach, but our army travels on its tires. We have rolled rapidly over France and are now smashing in the gates of the Fatherland. Without strong support from the rear, we cannot hope to continue to advance. Thousands of vehicles are needed to carry supplies to the front. Rubber is scarce, for Japan holds the world's supply of it.

Everyone must conserve. Ideas are needed to remind soldiers of the necessity of being careful. Write a short essay of one hundred words or less on tire conservation. It will help everyone concerned. As an extra incentive, a three day pass will be given for the best essay in each detachment. Here's your chance for a short leave and to also remind other GIs of the seriousness of the situation.

§3 §3 §3 A GI REMINDS US §3 §3 §3

Reprinted in the leading newspapers throughout the United States is a letter written by PFC Morris Litsky of Detachment "E". It is an appeal to the American people written while in a rest hospital after fighting with the "Rangers" in Normandy.

Landing with the first wave on D-Day, PFC Litsky lasted until D-14 when he collapsed. On behalf on his Company Commander and his comrades, he wrote the following plea.

"Oh, weary world, open your ears to our cries that rise from beneath the sand and earth. We hated to die. There was so much we wanted to do, but for us nothing can be done - only little white crosses and a woman's tears. But remember us and how dearly bought has been the liberty of which we so lightly boasted throughout our nation's life."

"We are not heroes. We are just plain dead Americans. We died prematurely. We can only rest in peace if we can be sure that we have not died in vain. If our death brings everlasting peace to this, our world, then it is worth the blood spilled."

"You that are left, the world over, turn to God and love. In God we trust and in humanity we can only hope that it has learned the lesson for which we have paid. Learn to be a little more kind, a little more gentle. Learn to love thy neighbor."

——— AFTERNOON EDITION ———

The "Stars and Stripes" has now become an "afternoon edition". This change is due to the late arrival of trains. In the past the delivery of this newspaper was made to this organization by vehicle, but a drastic reduction has been made in the "Stars and Stripes" personnel, and that service no longer remains. "Pre-breakfast" delivery cannot always be given; however, we will endeavor to get the papers to your detachment as soon as possible.

☆ DON'T MISS THESE!!! ☆

31 Dec. "Open House" Party, Holland Road Rec Hall
      9:00 - 12:30 AM
2 Jan. Town Hall Dance   8:00 - 12:00 PM
    Dets. C,D,Hqs, and WACs
3 Jan. USO Show   Holland Road Rec Hall
    8:00 PM
6 Jan. Town Hall Dance   7:30 - 11:30 PM
    Dets. B,E,F, and WACs

Anglo-American Forum

PATTISON'S CAFE, THE PARADE,
SUTTON COLDFIELD

THURSDAY, APRIL 19th

At 7-30 p.m.

"DUMBARTON OAKS
YALTA
SAN FRANCISCO
What they mean to you"

Opener :

Lieut. ANDREW P. ZIRPOLI
(U.S. ARMY).

ADMISSION, including REFRESHMENTS :
H.M. and ALLIED FORCES, FREE.
CIVILIANS, 1/-

JAMES UPTON, LTD., PRINTERS, BIRMINGHAM AND LONDON.

U.S. OFFICER EXPLAINS AMERICAN POLITICS

Addressing Sutton Coldfield Rotarians at their weekly luncheon on Wednesday, Lt. Zirpoli—welfare officer for American forces—spoke on the trend of American politics. Explaining that he was, personally, a "New Deal-er," and keen supporter of President Roosevelt, he said that it was his desire to be fair to all parties in his brief resume of his vast subject. In dealing with the origin and aims of the various parties, Lieut. Zirpoli gave an interesting word picture of the various personalities outstanding in the different parties, and engendered in his hearers, a lively interest in the forthcoming presidential elections.

The interest he aroused was demonstrated by the questions which were put to him by Rotarians at the end of his address. In both address and answers Lieut. Zirpoli showed himself to be a keen student of politics and possessed of a sound and extensive knowledge of his subject.

Some amusement was caused when, in answering one question, one of his colleagues—Lieut. Gill, who was present—felt he had been put "on the spot" by Lieut. Zirpoli's comments, as his views did not altogether coincide.

Proposing a vote of thanks, Mr. L. T. Howes commented on the number of addresses Rotarians had listened to during recent months which had a bearing on post-war conditions. He expressed the opinion that the outstanding fact that emerged from these various talks was that if we were to obtain the post-war conditions so much desired, the sure foundation on which to build was Anglo-American friendship. He commented on the fact that the speaker was doing so much in this cause, and felt that in giving Rotarians a clear understanding of American politics he had, by coming to address them, helped considerably to this end.

Sutton News 10/6/44.

AMERICAN OFFICERS RECEIVE SUTTON'S "FRIENDSHIP FILM"
U.S. FORCES "EXCEPTIONALLY KIND TO THE CHILDREN

COLONEL G. V. HERIZ-SMITH. Chief British Liaison Officer with the U.K. Base Headquarters, American Army, and Colonel J. Mallory, Deputy Chief of Staff at Base Headquarters, attended the July meeting of Sutton Coldfield Town Council at the conclusion of which the Mayor (Councillor F. W. Terry) made a presention of a coloured film taken during "Salute the Soldier" Week, in May, 1944, when American personnel took part in a procession and march-past. The officers had come from London in response to a special invitation.

The Mayor remarked that the people of Sutton Coldfield had made many friends with members of the American Forces, who had been exceptionally kind to the children. There had been happy parties, particularly at Christmas time, many of the officers became "uncles."

Accepting the film, Colonel Mallory said the American troops had been unusually happy in their contacts with the citizens of Sutton Coldfield. The coming to the town during the war years of a large number of American troops had meant a considerable burden and had resulted in hardship on the community; and the friendship, co-operation and cordiality received had been appreciated.

"Through our united efforts with our Allies we have finally overcome the Nazi tyranny which threatened for so long the fundamental principles of justice and fairness on which our two countries were founded, Col Mallory said.

He added that Americans all over the United Kingdom would take back with them happy memories; they hoped the memories of their visit would be equally as pleasant to Sutton folk. The presentation film would be regarded as a token of the friendship of the people of Sutton, which the American Forces had very much enjoyed.

Sutton News.

G.I.s awaiting the start of the Wings for Victory Parade (P. Tillar).

Lt. Col. Hartigan (front, centre) and officers of the F.B.P.O. (Illustrated).

Training for the G.I.s was not just for the mind. As soldiers the G.I.s also had to be trained in military skills such as shooting. This applied mainly to the guard detail. Most of the G.I.s had received some firearms instruction during basic training. Phil Tillar remembers using Springfields, M-1 Garands, Browning Automatic Rifles and Machine Guns. On travelling overseas the men were issued with pistols but no ammunition. On arrival at the Post Office they turned them in to the Commanding Officer and they were re-issued to the men (along with ammunition) only when they were on guard duty.

During the time when there was a threat of Nazi invasion the men were issued with rifles which were later traded in for carbines. When the threat of invasion was over these were handed in and from this time on it was mainly the guard detail who handled the firearms. The guard detail of the unit and the prison guards were regularly required to complete the carbine course at the Maney Hill Range. High scores were usually obtained and results revealed a good knowledge of marksmanship technique.

Marching was also part of the men's military training. Most mornings would find the men parading outside their messing centre before marching to work. The American servicemen were involved in several parades in Sutton. The first of these was the 'Wings for Victory March' on the 1st of May 1943. Many of the men had not taken part in formal parades since they left the States so a week before the event they practised marching with

*Passing the Empress Cinema in the
Wings for Victory Parade.*
(L. McDermott).

10th Replacement Depot Band leading the Wings for Victory Parade. (P. Tillar).

133

In front of Mere Green Mess Hall. (H. Brown).

Salute the Soldier Parade. (H. Brown).

the band in side streets near the Holland Road Barracks and in Sutton Park. Kate Kendall (an eight year old at the time) remembers watching them and her opinion was that they needed the practice!

Out of 2,000 people in uniform 7 officers and 200 enlisted men from the Post Office took part. Beside the G.I.s the R.A.F., Home Guard, A.T.S., W.A.A.F.s, Firemen, Air Raid Wardens, Nurses, Land Army, Boy Scouts and Girl Guides were represented. A Drum and Bugle Corps was loaned by the 10th Replacement Depot and on the day they marched at the front of the parade.

Leonard McDermott was one of the G.I.s that took part on this occasion. He noted in his diary that he and his colleagues followed a route from the Town Hall, down The Parade to the Odeon then back to the Town Hall where the marchers assembled in the square and listened to a short speech by the Lord Mayor who thanked everyone for their efforts to make the 'Wings for Victory' drive a success. Air Vice Marshall J. C. Andrews C.B., D.S.O., M.C. took the salute. Lieutenant Colonel E. E. Schroeder, Chief Postal Officer; Lieutenant Colonel Hartigan; Sutton's Mayor, Councillor W. Moss; the Town Clerk, Mr R. Walsh; and Councillor J. J. Ogley were also on the reviewing stand.

At the time Francis Sullivan thought:

"We looked poor excuses of soldiers compared to the disciplined trained Tommies that marched with us."

Phil Tillar, on the other hand, thought that they made a good impression. The men were complimented on their 'fine bearing and manner of marching'* by their superiors. On the men's return to Holland Road Barracks they were assembled near the auditorium to hear the announcement of promotions. Phil Tillar was one of the lucky ones to be promoted on this occasion.

On July the 10th the Suttonians had another chance to view the G.I.s in their official capacity at the Farm Sunday Service in Sutton Park. The postal workers were on parade at the pageant site and the residents gathered on the slopes to watch them. In August the park was again the scene of military activity, this time the Battallion Army Cadet Force were the soldiers in question. The U.S. Army's part in this was to provide the catering and 'cookies'.

On the 13th of May 1944 400 enlisted men and women from the Post Office participated in a 'Salute the Soldier' week parade. Again Leonard remembers the occasion in his diary:

"At 11:30 those of us who were to parade were let off from work and we rode up to Four Oaks for lunch. After changing into dress uniform we rode down to Holland Road Barracks to form for the parade. We started from the playing fields near Coles Lane and, under threatening skies, marched up to the Parade. Large crowds[†] were out to watch what was termed the biggest parade ever held in Sutton. It went off rather well as far as we were concerned and a few speeches in the park finished up the ceremonies."

The troops were reviewed by Brigadier General A. M. Ramsden O.B.E., T.D., A.D.C., of the British Army with Colonel Kilean of Whittington Barracks, Lieutenant

---

*F.B.P.O. Historical Report 1943.
[†]Sutton News reported that these numbered approximately 2,300 people.

Colonel Hartigan and Lieutenant Colonel Bacarach on the reviewing stand. The Lord Mayor expressed his appreciation for the cooperation extended by the United States forces in the area and for their part in making the observance successful.

On the 19th of June members of the unit participated in a similar 'Salute the Soldier' parade, this time in Erdington, and on June the 21st there was another one at Gravelly Hill. A coloured film was taken during the week and included shots of the processions. Later this film was presented by Mayor Terry to Colonel G. V. Herizsmith, who was the Chief British Liason Officer with the U.K. Base Headquarters American Army.

Chapter 16

Invasion Mail

D-Day came as no surprise to the majority of the postal workers. The men were aware of the intense training that the fighting units were undergoing. They also read in the English newspapers and the American publication 'Stars and Stripes' about the softening up of defences in Europe from the British night bombing and the American daylight pinpoint bombing.

Since April 1944 the 'Invasion Post Office' (17th B.P.O) had been working alongside the 1st B.P.O. The core of this unit had been formed from elements of the 8th B.P.O. (Cairo, Egypt) and the 4th B.P.O. (Pomona, California). It also incorporated men with limited postal experience. Colonel Harkins was the Commanding Officer of the unit which consisted of 31 officers and 824 enlisted men. The 17th B.P.O.'s assignment was to aid the 1st B.P.O. until they could move overseas with the invasion forces. Whilst in Sutton they were able to gain valuable mail handling experience as they worked alongside the 1st B.P.O. The unit was invaluable in Sutton as the volume of mail had grown to such great proportions that it was impossible for the regularly assigned personnel to deal with it all.

From the beginning of May 1944 the men at Sutton were waiting for D-Day to arrive. The following are extracts from Leonard McDermott's diary:

"Friday 5 May – The weather continues rather cool and showery and it begins to look as though the last fortnight in April would have been a good time for the invasion. Everyone is speculating on the time and place of the Big Event.
Monday 22 May – Another week begins and no invasion yet. Everyone is very impatient, yet have faith in Eisenhower and the other leaders, who must be 'sure' this time.
Tuesday 16 May – In the training programme this morning we had instruction on the carbine. Work at the P.O. continues about the same . . . 17th Base P.O. men still work with us. We did lose a few men recently . . . some cooks and some truck drivers. Everything seems to be just marking time until the big day.
Monday 22 May – Another week begins and still no invasion . . . the days are long now, but in a month we shall have the longest day of the year, so, if any move is to be made on the Western Front, now is the time. All we ever talk about at work is when the big push will start and when we shall go home.
Tuesday 23 May – The weather is much improved over last week . . . Plenty of work at the P.O. Units are beginning to move around . . . and all sorts of rumors are flying about. It begins to look as though the long awaited Second Front is not too far off.
Thursday 25 May – Still the days slip by and no invasion. Everyone talks about it and of when we are going home. The campaign in Italy seems to be going well, with the Anzio beachead boys being finally relieved.
Friday 26 May – My 29th birthday – my third in the army, and my second in England. The day passed much the same as all the rest in recent weeks. Plenty of work,

everyone still wondering when the invasion will take place and when we shall be going home.

Monday 5 June – The directory is spreading out some more at the P.O. and further changes are being made. In the war news today the Allied Armies marched in on Rome which had been evacuated by the Nazis without a fight.''

At the end of May representatives from the Post Office had to attend a conference at Postal Division Headquarters in London with regard to the handling of mail for troops in

Invasion mail being readied for transportation to units taking part in D-Day landings. (U.S. Army).

the marshalling areas and for other echelons which might move forward. A tentative plan was also outlined for the handling of mail for the invasion forces. In readiness several postal workers were sent to perform duty in the marshalling areas and some were transferred to quartermaster truck companies where they were needed.

Just before the Allies invaded Normandy the censors ordered outgoing mail to be halted. The men continued to work day and night. Mail was cased, tied up and sacked, and everything was ready for shipment. Francis Sullivan remembers that the sacks of air mail were piled up to the ceiling. Leonard McDermott recalls that at this time the Post Office was processing mail for upwards of two million people.

On the night of June the 5th Julia Goble remembers marching back to the barracks from the Post Office with a group of W.A.C.s. She noticed that the moon was particularly bright and whispered to her friend, Margaret Malloy, 'What a night for bombing.' The next minute they heard planes going overhead. The Commanding Officer gave the order to 'Halt', as the girls were so busy watching the planes and cheering them on that they were not keeping in formation. After a couple of minutes the C.O. quietened them down and brought them to attention. Back at the camp the girls couldn't sleep and spent most of the night talking about the night's events. Back at the barracks Janis Leonard remembers hearing the endless roar of planes overhead. When she went outside to take a look a guard reassured her with 'Don't be afraid, they're ours!'

David Turney remembers that he was drinking coffee with his billetters when he heard the noise of a number of planes going over. Everyone went out in the garden and listened and watched. When he heard the planes David knew in his heart what it meant and that this was the beginning of the end, or as Winston Churchill put it – 'the end of the beginning'.

Mrs B. Upton, who was a civilian worker at the Post Office also saw the 'planes going over on D-Day. When she arrived for work at the Post Office she noticed that the sentries had fixed bayonets on their rifles so she knew that something had happened. During the morning, while the men and women were working a G.I. came in and announced the news. Everyone was very excited and most thought that the war would soon be over. Later Mrs Upton found that her husband was one of the ones that had landed in France that morning.

The report that electrified the whole of Penns Lane Camp (occupied by the 17th B.P.O. men at the time) came over the radio at 09:45 a.m.:

" 'Hey you guys, the invasion began this morning,' yelled Bob Dencer to his tentmates in Detachment C.

'Go-wan. We've been hearing stuff like that for weeks. Get away and let us sleep,' retorted some of the unbelieving skeptical G.I.s

At 11 O'clock, while scores of us hovered over the radio in the day room, the announcement of General Eisenhower's confirmation of the invasion satisfied the most incredulous of us. This was it, the day we had looked forward to for so long. We knew it meant the beginning of the end of the 17th Penns Lane, but it also meant the beginning of the end of the enemy."*

Leonard's diary entry for the 6th of June reads:

June 6th – Today was the *big day*!! D-Day has finally arrived. The big push began about 6 a.m. Various reports began to trickle in from time to time and the P.O. was a-buzz with excitement. Not much detail yet. Today was also the day we had picked a few weeks ago to celebrate our second anniversary of overseas duty. The old original 32 planned to have a party, we also invited the second group of 19. Many have left, of course, but about 35 turned up at the White Lion Inn. Capt. Jordan took pictures before the party. The meal was marvellous! Absolutely the best I've had in England. Everyone made a speech, including Colonel Hartigan, who surprised eveyone by his humility. A good time was had by all and the party wound up with the usual community singing."

---

*17th B.P.O. The Invasion Outfit.

5 MONDAY (157-209)

Tough getting back to work after a pleasant eventful weekend. The directory is spreading out somemore at the P.O. and further changes are being made.

In the war news today, the Allied Armies marched in on Rome, which had been evacuated by the Nazis without a fight.

After supper this evening I went with George down to Doreen Andrew's house. Jim Stanmore, Robert's brother, was there, just back from India, Africa and other far off places. Maggie, Doreen's friend, also was there. We had a very enjoyable evening, spent mostly talking and playing Monopoly — with George emerging as the winner.

6 TUESDAY (158-208)
Trinity Law Sittings begin

Today was the big day!! D-Day has finally arrived. The big push began about six o'clock this morning. Various reports began to trickle in from time to time and the P.O. was abuzz with excitement, not much detail yet.

Today was also the day we had picked a few weeks ago to celebrate our second anniversary of overseas duty. The old original 32 planned to have a party; we also invited the second group of 19. Many have left, of course, but about 35 turned up at the White Lion Inn. Capt. Jordan took pictures before the party. The meal was marvelous! Absolutely the best I've had in England! Everyone made a speech, including Col. Hartigan, who surprised everyone by his humility. A good time was had by all, and the party wound up with the usual community singing.

Leonard McDermott's diary.

Although D-Day was a cause for celebration in the Post Office Kenneth Osgood remembers that the men had to wear battledress all that day and be alert for counter invasion. Chas Bubenas recalls that they were instructed to wear their helmets and carry their gas masks around with them.

Although prior to D-Day most of the men were kept in the dark as to the exact details of the invasion plan there were some bigotted officers who were privy to certain classified information. Unfortunately one of the bigotted officers of the 567th Postal Unit based at Sutton at the time disclosed the objectives of the U.S. Army's part in the plan to a member of the Adjutant General's department (who wasn't privy to the plan). For this breach of security he was convicted, dismissed from the service and sentenced to confinement with hard labour for one year at the U.S. Disciplinary Barracks, Greenhaven, New York.

After D-Day it was found that Sutton had had a bigger hand in the success of the invasion than was known at the time. A counter intelligence unit that had a hand in creating the deception that the invasion would be caried out at Calais instead of Normandy was based in Sutton.* Prior to D-Day the unit worked night and day to set up this myth. Even now it is hard to find exactly how big a part the unit in Sutton played in the deception although one of the officers says:

"I have frequently entertained the feeling that if it was not for what took place in Sutton the Normandy invasion would have been a slaughter."

After the invasion the word came in to release the mail and then it was shipped out by the fastest means of transportation posible. A completely new section called 'the French Section' had to be organised and this section handled the mail intended for dispatch to Normandy. The first dispatch to France was made on the 8th of June. A red and black colour code was used to represent the two established beachheads. Black signified the U.S. forces and red the British forces. The mail was packed into pouches with the appropriate colour code and shipped directly to the beachheads.

On the 12th of June Detachment B of the 17th B.P.O., which consisted of 96 men and was attached to Advance Section Communication Zone, left for France. They landed on the beaches on July the 3rd. On June the 14th Detachment A of the 17th B.P.O., which consisted of 99 men and was attached to the 1st Army, left Sutton for Tidworth Barracks. They arrived in France five weeks later.

Meanwhile on the 13th of June the first cards recording invasion casualties in France arrived from the Machine Record Unit. These represented the casualties of the 82nd Airborne Division who were amongst the first troops to be dropped in France and suffered heavy casualties. D-Day, like any major battle, was high in casualties and this meant that there was a large amount of redirected mail. Any G.I. who was wounded or transferred usually had his mail returned to the 1st B.P.O. It would then be held for a while and then resorted by the civillian workers in the hopes that a forwarding address had been filed in the meantime.

The Casualty Section was moved into a part of the new annex building, allowing room for the expansion which was urgently needed. Ten additional secondary sorting cases were installed and mail being returned to sender from this section was carefully processed. More civillian employees had to be assigned to this section because of the

---

* – See Chapter 8.

Crew working mail outside 1944. (H. Brown).

Loading invasion mail onto platform trucks. (U.S. Army).

Convoy taking 17th B.P.O. to France. (C. Abraham).

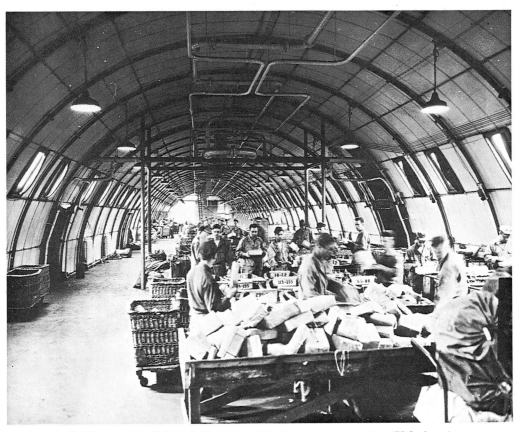

Civillian women, G.I.s and W.A.C.s working in the casualty section. (U.S. Army).

increase in mail. An intensive course of instruction was initiated to insure that each person in the section knew the exact procedure in handling Casualty Mail. Any errors here could cause untold upset to relatives back in the States. All K.I.A. (Killed In Action) or M.I.A. (Missing in Action) mail was held until the family at home had been notified, then the mail would be returned to sender.

On the Sunday after D-Day Henry Brown was concerned about a close friend of his who was in the 2nd Infantry division which had landed on the beaches of Normandy. When Henry looked through the files at the Post Office he found the K.I.A. stamp by his friend's name. As this information was confidential he could not let the family know that he knew, so he wrote a letter to the family asking how his friend was and mentioning that he had not heard from him for a while. The family, who had been notified by this time, then wrote and told Henry the circumstances of his friend's death.

In August the Casualty Section was moved from the annex back into the main building where a separate large room afforded better security provisions for this work.

The unit celebrated Independance Day in July. Phil Tillar remembers seeing the 'Stars and Stripes' flying from Sutton Town Hall's flagpole, replacing the Union Jack. On seeing this Phil assumed that at last all had been forgiven for the events of that day in 1776, the end of a very different sort of war to the one that England and America were now fighting hand in hand in Europe.

On July the 8th Detachment C of the 17th B.P.O. consisting of 223 enlisted men left Sutton for France. Some men from the 1st B.P.O. had been transferred into the 17th B.P.O. along with men from the replacement depots and other B.P.O.s. By July ten tons of letter mail were being dispatched daily to units in Normandy.

On the 24th of August Detachment D of the 17th B.P.O., which consisted of 100 men, was moved out to the marshalling areas for shipment to France to serve the troops there. On September the 20th H.Q. and the remaining detachments of the 17th B.P.O. left for France. Although the men were needed in France the work in England was still increasing and training activities had to be suspended so that there were more work hours to cope with the increase in mail volume. A swing shift had to be brought into temporary use.

Some of the troops that had been working at the Post Office were now being sent overseas to supplement the combat units. After D-Day Tom Morrissey was one of the G.I.s who was sent to Tidworth Barracks for intensive infantry training, where the men went through a hardening process as they prepared for combat. In September of 1944 Tom was sent to France to join General Patton's 26th Infantry Division, 104th Infantry Regiment, as a rifleman. Later he took part in the Battle of the Bulge where he was injured. He escaped death by about an inch when mortar fragmentation hit the left side of his head. From this time on many G.I.s were sent to Tidworth to retrain for combat. By Spring of 1945 only a small number of able bodied men were left working in Sutton. Don Whalen felt that if the war had lasted long enough most of the postal men would have been transferred into combat units.

This process worked in the reverse. Some of those who had been injured in the fighting in Europe or during their training in England were sent to rehabilitation centres in England where they were given a choice of various non-combatant units to transfer to.

Joe Gardiner's right ear drum had been damaged while training with the 29th U.S. Infantry Division on the Devonshire Moors in January of 1944. He remembers that:

17th B.P.O. Cherbourg, France August '44 (H. Brown).

"They were firing 105 Howizers over our heads and one fell short. The next thing I remember I woke up in the hospital in Tavistock at the 115th Station Hospital. They moved me from there to the 177th General Hospital in Taunton. After I recovered they sent me to the 1st B.P.O."

Many soldiers like Webb Armstrong chose to go to the 1st B.P.O. rather than a cook and bakers school or the like. Webb couldn't go back into combat as he had lost the hearing in his right ear and had been badly burnt. He was the only one to survive when his tank blew up while serving with the 749th U.S. Tank Battallion at St Lo.

In August 1944 a new airmail service was inaugurated at the Post Office to help with the incoming and outgoing mail to and from France. The service ran daily from Prestwick, Scotland, to Aldermaston via Fradley Airfield, Lichfield, and return. Mail to the States and the Continent were transported by truck from the Post Office to Fradley to make these connections. Mail to France would go via Aldermaston. Unfortunately this service did not run as smoothly as it might, this was due to the lack of flying equipment. This caused one incident where it was necessary to move 30,000 pounds of first class mail by train to Southampton where it travelled by ship to France. Air shipments to the continent were discontinued in February 1945 and a boat-train service was used instead.

145

Chapter 17

Base Post Office, France

Christmas 1944 was a busy time for the 1st B.P.O. with more troops in Europe to process mail for than in the previous year and less postal workers in Sutton to do the job. The first of the Christmas parcels began arriving in October. Men from the 11th and 12th Replacement Depots were attached temporarily to the base from this month onwards. Five hundred men from the Ground Force Replacement System were assigned for temporary duty at the base and two hundred extra civillians were requested to compensate for the large number of civillian absentees reported daily.

During November the post arrived in heavy volume. Simultaneous with the Christmas mail a large amount of mail for hospitalized personnel arrived. This mail had been returned from combat units without a hospital designation.

To store the mail 35,000 square feet of storage space was acquired at the Castle Bromwich R.A.F. station where a large hangar was made available for the purpose. This hangar was used for the alphabetizing of parcel post from the Directory Section and the separation of mail to replacement companies. The hangar was originally intended to be returned to the British before the end of December but this was impossible due to the large amount of 'No Record' mail on hand towards the end of the month. The Post Office had to ask for an extension of time, which was granted.

Men from the 10th Replacement Depot who had been hospitalized and were awaiting shipment back to the continent were asked to volunteer for work at the Post Office during November. The depot was able to supply about 200 casuals a day to help with the large influx of mail.

In December a further five hundred men from the 10th Replacement Depot were assigned to the Post Office to help during the rush period, which was expected to last until March. This group of men did night tour duty in the Directory Section. A group of National Fire Service men, who were no longer needed by the British Government, were also drafted in to help.

During December the Sutton G.I.s (enlisted men and officers) were working a seven day week while the W.A.C.s were working six days out of seven. In this month the largest amount of parcel post handled in the Parcel Post Section for a single day consisted of 9,100 sacks. During this month 1,114 railway carloads of mail were dispatched.

To make the G.I.'s job harder severe fog seriously interfered with the normal operation of the unit during December. At times all vehicles were grounded which meant that the mail and personnel could not be moved around and this held up operations for long periods at a time. During foggy days it was necessary for a man to walk in front of the vehicles waving a white hankerchief as a guide for the driver. In the evenings the man would carry a flashlight.

In this month Captain Jordan was transferred to H.Q. Normandy Base Section and Captain Bacon took over as H.Q. Commandant. Leonard McDermott has the following entry in his diary for December the 4th:

Civilian workers working through mail for hospitalized personnel. (U.S. Army).

"This afternoon all the 'old gang' got off at quarter past five to prepare for the party in honor of Captain Jordan. (A few days earlier we had learned that he was to be transferred out of our unit.) The party was held at the officer's quarters with 20 out of our original 32 present and 12 out of the next 19. We had a nice meal and Capt. Jordan 'let his hair down' and admitted to being very soft-hearted, as we had always suspected. A lot of us made a little speech expressing our regrets and extending our best wishes to 'Ol' Buck'. It was a swell party all around."

With the extra manpower in December the postal workers managed to wade through the bulk of the Christmas mail and most of the parcel post was dispatched to the units by

Christmas Day. (Although Kenneth Osgood remembers seeing packages at the Post Office in February 1945 that had been mailed in September of the previous year. These were the parcels that had come via North Africa.)

Part of the 1,867,810 Christmas parcels serviced through the Directory, Christmas 1944 (U.S. Army).

Christmas was a holiday well-earned by all the postal troops and it was celebrated with parties for all of the detachments. On the 16th of December there was a party at the 'rec hall' (Holland Road Barracks). The First Class Section held their party at the Four Oaks Day Room on the 17th. On the 20th the Front Office Staff also held their party at the Four Oaks Day Room. About 50 people attended for dancing and games. Francis Sullivan was the Master of Ceremonies and was, in Leonard McDermott's words, 'a riot'. On the 22nd of the month the Motor Pool held their party at the Four Oaks Day Room. The W.A.C.s had their party at the Holland Road Day Room on the 23rd of December and the officers held theirs on the 24th at Grey Friars Mess.

Many G.I.s celebrated Christmas with the families that they were billetted with as they had come to look on these as their second families. Dorothy and Sybil Grieg remember their house being full of females on Christmas Day so their mother sent the G.I. who was billetted with them, George Murphy, to bring some friends so that there would be some males in the company. George went and when he returned they opened the door to find a garden full of G.I.s. Sybil remembers that they had quite a party!

Jeanne Lidgate remembers her family inviting two G.I.s to her house for Christmas as her brothers were away and the family was depleted. The Americans arrived laden with such luxuries as tins of fruit, lipsticks and stockings. Jeanne's mother cooked a goose for lunch and her father, who she recalls was an expert on mixing cocktails, saw to the liquid refreshment. After dinner they roasted chestnuts on the open fire and sang songs around the Christmas tree. She remembers that everyone enjoyed that family Christmas.

On Boxing day the W.A.C.s held a Christmas Dance at the Holland Road Day Room with music furnished by the 77th Station Hospital Orchestra. Nearly 400 attended on this occasion. Ken Sell gives his account of the event:

> "The school auditorium was the recreation Hall of the W.A.C.s. It was decorated with holly from Sutton Park, courtesy of Mayor Terry. Refreshments were large tubs (10 gallons) of beer and tubs of lemonade. A British Unit from Sutton park had been invited. The band played loudly, the dancing was getting better all the time. I had been invited to have a Boxing Day dinner at the home of Eric and Clarissa Illife in Wylde Green. Sgt. Robert E. Dayo had been left in charge of the party. When I returned to the party after 10:00 p.m. Sgt. Dayo immediately told me that the party was getting to be 'too much'.

> "Pvt. Helen Cooney, a lively Irish girl with a great sense of humor, had her auburn hair done up in a bun-style. Three large rhododendron leaves resembling feathers stuck out from the bun. Helen was in charge of the refreshment serving crew. I told her that she looked like a wild Indian princess. After she laughed loudly she replied: "Yes, but just look at them. They are all getting plastered. They all want the beer and won't touch the lemonade, there is only a little beer left." I told her to have her W.A.C.s pour the lemonade into the beer and said: "They certainly will not want it and that will stop the drinking." A British Tommy observed the dumping of the beer into the lemonade and began to inform all the G.I.s and W.A.C.s around him that they should try a great drink – a shandy! "Dancers stopped and crowded around the refreshment booth clammering for this new drink. In a short time there was no more shandy. Pvt. Cooney loudly wailed: "Look at them, they're all getting drunker." Sgt. Dayo decided that the great British party had to end, so he stopped the music. Pvt. Cooney was told to phone the British camp to bring down their lorry and to load on their Tommies. We herded the G.I.s out of the barrack gates and the W.A.C.s back into their own barracks and the W.A.C. Broom Brigade* was alerted for duty. We had a smashing party and an introduction to the surprising 'shandy'."

On the 31st of the month a letter from Colonel Hartigan was sent to all the troops of the Command thanking them for their cooperation and good spirit during the Christmas rush. In it he promised that from now on they would be able to have one day off a week with the occasional privilege of a 24 or 48 hour pass. This was received with enthusiasm by the overworked troops.

It took until January the 24th for the working hours to change. Since November the 1st the men had been working from 7 a.m. to 6 p.m. on the day tour and from 9 p.m. to 7 a.m. on the night shift. This meant that that the men who were billetted at a distance from the Post Office were having to get up at 5 a.m. to be at work for 7. In January the hours were shortened by one hour so that the day tour began at 8 a.m.

Also in January 1945 a further five officers and fifty enlisted men were assigned to

---

*A duty list of W.A.C.s was posted each week. Straw brooms were placed at each barrack entrance. A W.A.C. was at each entrance ready to use her broom on any wandering G.I. who happened to stumble through the doors.

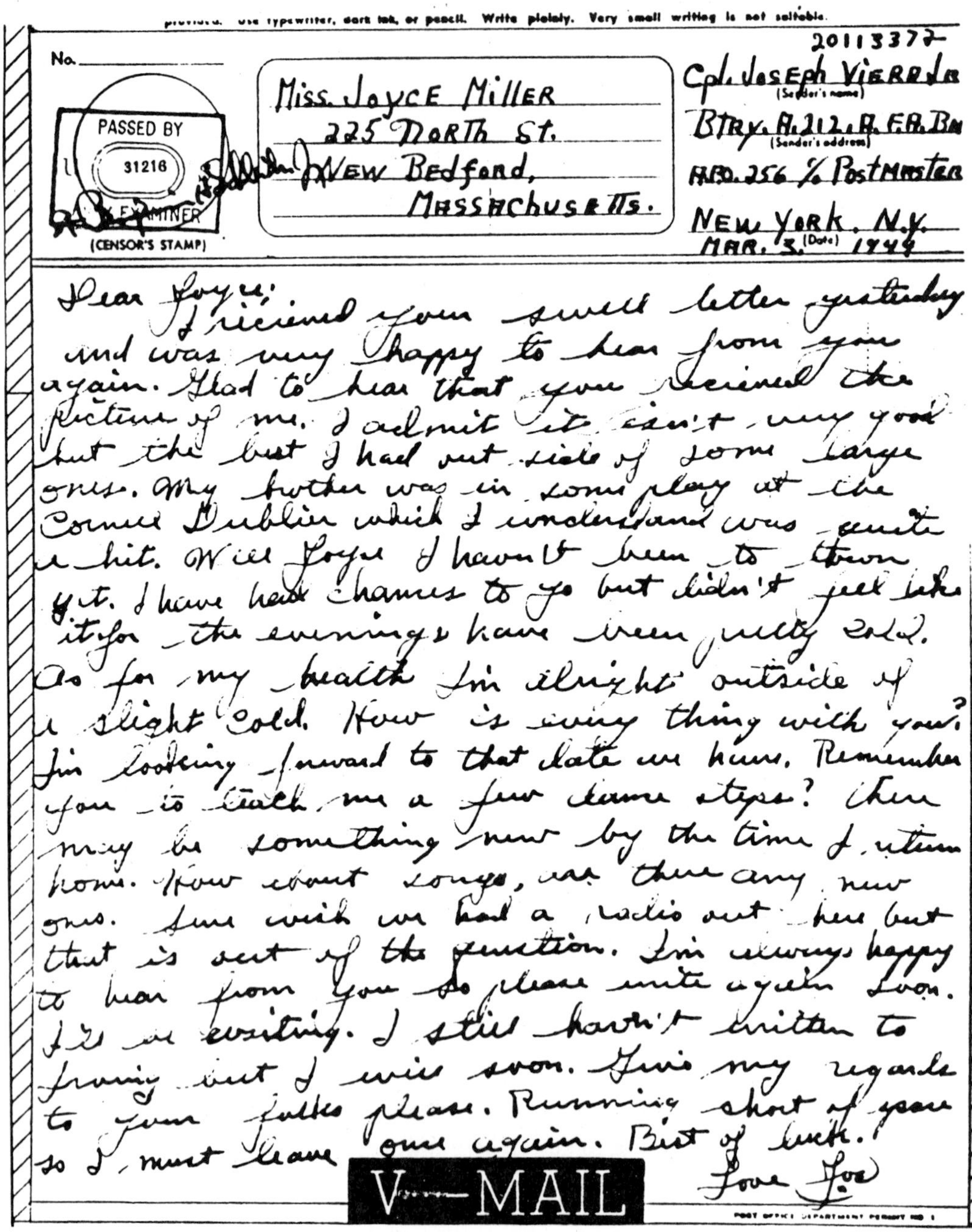

No. _____

PASSED BY
31216
EXAMINER
(CENSOR'S STAMP)

Miss. Joyce Miller
225 North St.
New Bedford,
Massachusetts.

20113377
Cpl. Joseph Vierra Jr.
(Sender's name)
Btry. A. 212. A. F.A. Bn.
(Sender's address)
A.P.O. 256 % Postmaster
New York, N.Y.
Mar. 3 (Date) 1944

Dear Joyce;
I recieved your swell letter yesterday and was very happy to hear from you again. Glad to hear that you recieved the picture of me. I admit it isn't very good but the best I had out side of some large ones. My brother was in some play at the Cornell Dublin which I understand was quite a hit. Well Joyce I haven't been to town yet. I have had chances to go but didn't feel like it for the evenings have been pretty cold. As for my health I'm alright outside of a slight cold. How is every thing with you? I'm looking forward to that date we have. Remember you is teach me a few dance steps? There may be something new by the time I return home. How about songs, are there any new ones. Sure wish we had a radio out here but that is out of the question. I'm always happy to hear from you so please write again soon. I'll be waiting. I still haven't written to Frank but I will soon. Give my regards to your folks please. Running short of space so I must leave once again. Best of luck.

Love Joe

V-MAIL

POST OFFICE DEPARTMENT PERMIT NO. 1

V-mail letter shown as it would appear when reproduced from microfilm.

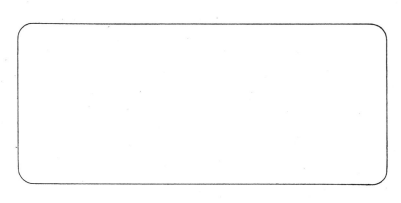

V ···— MAIL

See Instruction No. 5

V-Mail Service provides the most expeditious dispatch and reduces the weight of mail to and from personnel of our Armed Forces outside the continental United States. When addressed to points where micro-film equipment is operated, a miniature photographic negative of the message will be made and sent by the most expeditious transportation available for reproduction and delivery. The original message will be destroyed after the reproduction has been delivered. Messages addressed to or from points where micro-film equipment is not operated will be transmitted in their original form by the most expeditious means available.

INSTRUCTIONS

(1) Write the entire message plainly on the other side within marginal lines.

(2) PRINT the name and address in the two panels provided. Addresses to members of the Armed Forces should include rank or rating of the addressee, unit to which attached, and APO or Naval address.

(3) Fold, seal, and deposit in any post office letter drop or street letter box.

(4) Enclosures must not be placed in this envelope and a separate V-Mail letter must be sent if you desire to write more than one sheet.

(5) V-Mail letters may be sent free of postage by members of the Armed Forces. When sent by others postage must be prepaid at domestic rates (3c ordinary mail, 6c if air mail is desired).

Back of V-mail form. Where photographic facilities were unavailable this letter would fold in on itself to form its own envelope and so save postage weight.

151

Detachment A, which by now was operating the V-mail station located in London. V-mail was the solution to the problem of transporting large volumes of mail. This system meant that a ton of letters could be reduced to 25 lb. V-mail letters had to be written on special forms which permitted the letter to be photographed on microfilm. This was carried out by the personnel in London. The men would take the letters to the Kodak Plant to be microfilmed. The microfilm would then be put in a mail pouch and taken to Bovington Airfield in Hertfordshire, from where it was easily transported to the United States. Once in the U.S. the letters were reproduced and delivered. This system worked in reverse with incoming mail. Facilities for photographing V-mail were not always available so sometimes the original forms, which were light and easy to transport were sent directly to the recipient.

Although this method was better than the traditional way of writing letters, work was done to see if the system could be even more effective. Staff Sgt. Shaak and Pvt. Gunther of Detachment A were placed on detached service for a week in December 1944 to make a running test of a new type of folding-sealing machine for V-mail. This machine would eliminate the use of envelopes for V-mail facsimiles by folding and gumming the facsimile itself leaving only the address and return address exposed. Results were very satisfactory with a speed of 1,800 letters per hour per machine.

Don Whalen was in Detachment A. He recalls being billetted in a hotel in Park Lane, London, which had been hit by a flying bomb. Nine G.I.s had been awarded a Purple Heart* on this occasion. Don remembers that he was billetted on the fifth floor. He was relieved that he didn't sleep walk, as in his words:

"You could walk down to the end of the hall and step out into space."

Fortunately the building was repaired soon after Don had been billetted there.

Al Lucas was in charge of Detachment A for the latter part of the war. He remembers that the H.Q. building was a lovely building belonging to a Duke. It was near to Marble Arch, one block south of and parallel to Oxford Street.

The V-mail station was a sorting office and was run on similar lines to the Sutton Post Office. The men working there processed the V-mail and sent it directly to the unit concerned. Some problems did occur and sometimes V-mail letters had to be refilmed, but on the whole things went smoothly and the workload in Sutton eased as only insufficiently adressed V-mail had to be handled there.

At the end of January the Public Relations Section press men photographed the Detachment A staff while they were engaged in the process of recording letters onto V-mail microfilm. The special occasion was the processing of the 200,000,000th outbound V-mail letter. It was addressed to Franklin D. Roosevelt, The White House, Washington D.C. and was from 'G.I. Joe', European Theatre of Operations. The press men took photos of several operations in the Post Office and also some at the Kodak Ltd.Plant which was 12 miles from the V-mail Station. Photos were also taken at John Dickinson Paper Mills Ltd. (15 miles from the Kodak Plant) where the enveloping and distribution of facsimile letters was photographed.

Also in January a new Detachment B, consisting of Lieutenant Col. Hartigan and 17 enlisted men, was activated to set up a V-mail Station on the Continent.

---

*Purple Heart – medal awarded for injuries received in the course of duty.

Examining V-mail letters with magnifying glass to make out the address. (Illustrated).

Julia Lynch at Vitrie Sur Seine. (J. Goble).

Henry Brown's files awaiting shipment to France 22/7/ 45. (H. Brown).

Henry Brown, shortly after being presented the Certificate of Merit in Paris, France. 20/8/45. (H. Brown).

(Major Jernigin assumed command of the 1st B.P.O. in Sutton). The new type of V-mail machine was sent to the Continent to be used by this detachment. The Continental V-mail Station A.P.O. 887 handled 100 rolls of inbound V-mail per day. By the end of February 1945 66 A.P.O.s were operating in the U.K. and 229 A.P.O.s on the Continent.

A large group, which became the 23rd B.P.O. and included many of the W.A.C.s, moved over to France in Spring of 1945. Kenneth Osgood was in this party and remembers seeing much destruction on his way to Vitry Sur Seine, a quiet little village near Paris. Fifty men from the 1st B.P.O. were selected to establish a Hospital Directory in France through which all mail for wounded soldiers could pass. In Kenneth's words:

"It was a most successful operation employing 3,000 French workers."

German P.O.W.s were also employed in some of the sections to do the heavy work.

A party which included Technical Sergeant Henry Brown went to France in June. He carried on his work in the Troop Locator Section over there. He had bought a brand new bicycle while he was in England and instead of leaving it behind he took it to pieces and parcelled it up so that he could post it to his new Paris address, which was near to the Arc de Triomphe. Once in Paris he spent his free time cycling around all the famous sights and taking pictures.

In July 1945 Henry was presented with the Certificate of Merit by Major Gheesling (the Commanding Officer of the Post Office in Paris) at a formation called for that purpose. Henry received the award for meritrous service performed in maintaining the troop locator files at the 1st B.P.O. during the period May '44 to May '45. His efforts greatly aided the smooth flow of mail to the troops in the combat zone during this period.

Also in July a Headquarters was established in France with 13 enlisted men and one officer, the balance to arrive in small groups from day to day as shipments were made up and transported across the channel from England. The Headquarters set up their operations in the Citroen Garage alongside the 17th B.P.O. H.Q. The Citroen Garage, situated in Blvd. des Batignolles was a huge two storey building which consumed the complete block. The Headquarters was officially known as 'Base Post Office, France' and was assigned A.P.O. 350 as its serving A.P.O. From here an airmail service to Berlin was inaugurated, mail planes left Orly Field, Paris, daily with mail.

Once the men were settled in France the Special Service Section was set up to cater for their needs. As in England, sport played an important part in the men's leisure time. An outdoor basketball court was secured until an indoor gymnasium could be obtained. Basketball equipment was issued and practices were started.

The baseball team played at Orly Field against the 14th and 17th B.P.O.s. They also flew to St Andre to play the 442nd U.S. Troop Carrier team. After the match, which they won (the 442nd's first defeat on their home field), the Troop Carrier Group gave them an air tour over Paris in one of their C47's and then took them home.

Pfc. Lunger was able to set up his swimming club again in the Butte aux Cailles swimming pool, a far cry from Erdington Baths. Lunger excelled himself by being a double winner in the Com. Z. swimming championships held at Tourelles Stadium in Paris. He won in both the low board and high board diving competitions, and by doing so qualified to take part in the E.T.O. meet at Nuremberg which took place on the 28th and 29th of July 1945. Swimming parties and picnics were held by the personnel of the Post Office along the Rivers Seine and Marne.

An Enlisted Men's Club was organised and operated on the premises of the 'Florida

EUROPEAN THEATER OF OPERATIONS
UNITED STATES ARMY

HEADQUARTERS COMMUNICATIONS ZONE

This

CERTIFICATE OF MERIT

is awarded to

TECHNICAL SERGEANT HENRY W. BROWN, 35168258, AGD

IN RECOGNITION OF CONSPICUOUSLY MERITORIOUS AND OUTSTANDING PERFORMANCE OF MILITARY DUTY

Citation

As chief of the Troop Location Section, 1st Base Post Office, from 25 April 1944 to 15 August 1944, Technical Sergeant Brown was responsible for the plan of mail distribution to units in marshalling areas on the continent, and those enroute to the continent. His outstanding diligence, high degree of technical skill, and perseverance made possible the forwarding of mail without delay in spite of changes occurring in troop locations, thus contributing in great measure to the morale of invasion troops.

JOHN C. H. LEE,
Lieutenant General, U.S. Army.

Citroen Garage. (H. Brown).

Parcel Post Section in Citroen Garage. September 1945. (H. Brown).

Club' at 20, Rue Clichy. Dances and floor shows were given almost every night and the men's beer rations were sold through the bar at the club. Unlike British beer the beer in France was chilled, but by this time the Sutton G.I.s had become accustomed to 'warm' beer. Ken Sell of the Special Service Section remembers:

> "When the last large group of G.I.s to arrive for assignment to the 1st B.P.O. were finally billetted in homes or barracks at Penns Lane, the Special Services asked them how they liked England. The reply was 'We don't because we don't like warm beer! Beer in the U.S.A. was always served ice cold.'
> "After their long period in Sutton Coldfield they were finally transferred to the new 1st B.P.O. in Paris. Since their barracks were within several blocks of the Arc d'Triomphe one would have been pleased to be in such a beautiful city where the beer was served cold. When Special Services inquired how they liked living in Paris, the reply was, 'We don't, we want to go back home to Sutton Coldfield where the beer is warm.'

The Seine Section Special Service Section held 13 dances and 7 shows through the month of August. The officers held two dances and a floor show in this month.

Chapter 18

Roosevelt est Morte

While the main bulk of the work had been transferred to the Post Office operations in France the 1st Base Post Office was still carrying out its normal operations in England. In the first part of 1945 two tragedies hit the Sutton G.I.s.

On February the 2nd there was an unfortunate incident in Sutton when an American truck reversed into a G.I., Private Eugene Stanwich. He died three days later at the 33rd Station Hospital of a ruptured liver. The ill-fated G.I. had been earlier invalided out of combat to work at the Post Office. Like the W.A.C.s who had died a few months before he was buried at the Cambridge American Military Cemetary.

In April the Americans in Sutton were dealt a bigger blow. On April the 12th 1945 the President of the United States and Commander in Chief of the U.S. Military Forces, Franklin D. Roosevelt died of a cerebral haemorrage. His death was a terrible loss to Americans. Roosevelt had held the post longer than any man in history up to that date. He had served for twelve years and many Americans could not remember any other President.

Leonard McDermott was at Tidworth Barracks awaiting transportation back home when the news came through. His diary entry for April the 13th reads:

"Before we began our firing exercise on the Perham Downs range, we heard the fateful news of the death of our great leader, President Franklin D.Roosevelt. He died suddenly of a shock yesterday afternoon while at Warm Springs, Georgia. He was 63 years old."

Kenneth Osgood learnt the sad news while based at the Post Office in France. He noticed two Frenchmen reading a newspaper and saw the headline, 'Roosevelt est Morte.' At first he thought that it was a misprint but when he realised that it wasn't he was stunned. He remembers that all the Post Office G.I.s and W.A.C.s based in France at that time were saddened by the news.

Roosevelt's death did come as a shock to the U.S. troops, many of them had not realised how ill he was. Andrew Arden recalls that when he heard the news he felt as though he had been hit in the pit of his stomach and remembers a sense of gloom over the Post Office as many felt that a change in administration might lengthen the war. Phil Tillar remembers being shocked by the news, although with hindsight he realises that it was apparent from the pictures taken at Yalta shortly before his death, that Roosevelt was very ill.

An American flag was flown at half mast over Sutton Town Hall and Sunday the 15th of April was set aside as a day of mourning. Impressive services were held in the Congregational Church and Holy Trinity Church, with all detachments attending. Francis Sullivan remembers:

"This was one time when English and American grieved together. You could see some holding back tears while others wept openly."

Sutton Coldfield News

REGISTERED AT THE G.P.O.
AS A NEWSPAPER

Offices: GAZETTE BUILDINGS.
CORPORATION ST., B'HAM 4
'Phone: CEN. 6640

No. 2,312   SATURDAY, 14 APRIL, 1945   PRICE 2d.

PRESIDENT ROOSEVELT

BY PRESIDENT ROOSEVELT'S DEATH BRITAIN HAS LOST HER MOST VALUED FRIEND, ABROAD, AND THE WORLD ONE OF THE GREATEST STABILISING FORCES EVER KNOWN.

IN EVERY COMMUNITY THROUGHOUT THE LAND THERE IS A DEEP SENSE OF ALMOST PERSONAL LOSS AND A PROFOUND REGRET THAT HE HAS NOT LIVED TO SEE THE DAY OF FINAL VICTORY TO WHICH HE HAS SO GREATLY CONTRIBUTED.

THERE COULD BE NO FINER MEMORIAL TO HIM THAN THE PRESERVATION OF THE GREAT DEMOCRATIC IDEAL FOR WHICH HE LIVED AND DIED.

IN MEMORY OF THEIR PRESIDENT

American Service men and women filled Sutton Coldfield Parish Church on Sunday morning to pay final homage to President Roosevelt. The service, which was attended by the Mayor and Mayoress of Sutton (Councillor and Mrs. F. W. Terry)—was conducted by Captain Shelta M. Hutchison, a U.S.A. Army chaplain, assisted by the Rector of Sutton (Rev. J. H. Boggon). Major D. C. Jernigin led the U.S. uniformed personnel in mourning the loss of their President; and the American Anthem was sung.

The monthly church parade of Scouts and Guides, cubs and brownies, at Park Road Congregational Church, Sutton, on Sunday, took the form of a memorial service to President Roosevelt. Two members of the U.S. Forces presented the American and British flags.

The Minister (Rev. Glynmor John) spoke of the life and work of the late President.

Sutton News 21/4/45.

Many G.I.s mourned the fact that Roosevelt had not lived to see the end of the war in Europe, an event that came less than a month after his death. Meanwhile the fighting continued in Germany with the Allied Forces gaining ground. Many Prisoners of War were taken and sent over to England to work for the Allies.

In February 1945 700 Germans were part of a large group of 1,500 men who were sent to work at the postal sorting office in Taunton. A group of enlisted men from the 1st B.P.O. formed the nucleus of the group. They travelled to Taunton by train along with 186 railway vans which had been in storage at Castle Bromwich.

A new system was put into operation so that all future directory post was diverted to Taunton. Each day a courier had to travel between Sutton and Taunton taking new directory cards. He would return with incomplete directory cards which needed to be completed in Sutton.

The receipt of directory post at Taunton was discontinued after a month which meant that from March onwards a large volume of mail was received in Sutton. On April the 15th (the day of Roosevelt's Memorial Service) a record was set when 206 railway vans were on hand waiting to be unloaded.

Many of the parcels received required rewrapping, 11,358 man hours had to be spent doing this. Some of the mail received from Taunton had obviously been rifled as many parcels were incomplete and there were some wrappers with all of the contents missing. This was a problem that had occurred more than once. In this case it had to be reported to the Postal Division.

April the 27th saw the arrival of 150 German prisoners in Sutton. An enclosure was erected in Sutton Park and 30 enlisted men were selected to act as guards. On April the 30th the P.O.W.s started work at the Post Office. On May the 8th a further 348 Germans were attached to the Post Office for duty.

As the Germans arrived they were screened for their suitability to different types of work. Some were detailed to manual labour such as loading and unloading vans and cleaning details at the Post Office and the camps. This meant that the G.I.s who had previously carried out these jobs could be available for duty in sections where their experience could be used to better advantage. The main body of prisoners though, were used in directory work.

Megan Lewis, one of the civillian workers, remembers the Germans working at the Post Office as being particularly uncooperative and doing all they could to slow down the work. The prisoners would be punished for any misdemeanours. One of the punishments was that the culprit had to dig a foxhole and sleep in it for one or more nights depending on the severity of his wrongdoing.

The fact that a small minority of the Germans were uncooperative was not helped by the way some of the Americans treated them. Hilda Partlow remembers some of the G.I.s standing on the other side of the wire fence from the prisoners and lighting up cigarettes. They would inhale a couple of times, watching the look of longing on the prisoner's faces, and then drop them on the floor out of the prisoner's reach.

Not all of the German's were uncooperative. Don Whalen remembers them as being a contented lot. The provisions of the Geneva Convention were strictly adhered to in Sutton. The Germans had the same food as the Americans and their work hours were strictly held to 40 hours, a great deal less than the Americans were working.

Many of the Germans had a good knowledge of English and would talk to the G.I.s about the circumstances of their capture. Two teenagers told Phil Tillar how they had been made prisoner. Early one morning all the fifteen and sixteen year olds in their home

HQS., 1ST BASE POST OFFICE, APO 640, U. S. ARMY

MAJOR D. C. JERNIGIN, COMMANDING OFFICER

PRESIDENT ROOSEVELT MEMORIAL SERVICE

Parish Church, The Parade, 0900 hours, 15 April 1945

ORDER OF SERVICE

    I Prelude

    II Hymn — America The Beautiful.

    III Invocation and The Lords Prayer.

    IV Hymn — Be Still My Soul.

    V Responsive Reading — 23rd Psalm

    VI Hymn — Jesus Saviour Pilot Me.

    VII Remarks — Rev. John Boggon, Vicar.

    VIII Scripture Reading.

    IX Prayer.

    X Sermon — Chaplain Shelton M. Hutchison.

    XI Prayer.

    XII The Star Spangled Banner.

    XIII Recessional.

America The Beautiful

1. O beautiful for spacious skies,
For amber waves of grain,
For purple mountain majesties
Above the fruited plain!
America, America,
God shed His grace on thee,
And crown thy good with brotherhood
From sea to shining sea.

2. O beautiful for pilgrim feet.
Whose stern, impassioned stress
A thoroughfare for freedom beat
Across the wilderness!
America, America,
God mend thine every flaw,
Confirm thy soul in self control,
Thy liberty in law.

3. O beautiful for heroes proved
In liberating strife,
Who more than self their country loved,
And mercy more than life!
America, America,
May God thy gold refine,
Till all success be nobleness,
And every gain divine.

4. O beautiful for patroit dream
That sees, beyond the years
Thine alabaster cities gleam.
Undimmed by human tears!
America, America,
God shed His grace on thee,
And crown thy good with brotherhood
From sea to shining sea.   A-men.

Be Still, My Soul

1. Be still, my soul: the Lord is on thy side;
Bear patiently the cross of grief or pain
Leave to thy God to order and provide;
In every change He faithful will remain.
Be still, my soul; thy best, thy heavenly Friend
Through thorny ways leads to a joyful end.

2. Be still, my soul: thy God doth undertake
To guide the future as He has the past
Thy hope, thy confidence let nothing shake:
All now mysterious shall be bright at last
Be still, my soul: the waves and winds still know
His voice who ruled them while He dwelt below.

Be still, my soul: the hour is hastening on
When we shall be forever with the Lord,
When disappointment, grief and fear are gone,
Sorrow forgot, love's purest joys restored.
Be Still, my soul: when change and tears are past,
All safe and blessed we shall meet at last. A-men.

Responsive Reading - 23rd Psalm

The Lord is my Shepherd
I shall not want
He maketh me to lie down in green pastures
He leadeth me beside the still waters.
He restoreth my soul:
He leadeth me in the paths of right-
eousness for his Name's sake.
Yea, though I walk through the valley of
the shadow of death, I will fear no evil:
For Thou art with me, thy rod and thy
staff they comfort me.

Thou preparest a table before me in the
presence of mine enemies:
Thou anointest my head with oil, my cup
runneth over.
Surely goodness and mercy shall follow me
all the days of my life:
And I will dwell in the house of the
Lord for ever.

Jesus, Saviour Pilot Me

1. Jesus, Saviour, pilot me
Over life's tempestuous sea;
Unknown waves before me roll,
Hiding rock and treach'rous shoal;
Chart and compass came from Thee:
Jesus, Saviour, pilot me.

2. As a mother stills her child,
Thou canst hush the ocean wild;
Boisterous waves obey Thy will
When Thou sayest to them "Be still."
Wondrous Sovereign of the sea,
Jesus, Saviour, pilot me.

3. When at last I near the shore,
And the fearful breakers roar
'Twixt me and the peaceful rest,
Then, while leaning on Thy breast,
May I hear Thee say to me,
"Fear not, I will pilot thee." A-men.

The Star Spangled Banner

1. O say, can you see, by the dawn's early light,
What so proudly we hailed at the twilight's last gleaming,
Whose broad stripes and bright stars, through the perilous fight,
O'er the ramparts we watched were so gallantly streaming?
And the rockets' red glare, the bombs bursting in air,
Gave proof through the night that our flag was still there;
O say, does the Star spangled Banner yet wave
O'er the land of the free and the home of the brave?

3. O thus be it ever when free men shall stand
Between their loved homes and the war's desolation;
Blest with victory and peace, may the Heaven rescued land
Praise the Power that hath made and preserved us a nation.
Then conquer we must, when our cause it is just,
And this be our motto, "In God is our trust,"
And the Star spangled Banner in triumph shall wave
O'er the land of the free and the home of the brave.

161

Rear of Post Office German P.O.W. standing in doorway of the hut in foreground. (P. Tillar).

Rewrap Section. (U.S. Army).

town had been sent to the induction centre. There they were processed, put through a physical examination and sworn into the German Army. While they were there, waiting in line to receive their equipment, advance troops of Patton's 3rd Army stormed the town. After a short skirmish the Americans were victorious and took as prisoners all the German troops, including those who had not yet been issued uniforms or rifles. Although the two young Germans did not feel that this was fair they said that they were glad that it was the Americans who had captured them rather than the Russians.

Chapter 19

The End of the End

"*September 15 1944* – All the talk these days is of the lifting of the blackout restrictions. This is a good sign of the end of the end, we hope. Also the flying bombs have ceased to menace London, as the Allies have captured most of the bomb sites in France and Belgium.

September 17 – After supper Milton Abramowicz and I rode down to visit the Bathams. Mr B. was out on duty, but we had a nice chat with Mrs B. for a couple of hours. On the way home we stopped in at the Donut Dugout for coffee and donuts. Practically all of the local people (and soldiers) were out to see the 'big event' tonight . . . the lighting up of the streets after five years of blackout."*

As with D-Day the postal workers were awaiting V.E. Day long before it came. On September the 17th 1944 the blackout was ended. Many children from Sutton were allowed out late that night to see the lights switched on on the Parade. Most of them did not remember seeing them lit before. V.E. Day was expected to follow this event virtually straight away but the Battle of the Bulge, which started in September, was a tougher campaign to fight than the Allies had expected and Britain and America had to wait another eight months for an end to the war in Europe.

The work scheduled for V.E. Day and V.E. plus one was prepared and announced in advance. In the week preceding V.E. Day the British Liason Officer requested that U.S. personnel cover the work at Snow Hill Station in addition to New Street Station so that the G.P.O. staff could spend some time with their families.

All of the G.I.s were to be granted a holiday with the exception of a skeleton crew of enlisted men to maintain the necessary movement of mail at the Base and the railway stations. Also, perhaps forseeing that celebrations might get out of hand, 31 additional guards were to augment the regular M.P. patrol. These men would be granted compensatory time off.

May the 8th 1945 saw the surrender of the German troops to the Allies. This brought celebrations all over Europe and America. Sylvia Phillips was working at the Empress in Sutton Coldfield when the news was announced. She remembers someone coming into the cinema and shouting that it was all over. The cinema shut and everyone linked arms and marched up to the church where they danced around the flagpole. Phil Tillar remembers dancing, singing, music, yelling and generally a lot of noise in the streets of Sutton. Joyce Streib, who lived in Sutton at the time, remembers that V.E. Day celebrations took place in the Town Hall Square. It was crowded with people dancing and having a good time. In the evening bonfires were set alight in the fields around Sutton.

Tom Morrissey was recovering from his injuries sustained in the Battle of the Bulge and awaiting reassignment at the 10th Replacement Depot when Germany surrendered.

---

*Leonard McDermott's Diary.

Eugene Rothert with Angela and Claire Supple celebrating V.E. Day. (A. Andrews).

V.E. Day ceremony at Sutton Town Hall. (H. Brown).

Town Hall flying the flags of the Allied Nations on V.E. Day. (H. Brown).

V.E. Day celebrations in Paris. (E. Ward).

Eisenhower granted a 72 hour pass to all unassigned G.I.s so naturally Tom wanted to spend the time in his second home, Sutton Coldfield. He remembers it as an unforgettable time, when there was an outpouring of love that he never witnessed before or since.

Leonard Nole was stationed at the Transit camp, Tidworth Barracks, for the weeks preceding V.E. Day. A large number of G.I.s from the Post Office had been sent there to retrain for combat. At the end of the training they were given a three day pass and Leonard remembers that nearly all of the men used the pass to return to Sutton to see their friends. On the last day of the pass V.E. Day was announced.

Chas Bubenas was one of a later group of G.I.s who were retraining at Tidworth and it was there he heard the news. On receiving the 72 hour pass that he was due as an unassigned soldier he also travelled to Sutton to take part in the celebrations there.

David Turney, Don Whalen and Charles Watts were stationed in London when they heard the news. David and Don spent the whole afternoon and evening in Picadilly Circus with thousands of others. David remembers a small band leading the others in singing and dancing to 'Knees Up Mother Brown'. Don remembers the church bells ringing incessantly and complete strangers kissing each other. He comments that:

"Everyone drank too much and celebrated too much – and why not? It was a once in a lifetime event!!"

Charles Watts gathered, with many others, in front of Buckingham Palace to cheer the Royal Family. Then he returned to Sutton to join in an enthusiastic neighbourhood celebration. His wife's neighbours had been saving up tins, packets and even bottles of champagne for this glorious occasion.

During May 1945 Kenneth Osgood was stationed in France, a country that had perhaps even more to celebrate than Britain. The night of May the 7th saw fireworks over Paris. The men in France were given May the 8th and 9th off, those that could travelled into Paris to join in the celebrations up and down the Champs Elysees.

Jim Brady describes V.E. Day in France. It was:

"the day when Parisians, American and English went delirious with joy. The overcrowded jeeps and trucks that careered down the thickly lined, flag festooned avenues. The V-shaped searchlights that streaked across the sky in the evening. The boisterous, rollicking crowds that swarmed onto every street and danced on many corners all night long."*

After V.E. Day it was easier to get furloughs and many of the men took trips back to Sutton from their different bases in the U.K. or on the Continent. As Leonard Nole says:

"Sutton was definitely where our second home was located. If we couldn't get back to the U.S. for a while we wanted to be with our friends."

Following V.E. Day the workload at the Post Offices in Sutton and France eased, to the men's relief. The staff at Sutton was now much smaller than it had been. More men had been sent to aid Detachment A in London and the men who had the longest Army service

---

*17th B.P.O. The Invasion Outfit.

167

Local School Vacated By Americans

COMPREHENSIVE SCHEME CAN NOW BE COMPLETED

THAT the American military authorities vacated the Upper Holland Road Schools "towards the end of the week commencing June 4th" was reported by the School Management Sub-Committee to Sutton Coldfield Education Committee at their meeting on Tuesday, and Alderman A. E. Terry, chairman of the sub-committee, remarked that there was some hope that the premises would now be available—he could not say at an early date—for the purpose for which they were intended. It would be a very great thing for the children of the borough, because it would complete a comprehensive scheme which the Education Committee had in mind for secondary schools—what, in the early days they called senior schools. A great deal of money would have to be spent before the schools were brought up to the required standard.

Promotion Age

The School Management Sub-Committee also reported that, after consultation with H.M. inspectors, and to relieve the pressure on the accommodation in the junior department at Boldmere, they had decided that the age of promotion of scholars to the senior department shall be ten years as hitherto. On this basis it was estimated that the junior department would commence the school year on September 1st with a total of 398 children on the registers.

Councillor C. H. Dainty presented the report of the School Attendance and Medical Sub-Committee, which contained a statement concerning the meals supplied to school children during May—namely that 23,434 were served from Hill kitchen (4,079), Boldmere kitchen (11,927), Minworth kitchen (2,089) and the Borough Restaurant (5,339). He also mentioned that the children committed to the care of this authority under the Children and Young Persons Act, 1933, had been visited by the School Attendance Office, who had found them and the conditions satisfactory.

Child Workers

"It is my hope," Councillor Dainty remarked "that I, myself, will be able to visit them and know every child."

It was reported that the total number of boys and girls registered under the Employ ment of Children Bye-laws is 70 and 17 respectively—engaged in newspaper delivery, 80; by chemists, two; by grocers, five.

Mr. W. J. Gurney mentioned that the local branch of the National Union of Teachers were organising a public meeting (to be held in September) to popularise the Education Act, 1944; and he invited members of the Education Committee to support it and to be present.

Councillor W. Cobb, chairman of the committee, thanked Mr. Gurney for the invitation, saying that he was sure some of the members would attend the meeting.

Sutton News 23/6/45.

AMERICAN THANKS

Sir,—After being stationed in and around Sutton Coldfield since July 1st, 1942, I was transferred from there on the 14th of this month. My orders came so unexpectedly that it made it physically impossible to get around to tell each and everyone of my friends good-bye.

So I want to use this medium to say to the people of Sutton Coldfield and vicinity, especially Mr. and Mrs. A. Whitehouse, of 11a Cremorne Road, Four Oaks, with whom I was billeted for eighteen months, and to Mr. and Mrs. P. Marden, of 141, Mere Green Road, Four Oaks, with whom I was billeted two months, I sincerely appreciate the kindness and hospitality extended to me during my stay in your community.

I shall never forget and, in years to come, to me England will be Sutton Coldfield. If any of you are ever in the United States step around at the Post Office at Shellyville, Indiana, and ask for me.

Once again, thanks a million.—Sincerely,
S SGT. CHARLES W. CLOSE
(United States Army).

Sutton News 29/9/45.

AMERICANS' HAPPY MEMORIES OF FOUR OAKS

During the last few years many American soldiers have been billeted in private houses in Sutton Coldfield, and from time to time there have been partings after unforgettable friendships. Letters received from the men express appreciation of the kindness shown to them while they were stationed in all parts of the Royal town.

Among those who enjoyed the company of two Americans for 18 months were Mr. and Mrs. Allday, of Hartopp Cottage, Four Oaks, and they have received a letter from one of the men now in Germany.

The following are extracts from the letter: While in Paris I met some of the boys who were stationed in England with me. All were unanimous in their desire to return to Sutton; most of them had been in Four Oaks and have only kind memories of their life there. If the people of Sutton could have heard these boys talk of their billets and the soft spot they have in their hearts for the people who were so kind to them, it would make all the inconveniences they were put to worth while.

Oh! I almost forgot. How is the garden? I certainly miss it and all its colour. Did the cuckoo-bird come back this spring? I often think of it.

Mr. and Mrs. Allday say that they will never forget this lad and will remember him whenever the "cuckoo-bird" returns.

GARDEN PARTY

An enjoyable garden party, which was well attended in aid of the London Missionary Society, was held at the home of Mr. and Mrs. F. Rednall, "Beechwood," Boultbee Road, Wylde Green, on Saturday, and about £7 was raised. The organisers were the Missionary Committee of Erdington Congregational Church, and the catering was done by the ladies of the committee. Mr. W. Sherlock, of Smethwick, gave an address, and the minister of Erdington Congregational Church, the Rev. W. E. Harding, was in the chair.

Sutton News 30/6/45.

AMERICANS IN THE MAYOR'S PARLOUR

At the invitation of the Mayor of Sutton Coldfield (Councillor F. W. Terry), several officers of the American Army were introduced to members of the Town Council in the Mayor's Parlour after last week's meeting.

Major Gheesling (Commanding Officer) said the 1st Base Post Office was in process of moving to Paris. He had been in Sutton Coldfield only a few weeks, but for a long time he had heard about the hospitality of the people of the town to the American Forces. He wished to express the appreciation of "the boys," who would take away with them very pleasant memories of their associations with Sutton. Friendships had been made which would serve to promote a better understanding between the two countries.

Lieut. Zirpoli remarked that as public relations officer, he was grateful to the present Mayor and those who had immediately preceded him for their interest in the American Forces; he trusted that the ties of friendship would bring the two great nations closer together.

The Mayor thanked the Americans for the hospitality they had extended to many persons in Sutton, especially to the children. "We have had some happy times and have cemented a friendship which is for the good of mankind," he said.

Central Postal Directory buildings, 1945 (P. Tillar).

records were being sent to transit camps to await rotation to the States. The few remaining men who were still billetted with Sutton householders were moved out of their billets around June the 14th 1945 and into Streetly Camp under the command of 1st Lt. Thomas F. Bradley.

The first building to close, at the end of May 1945, was the Holland Road Barracks. The 51 remaining W.A.C.s were posted to London. From June all first class mail was forwarded to Detachment A for processing. The night crew in Sutton were able to terminate their tour in this month after having worked off the bulk of the parcel post. It was now possible to work all the casualty mail on the day tour by the civillian personnel. Several civillain employees were discharged and by the end of the month there were only 95 working at the Post Office, these were either old employees or discharged veterans.

At the end of June Detachment B was activated as the sole Sutton detachment and the remaining personnel were quartered at Penns Lane Camp so that everything could be centralised. The officers had their last meal at Grey Friars mess on July the 9th and then vacated the building. They moved their quarters into Glenfield House but agreed to eat with the enlisted men at Penns lane to make messing arrangements easier.

Streetly Camp and White Lodge were derequisitioned in July. The Message Centre and the Supply and Personnel Sections were moved from Green Gables into the H.Q. offices in the main Post Office building as these had been vacated when the H.Q. detachment moved to France. Francis Sullivan remembers that by this time the 1st B.P.O. was a skeleton of its former self:

"Whenever you spoke words sounded hollow. You could feel the emptiness whenever you walked."

The task of reorganising and administrating Detachment B fell on the shoulders of the four officers who remained. By the end of July most of the activites had been consolidated. The N.C.O.s also found that their job was far from easy. The remaining enlisted men worked reluctantly and moaned about the system that had sent their colleagues home while they remained overseas.

News of Japan's surrender reached Sutton at midnight on August the 15th 1945. Most of the men were in their barracks at Penns Lane Camp when one of the members burst into Phil Tillar's hut with the news. The majority of the men got up and went into the town to join in the celebrations, which were similar to those of V.E. Day. Joyce Terry remembers a jeep full of G.I.s and goodies pulling up outside her house later that day. The G.I.s and the family were then able to celebrate in style.

Immediately following V.J. Day the Redeployment Programme for the troops was accelerated and more of the Post Office personnel were sent back to the States. In September all the N.C.O.s of the first three grades had earnt enough points (85) to be placed on orders to be returned to the U.S. Francis Sullivan was one of those N.C.O.s and was very glad to be going home as he says:

"Forty months overseas was more than enough for me."

He went home with thousands of others aboard the Queen Mary.

Phil Tillar had mixed feelings when he left. He had been 39 months overseas and was anxious to return to his family. On the other hand he had found the locality of Four Oaks to be pleasant, quiet and peaceful. If it hadn't been for missing his family (and major

Dooley, Griffin, Levesque and Daugherty on the 'truck and mule' near the directory door. January 1945. (H. Brown).

'Going home' November 1945. (H. Brown).

league baseball) he would have been happy to have stayed there for much longer. Phil left for home aboard the U.S.S. Europa. This German ship was the third largest passenger ship in the world at the time. The whereabouts of the 936 foot long luxury liner had been a mystery throughout the war but it was found, superbly camoflauged, when the American troops entered Bremenhaven. After V.E. Day the ship was taken to the U.S. where it was converted to a troop ship.

On the 10th of September the Base Post Office in France turned over the Citroen Garage and the work handled there to the 17th B.P.O. Some of the personnel were transferred from the 1st to the 17th B.P.O., just leaving the necessary men in the 1st to carry out the adminstration, transportation, supply, guard and other minor duties. Headquarters moved to the Royal Garage at 59, Rue de Courcelles, adjacent to the enlisted men's billets. This garage was originally one of the largest garages in Paris. It had been taken over by the Germans during their occupation for the use of their vehicles. The buildings around the garage had been used to billet S.S. men.

On the 19th of September in Sutton there was a 'marching out ' from the three romney huts formerly used by the Directory and they were returned to the engineer. This meant that there was approximately 40,000 square feet of floor space along with considerable equipment for return to the British. At this point the detachment was still operating the main Post Office buildings, Penns Lane Camp, East Croft Garage, Glenfield House and the P.O.W. enclosure in Sutton Park. In this month the W.A.C. Detachment in London was disbanded and all personnel were transferred to other units.

In October there was a 'marching out' from the three buildings at the rear of the Post Office which had been used as kitchens and a dental clinic. By this time all men of 65 points or more had been transferred either to reinforcement companies or to units that were being shipped to the States. Those who wished to remain could do so. Discipline in this month was made difficult because of the lack of qualified personnel and N.C.O.s of rank and experience. The Post Office was given the date of the 15th of November for the ceasing of operations so a Halloween Farewell party was planned for the 31st of October.

Detachment B, 1st Base Post Office officially ceased mail operations on the 15th of November 1945. The receipt of mail did not cease on the 15th as there were some dispatches that had been received late. The U.K. Base Signal Officer was contacted by telephone to discontinue the telephone service as of the 28th of November and the British G.P.O. were instructed to collect their equipment. The Q.M. Supply Officer was also contacted to cancel the laundry and dry cleaning contract with Sutton Laundry and Dry Cleaning Company.

The Birmingham G.P.O. was instructed to send all mail that came to them labelled 'Birmingham Z' to U.S. Army Mails, London. Daily dispatches were discontinued on the 28th of November although the last official dispatch of two vans, one to London and one to Southampton was made on the 30th of November. By the 10th of December Birmingham Z mail was no longer being received.

The orders came for Detachment B with one officer to move on or about the 5th of December from Sutton Coldfield to Paris. By this time the H.Q. Office had been moved back into the 17th B.P.O. building in the Citroen Garage. The officers were billetted with the 17th B.P.O. officers at the Hotel Atlantic 44, Rue de Londres, and the enlisted men were billetted at the 17th B.P.O. billet in Magasin Dufayel which had been a large department store in prewar days but was now known as 'The Barn'.

From France many of the men went straight home. Joe Gardiner remembers sailing from Lehavre in December 1945. The fourteen day long voyage in the Lee High Victory

Ship was extremely rough. As Joe sailed at Christmas time the crew served up turkey leg which was covered with grease. None of the men could touch it as they were so seasick.

The Americans took back with them many happy memories of their time in Sutton. They had been made to feel welcome by the inhabitants and many regarded it as their second home. For some, who married English girls and settled down here, it became their first home. Many grateful letters were sent from the G.I.s to those who had befriended and billetted them, some were printed in the Sutton News shortly after the war. The correspondence in many cases was kept up and many airmail letters still pass between America and Sutton.

Joyce Terry sums up the G.I.s in Sutton as:

" . . . strangers in a strange land, generous and kind hearted to a fault — they made the world a better place for us and if a 1st B.P.O. opened up again I would be first in the queue for a job."

Leonard McDermott sums up the feelings of most of the Americans:

"How did I feel when my time came to go back to the States? That's an easy one!! Delighted, excited, thrilled, ecstatic, — all of those!!! . . . I had been overseas for more than 38 months. There was no such thing as a furlough to go back home, nor was there even any chance to telephone to the folks at home. Our only contact was through the mail. So, all of us were most anxious to go back home. At the same time, however, we did have a tinge of regret at leaving the many friends we had met in Sutton. They had been so kind, hospitable, generous and patient with us that we could never forget them. . . All of us who had been stationed in Sutton know how lucky we were."

Chapter 20

Farewell to England

The 1st Base Post Office was officially closed and the G.I.s had gone from Sutton Coldfield but this was not the end of the story for those Sutton Coldfield girls who had married G.I.s and were awaiting transportation to America where they could be reunited with their husbands.

Before Ray Lasker returned to America he had to take his bride, Jean to the U.S. Embassy in Birmingham to register her for an American visa. Once this had been done he went back to the States while Jean had to wait for the visa to be granted. Notification of this came in March 1946 while she was taking a holiday in Blackpool with her sister. It was then necessary for her to cut short her holiday, come home and travel first to Waterloo Station in London and then to Salisbury Plain.

At Tidworth all the girls were put into barracks according to the alphabetical order of their surnames. They were generally treated like the soldiers who had been billeted there before them. It was even necessary for them to get a pass if they wanted to go off the camp.

Whilst in the camp the girls were introduced to what life in America might be like. They also had to undergo medicals, fill in endless forms, have their luggage examined and be fingerprinted. Pearl Lucas remembers being fingerprinted by the German P.O.W.s that worked there. She says:

"I cringed. I suppose that was understandable after the years we had been at war with them."

The P.O.W.s were also used in the camp for cleaning and waiting on tables.

Betty Sullivan travelled to the United States on the first Warbrides ship. She tells her story:

"My son, Tom, and I kissed my mother goodbye. It was cold and foggy when the train pulled out for Tidworth. My son became listless and feverish on the way. He just laid on my lap, not moving. U.S. Army buses met the train and we were driven to Tidworth. The rooms held about half a dozen beds.

"As soon as I arrived I asked to see a doctor. I was told there was no doctor, so they sent an American nurse who was heavily made up and had long, red fingernails. I asked her for something for my baby's fever, since they had no doctor. She told me she was just a nurse and couldn't prescribe anything for children and that I had to wait until I got on a ship. I asked her for food for Tom. She told me that she wasn't in the room service business. When I told her I couldn't leave my son for fear he'd go into convulsions, she told me to get one of the other wives to watch Tom for me. They had babies of their own and were afraid they'd get sick. So, for three days Tom became very feverish and listless, and I worried. I did manage to get something for us to eat, but I couldn't eat anyway. Tom managed to hold down some warm milk.

173

Self-Service Stores, Dress Styles, Amaze British War Bride Here

'Can't Get Over It,' Betty Sullivan Says

By KEN MAXCY

Betty Sullivan and her son Tommy from England who rejoined her husband, ex-Technical Sgt. Francis J. Sullivan, 326 Station St., here Monday, have been busy becoming accustomed to life in Aliquippa this week.

Mrs. Sullivan and Tommy arrived Sunday on the U. S. Army Transport Argentina, the first "brideship" from overseas.

The freedom from rationing has been the most surprising thing to Mrs. Sullivan. They have been going on shopping tours every day.

"There are so many things to buy" Mrs. Sullivan said in her soft English accent. "I really can't get over it. We really have nothing like this in England."

Dept. Store Experience

She related her experiences in a downtown department store, where "I was buying so many things I used all my money up and had to leave the store."

In England the rationing of clothes is very strict. Citizens are only allowed a few coupons. With these they can buy only "utility" clothes which are of one general pattern.

"I like all the American styles," she said. During the shopping tours she has to keep asking her husband: "How much is that in English money?"

Visits Grocery

She had another new experience at the self-service grocery. "They do not have self-service grocery's in England, and I was waiting for an assistant to help me," she said.

"There again, we had the same trouble," Mrs. Sullivan said, "there were so many things to buy, that I was taking more than we could carry".

Meanwhile the Sullivans have been entertaining many guests this week. "We have been receiving so many gifts we're really embarrassed." Mr. Sullivan said.

Francis and Betty, united again

Receive Gifts

"Little Tommy has received so many toys, we're afraid of spoiling him," Mrs. Sullivan added.

Tommy was just getting ready to take a walk in his Taylor-Tot which he calls a "motor" this morning, looking very sharp in an English knitted wool cap, when we called.

"Tommy is busy playing with all the gadgets around the house," Mr. Sullivan said. He plays with the radio dials, and the light switches."

Tommy still calls a locomotive by the English term "Puffer-billy," and when he says thank you he uses the English word "ta."

"We're transferring our savings account for Tommy which we had in England, here today," Mr. Sullivan said.

Likes Bananas

Tommy has been fascinated by bananas which he peels and then throws the skin away, and after a few bites, the banana also.

"He gets a big kick out of peeling them," Mr. Sullivan said. "He only saw two while he was in England."

Mrs. Sullivan is sending home a "parcel" of nuts to her Mother in England. "We can't get any over there you know, and Mother asked me to send her some," she said.

Tommy — toy collector.

lunteered. Mr. and Mrs. Sullivan looked extremely happy themselves.

The same happiness pervaded the Sullivan household this morning as when she and her son arrived. "They have really brightened up our home." Sullivan brothers, Emelio and Mario

Agents for
THE UNITED STATES WAR SHIPPING ADMINISTRATION

⚓

AMERICAN REPUBLICS LINE PACIFIC REPUBLICS LINE
AMERICAN SCANTIC LINE

*May all Your Troubles Be little Ones
(Not less than eight pounds) Marnie M. Leadon*

CAPTAIN'S DINNER

ON BOARD THE

T.E.S. URUGUAY

ARTHUR W. PIERCE, *Master*
Commander, USMS

STAFF

WILLIAM O. CRAMER - - - - - - - *Chief Officer*
Commander, USMS
WILLIAM N. MATCHES - - - - - *Chief Engineer*
Lieutenant-Commander, USMS
NICHOLAS R. SENA - - - - - - *Chief Purser*
Lieutenant-Commander, USMS
JOSEPH C. NUNN - - - - - - - *Chief Steward*
Lieutenant-Commander, USMS

ARMY STAFF

LIEUT.-COL. F. A. GOLDMAN - - *Transport Commander*
LIEUT. EVELINE HERTZ - - *Asst. Transport Commander*
CAPT. H. W. CARRINGTON - - - - *Transport Surgeon*
CAPT. J. C. HAVENS - - - - - *Transport Chaplain*
CAPT. M. C. EVANS - - - *Transport Dental Surgeon*
LIEUT. ROSE E. WATTERSON - - - - - *Chief Nurse*
LIEUT. V. L. ROGERS - - - *Transport Services Officer*
LIEUT. O. W. JOENS - - - - *Commissary Officer*
MISS RUTH E. CURTIS - - - *American Red Cross*

At Sea - - - - - - - *April 4th, 1946*

MENU - - -

⚓ ⚓

Green Olives   Dill Pickles
California Fruit Cocktail

●

Cream of Tomato Soup

●

Fried Filet of Cod Fish, Tartar Sauce

●

Baked Virginia Ham, Raisin Sauce

●

Boston Baked Beans   *Garden Green Peas*
Mashed or Roast Potatoes

●

Potato Salad, Mayonnaise

●

Ice Cream and Cookies   *Preserved Pears*
Cheese and Crackers
Coffee   *Tea*

Menu on board T.E.S. Uruguay signed by friends of Jean Lasker.

175

Barbara P. Baker all;

Best of Luck
Frederic A. Goldman
2414. P.C.

God Bless You Better Know Maria M. Landers.
J. P. Hamm - Chaplain

Mary R. Elley;
"First to you;"

movie scenim
understudies
friend from
Junior Gene

Selvin Segamosky
(for a grand girl)
Andover to New York

Home's Lookslie
New York State;

Jackson L. Darlich;
O. Gene

Best of Luck to the
"Super man"
Shirley Landau

Marjorie D. Hakesbergt;
249. V. Plumstead Ave;
Lansdowne, Pa;

Your Stokie;
Piedmont Calif;
Your pal from good ol' Brum.

All good wishes.
Joan O. Lons,

With all Good Wishes —
yours sincerely
Ethel Hutzler
5/4/46.

Best wishes for a happy
future
Iris K. Luis
Brum. to Michigan

176

Betty left the camp at the end of January 1946. She continues:

"Then we were boarded on a train and taken to the U.S. Argentina, the first bride ship. As soon as I got on board I asked to see the doctor 'right now'. So I was taken to the doctor who examined Tom. He agreed with me that Tom had a high fever, but he couldn't tell what was wrong with him. Since there were a lot of war brides and babies on the ship the doctor said Tommy would have to be isolated as he didn't want to take any chance on the others getting sick.

"The ultimatum given me was this: stay isolated with your son or be separated from him for the rest of the trip. I told the doctor I wouldn't leave my baby, not even for an hour. So we were given a cabin by the nurses station. Whatever medication the doctor gave Tommy worked. Within three or four days he started getting better.

"The food they brought us in the cabin was out of this world. I had not seen food like this for years. However, with the severe rationing of food in the war my stomach had shrunk. Plus I was terribly worried about Tom. So I was unable to eat too much. One day the doctor came to me and said,

'Mrs Sullivan, you have been very valuable to us. You have taken care of your son, watched over him, bathed him, and you never complained. But we want you to eat. We don't want you to get sick.'

I told him I would try although it was very hard for me to swallow food. The doctor wanted me to exercise on the officer's deck, get some fresh air and to get out of the cabin. However I wouldn't leave Tom. So they sent some young medics to watch him while I went to exercise.

"We reached New York about four in the morning. Over the loudspeaker came a message:

'If you want to see the Statue of Liberty we advise you to put on your coats and blankets.'

Again I wouldn't leave Tom alone so they sent some young medics to watch him. That's how I was able to see the Statue of Liberty.

"In due time we were processed and taken off the ship.

'Where are you going?' someone asked me before I got on the train.

'Aliquippa, Pa.' I said. The man scared me good when he said there was no such place. I told him there was and that it was near Pittsburgh. That's how I got on the train doubting, yet believing.'

Meanwhile Francis Sullivan, at home in Aliquippa, received word that Betty and Tom would be arriving at Aliquippa Station at 12:30 p.m. on February the 6th. He and his brothers went to the station and waited. The train arrived without Betty and Tom. So Francis went back home, planning to return to meet the next train. Francis hadn't been home ten minutes when a taxi pulled up at the house with Betty and Tom in it. Betty had got off the train at Pittsburgh to travel by taxi to Aliquippa.

Betty was a little homesick at first but she soon found that, 'The grass was greener on this side of the ocean'. One thing she couldn't get over was the vast amount of food in the stores.

It was normal for foreigners applying for citizenship in the United States to have to reside there for five years, but because Betty's husband, Francis, had served overseas she only had to wait two and a half years. This applied to all the G.I. brides from Sutton that went to live in America.

ENGLISH BRIDE ARRIVES

Monday Mr. and Mrs. C. D. Watts arrived at their home, 412 Oktibbeha Gardens from New York where they have been for a short time. Mr. Watts met his wife there as she arrived on the Vulcania from her home in England. On October 7, 1944 Mr. Watts was married to Bessie Gardner at Four Oaks, Warwickshire. He was returned to the States last December and Mrs. Watts came on the first boat bringing brides from all over Euorpe. There were 300 from England and 600 from various countries. Mrs. Watts says there were many charming girls in the group. She was impressed with the tall buildings in New York and thinks it is not a bit like London. Already she feels quite at home in Starkville. She remarked that though she had never seen her husband in civilian clothes she had no trouble recognizing him at the dock.

Starkville News March, 1945.

New York Harbor. (J. Lasker).

Eventually Jean Lasker set sail from Southampton, experiencing a rather rough voyage on the T.E.S. Uruguay, where she shared a cabin with some of the other girls she had been billetted with at Tidworth. After three weeks Jean's ship docked at New York Harbor where she was surprised to find that neither Ray, nor his family were there to meet her.

Immigration officials directed Jean and the other girls to New York Central Station. Jean remembers passers by staring at the English girls as they made their way there. She tried to phone Ray's family from the station but there was no answer so she boarded the sleeper that went to Cleveland, Ohio. (Ray lived in Cincinnati) expecting to meet Ray there. To her disappointment she saw no familiar faces when she arrived at Cleveland Station so she tried to phone Ray's family again. Again there was no answer, but eventually the family turned up and Ray and Jean were reunited. The family had been told that Jean would be arriving at the other station in Cleveland and so they had been waiting there.

Betty Watts remembers her journey to the States. She caught her train in Birmingham and sat next to a petite lady called Hazel. From that point until she docked at New York Harbor this tiny woman took Betty under her motherly wing and looked after her. After staying at Tidworth for a week or two they left for Southampton where they embarked on a ship that would take them to their new homes.

Betty and the girls with her were meant to be sailing on the Queen Mary (the biggest and fastest ship in the water at the time), but an earlier ship had had problems so the G.I. brides aboard this ship changed to the Queen Mary while Betty and her companions travelled on the Vulcania, a former Italian cruise ship which had an Italian speaking crew. Betty remembers very little of the sea trip as she spent seven days suffering from seasickness in the sick bay while the admirable Hazel looked after her.

When they reached New York, in March 1946, Hazel and Betty's husbands were waiting for them. The girls parted there as Hazel's new home was to be in Birmingham,

178

Frank and Joyce Casso.

Alabama, while Betty was bound for Starkville, Mississippi. She had to endure a 24 hour journey on an uncomfortable train, with wooden seats, to get there. Betty's new brother in law met her and Charles at the station and took them to their house. Fortunately Charles had bought his own house before war broke out so he had somewhere to take his bride.

A memory that still stands in Betty's mind is the 'refreshing' (so her brother in law thought) cup of buttermilk she was offered on her arrival at the house. Even now she hates buttermilk and still associates it with that time that she arrived tired and hungry at her new home.

Pearl Lucas departed from Southampton on the American ship S.S. Washington and arrived in New York in April 1946. Her husband, Al, had preceded her by only six weeks. Pearl remembers travelling along with several girls in a state room which had been previously converted to carry U.S. troops. She remembers being treated very well and being served the sort of food that she hadn't seen since before the war. Unfortunately she couldn't enjoy it, as, like Betty, she was seasick for the whole trip. She remembers entering New York Harbor to a reception of tug boats with bands playing and flags waving. Al was awaiting her on the pier.

A month later Celia Whalen travelled to New York aboard the S.S. Washington. Like Betty and Pearl she remembers being seasick for the whole of the voyage and spending most of the time in bed in her cabin.

Celia's first impressions of America were of its size and the plentifulness of things the people in Britain were so short of. When she arrived at New York she and her husband, Don, stayed for the first few nights on the 50th floor of a tall hotel. Celia had never been that far away from the ground before. To get to Celia's new home in Michigan the couple drove a roundabout way so that Celia could see some of the different States of America. They completed a journey of about 1,500 miles. Celia was amazed that there was no problem in buying the petrol for this trip.

Celia missed her relatives and friends but Don's family made her feel very welcome. Sutton Coldfield and her new home town of Niles were similar in size so she adapted well to the way of life there. A Warbrides Club sprang up in the Niles area and she became a member. The club consisted of several English girls, a couple from Australia, and at least one each from France and Belgium. Not all of the girls in the club remained in America. Some had ill-fated marriages and others were just too homesick.

Joyce Streib also sailed from Southampton on the S.S. Washington in May 1946, just two months after her wedding. She felt very fortunate that she was able to travel to join her husband so soon. Many brides had to wait a year before they could travel to their new homes. Her first memory of America was of seeing men that were there to meet their wives, wearing loud ties and wide brimmed hats. Quite a change from the olive drab the women were used to seeing their husbands in.

Joyce left the ship on May the 18th and began her four day rail journey to the state of Washington travelling through Chicago (Illinois), St Paul (Minnesota) and Portland (Oregon). She finished her journey at Kelso (three miles from her new home town of Longview). Her father in law met her train as her husband, Roy, was at Fort Lewis, 75 miles away and couldn't be there until the next day.

She found Longview very different to Sutton Coldfield. Everywhere there were wide open spaces. The homes were constructed of lumber and heated with wood burning stoves, which were also used for cooking. She found things rather outdated as she had been used to a gas cooker at home.

Like Celia Whalen Joyce joined a warbrides club:

"In 1949 I became aquainted with two more English girls and we founded a club 'The British Brides Club'. We had quite a number of girls and it helped to relieve some of our homesickness. After we left the area in 1959 it was renamed 'The Daughters of the British Empire' since the girls were coming from countries other than Britain. It is still going, though many moved on or passed on, we came in all ages and sizes, but had some fun times together."

Joyce Casso, another bride from Sutton, travelled to meet her husband, Frank, on the Thomas H. Barry. She left Southampton in May 1946. She remembers the Canadians at the docks quizzing the girls on their destination. When they heard that it was the U.S.A. they warned them that they'd be sorry. Unlike Betty and Pearl Joyce enjoyed the cruise, sharing a cabin with other G.I. brides and taking part in pillow fights and the like.

The boat docked in new York where Frank, who had returned to his home six months earlier, was there to meet her. They spent three or four days in New York before travelling to Texas, to Frank's home town, Laredo. America semed so different to the dreary wartime England and Joyce's first impressions were of bright lights and wonderful food, especially ice cream. At Laredo Joyce met Frank's large family (he was one of eight). They welcomed her and she soon felt at home, she was one of the lucky ones who didn't suffer from homesickness.

Epilogue

In September 1992 a ceremony was held for the unveiling of two plaques to commemorate the work of the men and women of the First Base Post Office. The first at the Post Office site and the second at Plantsbrook Comprehensive School.

Five G.I.s (Leonard McDermott, Francis Sullivan, Henry Brown, Kenneth Sell and Joe Gardiner) and a W.A.C. (Janis Leonard) were able to travel to England for the ceremonies. British men and women who had worked at the Post Office during World War Two attended the ceremony at the Post Office where the Lord Mayor of Birmingham, Councillor Peter Barwell unveiled the plaque. Those who had billetted G.I.s, were related to G.I. brides or simply had fond memories of the Americans that worked in Sutton Coldfield during the war attended the ceremony at the school where the Lord Mayor and Leonard McDermott jointly unveiled the plaque. Both ceremonies were very nostalgic. Old friendships were renewed and new ones made.

L-R. Leonard McDermott, Grace McDermott, Betty Sullivan, Francis Sullivan, Henry Brown, Janis Leonard, Kenneth Sell, Frances Brown, Buzz Leonard, Joe Gardiner at the Post Office Site 27/9/92.

Although some of the Americans had attended small reunions in the United States and one or two of them had travelled back singly to Sutton Coldfield to visit their old haunts this was the first time that members of the First Base Post Office had come to England as a group for a reunion.

Appendix A

List of the 32 enlisted men with their ranks made in August/September 1942 by Leonard McDermott.

First Base Post Office.

Master Sgts:	John C. Holden	Cuba, New York
	Thomas A. Land	Pittsburgh, Penn.
Technical Sgt:	Clyde W. Jones	Texas
Staff Sgts:	Robert J. French	Schenectedy, New York
	Earl E. Griffin	Griffin, Georgia
Sergeants:	Jerome Deuschberger	New York, N.Y.
	John J. Dooley	Bridgeport, Conn.
	John C. Hay, Jr.	Texas
	John J. Kallay	Detroit, Michigan
Tech. 4th Gr.	William R. George	Nanikoke, Penn.
	Francis J. Sullivan	Aliquippa, Penn.
Corporal	Marion A. Puccine	Philadelphia, Penn.
Tech. 5th Gr.	Charles W. Close	Shelbyville, Indiana
	Edmund A. Cullen, Jr.	Los Angeles, Calif.
	John A. Habel	Garrett, Penn.
	Joseph F. Kelleher	Canton, Mass.
	George H. King	Washington, D.C.
	Paul M. Lampl	Pittsburgh, Penn.
	Ben F. Rainwater, Jr.	Augusta, Georgia
	Edward J. Russell	Boston, Mass.
	Hugo Schefcak	Dallas, Texas
	Alexander Lucas	Bridgeport, Conn.
Privates 1st Cl.	Armand E.Levesque	Windsor, Vermont
	Leonard W. McDermott	Belmont, Mass.
	James M. McFarland	New Haven, Conn.
	Paul E. Menges	Indianapolis, Indiana
	Rudolph Niederle	Cleveland, Ohio
Privates	Leon Fefer	Chicago, Illinois
	Donald W. Fraser	Oakland, Calif.

Monette Gunby	Mississippi
Benjamin D. Loewinsohn	Atlanta, Georgia
Christian O. Resseth	Detroit, Michigan

Leonard remembers that the three officers were:

Major Robert E. Hartigan (within the first year to become Lieutenant Colonel).

1st Lieutenant Fred W. Jordan (to become Captain and later Major).

2nd Lieutenant – Kite (with the unit only a few months before being transferred to another unit).

Appendix B

from Historical Report, F.B.P.O. 1944

Comparison of necessary personnel assignment
1st Base Post Office, 1 September 1944
Illustrating T/O deficiencies

DUTY	ASGD EM	WAC EW	ATCHD	TOTAL NECESSARY	ALLOWED BY T/O
1st Sgt (Detachments)	3	1	0	4	1
Detachment Clerks	4	1	0	5	0
Clerk General	16	2	0	18	32
Telephones	1	7	0	8	0
Typists	0	5	0	5	9
Mess Sergeant	5	1	0	6	1
Cooks	32	15	0	47	17
Dining Rooms					
Orderlies	2	2	0	4	0
Permanent K P	24	0	0	24	0
Central Mess	7	0	0	7	0
Ration Detail	2	0	0	2	0
Garbage Detail	1	0	0	1	0
Firemen (Basics)	8	0	0	8	11
Orderlies	6	0	0	6	6
Table Waiters	4	0	0	4	0
Guard NCO	7	0	0	7	0
Guards	48	0	1	4	0
Truckmaster	2	0	0	2	0
Dispatcher	2	0	0	2	0
Drivers	20	2	0	22	10
Mechanics	3	0	0	3	1
Supply Sergeant	1	1	0	2	1
Supply Clerks	9	1	0	10	0

DUTY	ASGD EM	WAC EW	ATCHD	TOTAL NECESSARY	ALLOWED BY T/O
Carpenters	3	0	0	3	0
Post Utilities	6	1	0	7	0
Police Details	10	0	0	10	0
Barbers	3	1	0	4	0
Post Exchange	5	2	0	7	0
Special Service	2	0	0	2	0
S-3 Training	4	0	0	4	0
Postal Supply	8	0	1	9	0
On Detached Service	57	0	0	57	0
Medics	0	2	5	7	0
Film Service	0	0	1	1	0
Total Non-Postal Duty	305	44	8	357	89
Total Postal Duty	519	236	12	767	735
TOTAL	824	280	20	1,124	824

Appendix C

A roster of the officers of the 1st Base Post Office and their duties September 1944.

Lt. Col. Robert E. Hartigan	AGD. 0445354	Commanding Officer
Major Benjamin F. Hartl	AGD. 03474147	Executive Officer Unit Historian Unit Claims Officer Survey Officer
Captain Herbert F. Bisig	AGD. 0489574	Motor Transportation Officer Mess Officer Assistant Unit Claims Officer Agricultural Officer
Captain Fred W. Jordan	AGD. 0444391	Headquarters Commandant Agent Finance Officer Soldier Voting Officer
Captain Jess Poffenbarger	AGD. 0485427	Chief of Mails Intelligence Officer
Captain Walter F. Siders	AGD. 0497167	Night Crew Chief
1st Lt. Robert W. Barkhoz	AGD. 01179013	Post Utility Officer Fuel Officer Bomb Reconnaisance Officer
1st Lt. William R. Brogan Trial Judge Officer	AGD. 01174240	Personnel Officer
1st Lt. Victor H. Galvani	AGD. 01001562	Assistant Postal Officer First Class Section
1st Lt. George V. Kartozian	AGD. 1300809	Summary Court Officer Supply Officer
1st Lt. Earl M. Kooyman	AGD. 1313617	Adjutant Personnel Control Officer Security Officer
1st Lt Henry P. Quenelle	AGD. 02041050	Message Center Officer

1st Lt. Harry R. Waters	AGD. 01175352	Chief of Directory
2nd Lt. Thomas F. Bradley	AGD. 01060022	Assistant Postal Officer Night Crew
2nd Lt. Charles E. Callaway	AGD. 01058937	Assistant Postal Officer Parcel Post Section
2nd Lt. John Crisona	AGD. 01002895	First Class Section C.O. Det. B. Unit Gas Officer
2nd Lt. Russell W. Fisher	AGD. 01017390	C.O. Det. D. Prison Officer Laundry Officer Plans and Training
2nd Lt. Jerome J. Jasko	AGD. 01002655	Assistant Unit Censor
2nd Lt. Milton Maimon	AGD. 01646825	Night Crew
2nd Lt. Max I. Mannerow	AGD. 01321247	C.O. H.Q. Det. Officer of the Guard Fire Marshall
2nd Lt. Ralph R. Norton	AGD. 01546271	Unit Censor
2nd Lt. Thaddeus S. Paszkiewicz	AGD. 01173414	New Street Detail Officer Rail Transportation Officer Salvage Officer
2nd Lt. Edgar M. Peacock	AGD. 0153 5514	C.O. Det.E Control Section
2nd Lt. Casimir Roskowski	AGD. 01296263	C.O. Det. C. Casualty Section
2nd Lt. Andrew P. Zirpoli	AGD. 01016423	Post Exchange Officer Special Service Officer Public Relations Officer Education Officer

The following officers of this organization are assigned to Detachment 'A'. 1st Base Post Office, A.P.O. 413.

Major Dudley C. Jernigin	AGD. 0495873
1st Lt. Charles M. DuVernet	AGD. 0482371
1st Lt. Walter Lapinsky	AGD.0482363
1st Lt. Charles C.Labauch	AGD. 01294325
2nd Lt. Howard E. O'Dell	AGD. 0336765

Appendix D

Some Important Do's and Don'ts.
(from 'A Short Guide to Great Britain' by the U.S. Govt. Printing Office.)

Be friendly − but don't intrude anywhere it seems you are not wanted.
You will find the British money system easier than you think. A little study beforehand on shipboard will make it easier.

You are higher paid than the British 'Tommy'. Don't rub it in. Play fair with him. He can be a pal in need.

Don't show off or brag or bluster − 'swank' as the British say. If somebody looks in your direction and says, "He's chucking his weight about." You can be pretty sure you're off base. That's the time to pull in your ears.

If you are invited to eat with a family don't eat too much. Otherwise you may eat up their weekly rations.

Don't make fun of British speech or accents. You sound as funny to them but they will be too polite to show it.

Avoid comments on the British Government or politics. Don't try to tell the British that America won the last war or make wisecracks about the war debts or about the British defeats in this war.

Never criticise the King or Queen.

Don't criticise the food or cigarettes to the British. Remember they have been at war since 1939.

Use commonsense on all occasions. By your conduct you have great power to bring about a better understanding between the two countries after the war is over.

You will soon find yourself among a kindly, quiet, hardworking people who have been living under a strain such as few people in the world have ever known.

In your dealings with them let this be your slogan:

It is always impolite to criticise your hosts.

It is militarily stupid to criticise your allies.

Appendix E

WHEN YOU ARE OVERSEAS

THESE FACTS ARE VITAL

PAMPHLET NO. 21-1

WRITING HOME

THINK! Where does the enemy get his information—information that can put you, and has put your comrades, adrift on an open sea; information that has lost battles and can lose more, unless you personally, vigilantly, perform your duty in SAFEGUARDING MILITARY INFORMATION?

CENSORSHIP RULES ARE SIMPLE, SENSIBLE.—They are merely concise statements drawn from actual experience briefly outlining the types of material which have proved to be disastrous when available to the enemy. A soldier should not hesitate to impose his own additional rules when he is considering writing of a subject not covered by present regulations. He also should be on guard against false rumors and misstatements about censorship. It is sometimes stated that censorship delays mail for long periods of time. Actually all mail (with certain nominal and very unusual exceptions) is completely through censorship within 48 hours.

THERE ARE TEN PROHIBITED SUBJECTS

1. Don't write military information of Army units—their location, strength, matériel, or equipment.

2. Don't write of military installations.

3. Don't write of transportation facilities.

4. Don't write of convoys, their routes, ports (including ports of embarkation and disembarkation), time en route, naval protection, or war incidents occurring en route.

5. Don't disclose movements of ships, naval or merchant, troops, or aircraft.

6. Don't mention plans and forecasts or orders for future operations, whether known or just your guess.

7. Don't write about the effects of enemy operations.

8. Don't tell of any casualty until released by proper authority (The Adjutant General) and then only by using the full name of the casualty.

9. Don't attempt to formulate or use a code system, cipher, or shorthand, or any other means to conceal the true meaning of your letter. Violations of this regulation will result in severe punishment.

519309°—43

192

10. Don't give your location in any way except as authorized by proper authority. Be sure nothing you write about discloses a more specific location than the one authorized.

INCLOSURES IN LETTERS.—Do not inclose anything in a letter that would violate any of the foregoing rules.

PHOTOGRAPHS, FILMS.— Special rules apply to the transmission of photographs and films. Do not send them until you have ascertained what regulations are in effect in the area.

POST CARDS.—The use of post cards may or may not be authorized. Find out first, and then be sure that the picture or printed part of the card does not violate censorship regulations.

LETTER ADDRESSES

ADDRESS.— Always leave room for a forwarding address to be written in.
On mail to civilians.— Use normal address and form.

On mail to military personnel.— Give name, grade (rank), Army serial number (if known), unit and organization, and location if in United States. If addressee is also overseas use his APO number c/o Postmaster ——. If in the same general locality as the sender see Army Postal Service for authorized address.

On mail to prisoners of war held by enemy.— Obtain full information from local Army Postal Service.

RETURN ADDRESS. Every letter or post card must have a return address. Place it in the upper left hand corner, leaving a margin of ½ inch for resealing in case of censorship beyond the unit censor. The ½-inch margin rule applies equally to mail from officers and from enlisted men. Both are subject to examination by base censorship detachments.

```
Sgt. John Smith, 6719318,
Co. C, 299 Inf., A. P. O. 1005,                        Free
c/o Postmaster, New York City, N. Y.




                        Mrs. John Smith,
                        123 First Avenue,
                        New York City, N. Y.



```

193

The return address must include (1) full name, including grade (rank), (2) Army serial number, (3) unit (company, battery, etc.), (4) organization (regiment), (5) APO number, (6) % Postmaster (<u>city assigned</u>).

Return addresses on mail written to prisoners of war are subject to specific regulations. Obtain information locally.

No geographical location of sender may be shown on an envelope or other outside cover.

OFFICIAL MILITARY MAIL

Special regulations are provided for official military mail. They are not covered herein.

MAILING YOUR LETTER

Reread your letter to be sure you have complied with all regulations. This will protect you and assure the most expeditious delivery of your letter. Five minutes now will save later delay and prevent possible suppression of the letter. It will protect you from punishment for unintentional violations.

ENLISTED MEN.—Place your letter unsealed in your organization mail box, never in any civil post office box. *You are required to use the Army Postal Service, and the Army Postal Service only.*

OFFICERS.—Seal the envelope, sign your name without comment in the lower left-hand corner to indicate your compliance with censorship regulations (your letter is subject to further censorship examination by base censorship detachments), and deposit in the organization mail box. *Use only the Army Postal Service.*

V-MAIL

This is an expeditious mail program which provides for quick mail service to and from soldiers overseas. A special form is used which permits the letter to be photographed on microfilm, the small film transported, and then reproduced and delivered. Use of V-MAIL is urged because it greatly furthers the war effort by saving shipping and airplane space.

Censorship rules apply to V-mail with such adjustments as are necessary due to the form used and special processing features.

BLUE ENVELOPES

Enlisted men who wish to write of private or family matters and who feel that censorship of a specific letter by their unit censor would cause embarrassment may be authorized to use a blue envelope which will allow censorship action to be taken by the base censor rather than the unit censor.

Blue envelopes should be obtained from your organization and must be addressed to the final intended recipient. Only one letter may be placed in each envelope and the envelope should be sealed prior to mailing.

Censorship regulations apply to blue envelopes as well as to all other communications.

WARNING

Written communications may be sent only through the facilities of the Army Postal Service. Any attempt to avoid this restriction by mailing letters in civil postal systems or by having travelers transport communications will result in severe disciplinary action against both the sender and the intermediary.

CABLES; RADIOGRAMS

Every cable message goes through the hands of at least 12 people. Radiogram messages are available to all who wish to "tune in," including the enemy!

Constant effort is being made to provide you with approved, rapid, cheap electrical communication.

Under no circumstances can cables be sent over commercial or foreign outlets until their use is authorized by proper military authority. "Safe Arrival" messages, identifiable as such, are prohibited at any time. There are two types of electrical messages generally available: Senders' Composition Messages (SCMs), which are like the cablegrams and radiograms you know at home, and Expeditionary Force Messages (EFMs) which are fixed text messages sent at a very low rate, much like Christmas and birthday telegraph messages in use in the United States, but with set messages composed to meet your normal requirement.

As soon as safety allows you will be assigned an APO *cable* address. Until it is assigned only serious, emergency messages may be sent, and then only if first approved in writing by the theater or area commander or his authorized representative. The Red Cross can handle certain extremely urgent personal matters by cable.

Ask your unit censor how to send messages, either SCMs or EFMs.

CABLE ADDRESSES

Outbound.—First give *your* cable address; next, the full name, street address, city, and State of the person for whom the message is intended; then the message, and finally sign your full name. Example:

AMTRAG (typical APO cable address)
Mrs. John Smith, 1616 Main St.,
Zenith, Ohio.
    XXXXXX Message XXXXX
    XXXXXXXXXXXXXXXXXXXX
               John T. Smith.

Note that there is no Army serial number, no unit nor organization, and no mention of your location.

Inbound.—Cables and radiograms should be addressed to you, giving your full name, Army serial number, and *cable* address, but not your unit nor organization.

TALK

SILENCE MEANS SECURITY.—If violation of protective measures is serious within written communications it is disastrous in conversations. Protect your conversation as you do your letters, and be even more careful. A harmful letter can be nullified by censorship; loose talk is direct delivery to the enemy.

If you come home during war your lips must remain sealed and your writing hand must be guided by self-imposed censorship. This takes guts. Have you got them or do you want your buddies and your country to pay the price for your showing off? You've faced the battle front; it's little enough to ask you to face this "home front."

CAPTURE

Most enemy intelligence comes from prisoners. If captured, you are required to give only three facts: YOUR NAME, YOUR GRADE, YOUR ARMY SERIAL NUMBER. Don't talk, don't try to fake stories, and use every effort to destroy all papers. When you are going into an area where capture is possible carry only essential papers and plan to destroy them prior to capture if possible. Do not carry personal letters on your person; they tell much about you, and the envelope has on it your unit and organization.

BE SENSIBLE; USE YOUR HEAD

U. S. GOVERNMENT PRINTING OFFICE: 1943

Appendix F

Postmarks used at the 1st B.P.O.

The First Base Post Office used several different postmarks. From July the 1st 1942 to March the 10th 1943 the War Department directed that the A.P.O. number be not included in the postmarks. During this period there were three different types of postmark.

The first type to be used by A.P.O. 640 was a handstamp, it had a date in the upper three centre slots and the left ends of the killer bars formed a straight line. The second sort was also a handstamp. This time the left ends of the killer bars formed a curve corresponding to the circle of the postmark. The date inserts were usually in the first, second and fourth centre slots. The third type, which was used from January 1943, was a machine cancel. The time was featured in this postmark. After March 1943 an A.P.O. or B.P.O. number figured in the postmark.

e.g. of a handstamp A.P.O. 640. December 1944.

e.g. of a machine stamp. February 1944.

Appendix G

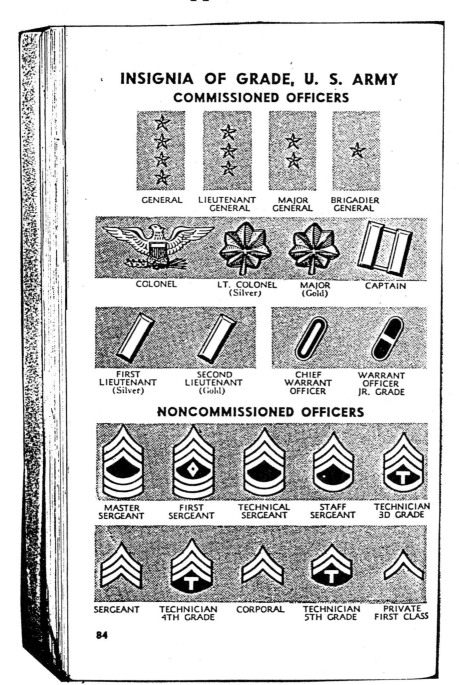

INSIGNIA OF GRADE, U. S. ARMY
COMMISSIONED OFFICERS

GENERAL   LIEUTENANT GENERAL   MAJOR GENERAL   BRIGADIER GENERAL

COLONEL   LT. COLONEL (Silver)   MAJOR (Gold)   CAPTAIN

FIRST LIEUTENANT (Silver)   SECOND LIEUTENANT (Gold)   CHIEF WARRANT OFFICER   WARRANT OFFICER JR. GRADE

NONCOMMISSIONED OFFICERS

MASTER SERGEANT   FIRST SERGEANT   TECHNICAL SERGEANT   STAFF SERGEANT   TECHNICIAN 3D GRADE

SERGEANT   TECHNICIAN 4TH GRADE   CORPORAL   TECHNICIAN 5TH GRADE   PRIVATE FIRST CLASS

84

Acknowledgements

In grateful acknowledgement of the following people and sources:

Great Britain

Doreen Andrew M.B.E., Angela Andrews, Dorothy Anwyl, Eva Attree, Mr Arblaster, Lily Bagshaw, Joan Bashford, Dawn Bibby, Lil Brown, Grace Collins, Anthony Dollman, Megan Cox, Vic Cox, Sheila Farrah, John Field, Ethnie Frost, Dorothy Grieg, Sybil Grieg, Doris Hendley, Patricia Hickson, Dolly Higgins, Derek Hudson, Wendy Hunt, Dennis Hurley, Irene Hurley, Clarice Illiffe, Edna Jennings, Kate Kendall, Julie Knight, Pat Knight, Jean Lasker, Megan Lewis, Jeanne Lidgate, Frances Lines, Mrs D. Lutz, Betty Mason, Violet Nicholls, William Orton, Mr J. Overend, Hilda Partlow, Sylvia Phillips, John Ravenscroft, Mrs Redfern, John Riley, Pat Sinsheimer, Veronica Smith, Joyce Terry, Mrs B. Upton, Jean Wilson.

United States of America

Cecilia Abrahams, Andrew Arden, Wilbur Armstrong, Carl Berkowitz, Thelma Brands, Henry Brown, Chas Bubenas, Betty Buck, William Ciolko, Joe Gardiner, Julia Goble, Art Johnson, Janis Leonard, Al Lucas, Pearl Lucas, Gladys MacDonald, Leonard McDermott, Tom Morrissey, Leonard Nole, Kenneth Osgood, Ike Osteen, Joyce Parr, Margaret Pedlar, Helen Sprava, Kenneth Sell, Ernie Stoeckal, Joyce Streib, Roy Streib, Betty Sullivan, Francis Sullivan, Phil Tillar, Charles Trimpin, David Turney, Andrew Vavreck, William Walter, Elizabeth Ward, Betty Watts, Charles Watts, Don Whalen, Andrew Zirpoli.

U.S. Army Publications

Army Life – W.D. Pamphlet 21 – 13.
Short Guide to Great Britain
When You are Overseas Pamphlet 21 – 1.
U.S. National Archives: History of the First Base Post Office and 640th
   A.P.U. Calendar year 1942 – 1943.
   Historical Report First Base Post Office Year 1944
   and negatives of photos with captions.
   Historical Report First Base Post Office Jan – May
   1945
   Historical Report First Base Post Office May – Dec
   1945

Other Publications

After the Battle Magazine
Beaver County Times, Beaver, P.A.
Birmingham Post and Mail
Illustrated.
Starkville News
Stars and Stripes
Sutton News
17th B.P.O. – Invasion Post Office by James R. Brady.

Also:

National Maritime Museum, Greenwich
We are grateful to Martin Harris and the staff of the Royal Mail International Foreign Postal
Depot, Sutton Coldfield for their cooperation.
Thanks are due to Tim Jebbit for his photographic expertise and help.